REBELS TO RULERS

REBELS TO RULERS

The Rise of Jat Power in Medieval India c.1665–1735

R.P. RANA

MANOHAR
2006

First published 2006

ISBN 81-7304-605-0

Published by

Ajay Kumar Jain for
Manohar Publishers & Distributors
4753/23 Ansari Road, Daryaganj
New Delhi 110 002

Typeset at

Digigrafics
New Delhi 110 049

Printed at

Lordson Publishers Pvt. Ltd.
Delhi 110 007

Distributed in South Asia by

FOUNDATION
BOOKS

4381/4, Ansari Road
Daryaganj, New Delhi 110 002
and its branches at Mumbai, Hyderabad,
Bangalore, Chennai, Kolkata

Contents

Preface

In the following pages I have tried to sketch the character and the contours of social and economic change in the central regions of the Mughal empire during the late seventeenth and early eighteenth century. The central regions of my study comprises the area between Agra, Delhi and Ajmer. The focus of discussion is on the tumultuous events that took place in the Braj, Mewat and Dundhar territories. These regions overlap and it is difficult to say with precision where Braj, Mewat, and Dundhar begin and end; yet their distinctiveness has been underlined. I have envisaged this as the central area of the Mughal empire

I explore the interaction between the material environment brought about by Mughal taxation policy and the events triggered off by the ratchet effect of those policies. In addition to that, the survival strategies devised by the peasantry in the face of famine and fiscal pressures of the state are also discussed. As the state proceeded to crush the zamindars and bring about alteration in the local power equations, a clash between local and central politics became inevitable. The process through which the zamindars transformed their defensive resistance into an open challenge of the empire and its agents is covered in this book. The net outcome of the political struggle between zamindars and the empire was a considerable enlargement of the zamindaris of the rebels and the erosion of imperial control on the region. The Jats, being the main driving force of these revolts, succeeded ultimately in carving out a state in the vicinity of imperial capitals of Agra and Delhi.

The volume covers the period from 1665 when reports of peasant and zamindar unrest began to reach the imperial capital to 1735 when Badan Singh formed his kingdom with Bharatpur as its capital and consolidated Jat power.

The Dundhari rendering of names and terms has been retained throughout this book. For instance *dastur amal,* as written in the archival documents, has been retained instead of the proper *dastur amal.* Similarly the *bhomia* of our documents has been kept instead of the correct Hindi word *bhumia*. Lineage names such as Khangarot or Kalyanot of Dundhari have been used instead Khangarvat or Kalyanvat in Hindi.

R.P. RANA

Acknowledgements

This book is an enlarged and revised version of my Ph.D. thesis 'Social and Economic Background of the Rise of Bharatpur Kingdom', Jawaharlal Nehru University, New Delhi, 1984. I express my deep sense of gratitude to Professor Harbans Mukhia for providing constant encouragement and guidance during the various stages of preparing the thesis. I also wish to thank Professor Dilbagh Singh for introducing me to the treasure trove of medieval Rajasthani literary and archival sources.

Many thanks also go to my colleagues, Suhas Chakrabarty, T.K.V. Subramanian, B.P. Sahu, S.Z.H. Jafri, R.C. Thakran and Dilip Menon for helping me in numerous ways. Their incisive comments and valuable suggestions were of critical importance in developing various arguments. I owe a special debt to my friends R.P. Bahuguna and S.B. Bhardwaj who offered useful correctives to the erratic development of some themes. I thank J.S. Grewal and A.R. Kulkarni for offering many useful insights while examining my Ph.D. thesis. I gratefully acknowledge the assistance offered to me by Bipan Chandra and D.R. Chaudhary at various stages of my studies.

I shall always remember the hospitality and assistance offered to me by the staff members of the Rajasthan State Archives in Bikaner. Many thanks are due to R.K. Gupta who meticulously converted the manuscript into a typescript. I also thank Yashpal and Narander Daraal for preparing the maps at short notice. None of those who have helped me in various ways, is responsible for any errors in this book.

R.P. RANA

Abbreviations

IESHR	*The Indian Economic and Social History Review*
IHR	*Indian Historical Review*
PIHC	*Proceedings of Indian History Congress*
JAS	*Journal of Asian Studies*
MAS	*Modern Asian Studies*
VS	*Vikrami Samvat*

Introduction

The fall of the Mughal empire as an organized polity and, along with it the dismantling of its support structures, had far-reaching consequences for the history of India. The empire was sustained by various systems—revenue, *mansab, jagir* and currency—that, with Akbar's stamp on them,[1] had an almost all-India spread and penetration.[2] The Mughal empire also commanded a fair degree of allegiance and legitimacy from among its subjects.[3] Nevertheless, towards the end of the seventeenth century a process of internal decay had set in. The disintegration of the empire became a turning point in the fortune of many imperial nobles, local zamindars, and rural communities. Its collapse pushed India into a prolonged period of political turmoil, agrarian dislocation, and contraction of commerce.[4] Elements that had done so much to destroy the Mughal state battled among themselves and scrambled for the legacy of the moribund empire. Thus the eighteenth century unfolded as a chronicle of the physical elimination of a large number of high-born nobles (*umaras*).[5] In this period of rapid change many high-ranking families were pushed to the wall. Only a few, though outmanoeuvred in the imperial court that was trapped in the cusp of history and ambition, made timely moves to the provinces where they founded the successor states of Awadh,[6] Bengal,[7] Hyderabad,[8] and Jaipur.[9]

The locus of political power was shifting from the court to the countryside. In this shift a mixed array of lower-caste zamindars and military adventurers became rulers of vast territories of the subcontinent.[10] Similarly, a wide spectrum of village headmen grew into zamindars.[11] Coeval with, and contributing to, the crisis of the empire was the phenomenon of heightened militancy among many subaltern castes.[12] This militancy was sustained by a proliferation of muskets as the weapons of the weak.[13] The easy acquisition and effective use of muskets by the peasantry whereas earlier the sole preserve of the nobility, democratized warfare. In short no matter how we account for it, the eighteenth century was awash with social churning and political re-alignment.

The decline of the Mughal empire has been a cornucopia for historians. William Irvin and Jadunath Sarkar sought to explain the decline in terms of a degeneration in the calibre of the rulers.[14] Sarkar, highlighting Aurangzeb's failure to maintain law and order, found the Emperor reneging on the well-established Mughal tradition of religious tolerance and thereby provoking a 'Hindu reaction'.[15] In support of his argument he says that the Rajputs, once politically side-lined, were no longer ardent supporters of the Mughal cause. Similarly, the Sikhs, Jats, and Marathas also revolted against Aurangzeb's policy of religious persecution. Sarkar's skewed approach to these events immensely strengthened communal interpretations of medieval history. Consequently a genre of history writing came into being in which too much attention was paid to Aurangzeb as cause of the subsequent woes of the country.

Subsequently more pellucid explanations arose for the decline of the empire. In his pioneering *Parties and Politics in the Mughal Court, 1707-1740*, Satish Chandra made a major breakthrough by shifting the focus of study from the failure of individuals to the working of institutions. The efficient working of the *mansab* and *jagir* systems were crucial for the maintenance of peace and collection of revenues, but the *mansab* and *jagir* systems were subjected to strains and stresses when Aurangzeb, in pursuit of his expansionist designs, began to recruit large numbers of Dakhani *sardars*. Their intake was not matched by a corresponding increase in the financial resources of the empire. A situation of acute shortage of *jagirs* (*bejagiri*) was created, with more claimants than *jagirs*. With frantic searches for lucrative *jagirs*, there was growing factionalism in the imperial court, each faction tugging in a different direction. This affected the unity of the ruling class. M. Athar Ali's seminal work on the nobility of Aurangzeb was not only congruent with Satish Chandra's conclusions but provided profuse statistical evidence to boot.[16] Later, taking cognizance of fresh but contrary evidence, Satish Chandra undertook a partial revision of his original thesis. He came to the conclusion that the non-functionality of the *jagirdari* system was central to the crisis. The increasing inability of the *jagirdars* to resist the growing assertiveness of the zamindars and to protect the interest of the peasantry, gave an impetus to a crisis which was essentially an interplay of social and administrative factors.[17] Both Satish Chandra and Athar Ali not only provided persuasive explanations of the decline of the Mughal empire, but also made lasting contributions in destroying some communal interpretations.[18]

The publication of Irfan Habib's *The Agrarian System of the Mughal Empire I (1556-1707)*, in 1963 was a landmark in Mughal studies. It not only provided insights into the working of the Mughal administration, agrarian economy, and village society and gave a new analytical framework for understanding the crisis of the empire. Habib dispelled the prevailing nobility–centred focus in the debate and emphatically brought out the agrarian aspects of the revolts that had shaken the Mughal empire to its roots. The core of his argument is that there was an intimate link between the highly exploitative pressures of the Mughal state apparatus and the escalating socio-economic tensions and political upheavals of the late seventeenth century.[19] According to Habib the Mughal state, taking into consideration its long term interest, fixed the land revenue demand at a level where agricultural production could both generate the maximum revenue and provide the necessary subsistence needs to the peasantry.[20] This cardinal principle guided the formulation of all imperial taxation policies. But each *jagirdar*, conscious of his impending transfer, after a routine cycle of 3 to 4 years exerted himself to extort from the peasants as much as he could.[21] Thus excessive and unauthorized fiscal demands from the peasants were on the rise. As a result large numbers of peasants were impoverished and forced to abandon cultivation.[22] In the process the revenue paying capacity of large areas was ruined. The imperial rules and regulations which were meant to check the recklessness of the *jagirdars* were often thrown to the winds.[23] Cumulatively, everything concurred to produce an agrarian crisis, during late seventeenth century giving birth to large scale social upheavals that ultimately engulfed the empire.[24] Habib's book not only redounded to a better understanding of the crisis of the Mughal empire, but also became a bench-mark for subsequent research on medieval Indian history.

M.N. Pearson and J.F. Richards each made a critical appraisal of the existing historiography of the imperial decline and concluded that Mughal involvement in the Dakhin was symptomatic of the derangement of the empire.[25] Pearson is of the view that the decline can be traced to what he calls the Shivaji factor.[26] In response to the military challenge posed by Shivaji, Aurangzeb marched to the Dakhin where he compromised Mughal prestige and the armies lost their way. The Mughals had already been overwhelmed by the callow Marathas in a number of encounters. J.F. Richards, correcting a longs held view that the Dakhin was a deficit area, highlights the point that political mismanagement by Aurangzeb led to the squandering of available resources. In Richards' view the emperor miscalculated in keeping the productive lands under the *khalisa*. Earmarking the disturbed areas to the *jagirdars* caused widespread disaffection among the nobles. As an increasing number of zamindars were taking to banditry, it became impossible for the empire to relcaim their allegiance. Richards terms the emperor's reluctance to accord respectable place to the frontier aristocracies in the Mughal political system, as another instance of imperial failure in the Dakhin.[27] P. Hardy, commenting on these generalizations, finds both Pearson and Richards's operating within the boundaries of a 'plane of thinking set by the Aligarh historians'. He underlines the need for research on some other facets of the problem, such as Aurangzeb's failure to eliminate or accommodate Shivaji, the court ethos, Mughal military demoralization etc.[28]

Karen Leonard in an impressive debut in the debate assigned a crucial role to the bankers. They influenced the course of political change between 1650 and 1750.[29] She argues that the bankers diverted financial support from the Mughals to the nascent states, thereby causing the fall of the empire. The increasing political clout and economic role of the bankers in some of the eighteenth century successor states may not be doubted,[30] but the central role that Leonard ascribes to the operation of the 'Great-Firms' in determining the fortunes of the Mughal empire is highly overdrawn. M. Athar Ali in a stimulating paper tried to trace the waning of the Mughal empire to India's cultural crisis, i.e. to a societal failure.[31] In the opinion of C.A. Bayly the empire became a 'victim of its own success in promoting agricultural and commercial growth'.[32] Recently, J.F. Richards has suggested that the empire fell prey to the prosperity of certain classes patronized by the Mughals in their heyday.[33] All these works indicate new perspectives for research, and reveal also the limitations of the research carried out so far on various facets of the crisis of the empire.

There is no gainsaying the fact that the Mughal empire was riven by mounting difficulties towards the closing decades of the seventeenth century. With the unfolding of the eighteenth century the empire, despite some spurts of recovery, was on an irretrievable path of faltering and withering. The basic rules and conventions crafted under the Great Mughals[34] had either fallen into disuse or could not any longer cope with emerging challenges.[35] The later Mughals were woefully devoid of innovative ideas in matters of governance[36] and military warfare.[37] There is plentiful evidence of chaos and corrupt administration at all levels.[38] Emperor Bahadur Shah, a man of many parts, unfortunately displayed more pomp than purpose. Barring a brief period of brilliance under the Saiyid Brothers who strove to firm up a more broad based state,[39] there was no trace of the Great Mughals' tact, spunk, or awe. A miasma of mutual distrust stalked the precincts of power. In such an ambience of uncertainty one emperor died violent death, others were rapidly ousted, and the rest lived with the crippling fear of assassination. The debacle of 1739 at Karnal and its aftermath exposed the military debility of the Mughals. In the autumn of its career the empire was headed by Muhammad Shah whose reign witnessed a pervasive breakdown of the political order. Whether there was a replication of the institutional framework of the empire in its former core areas or a staggered ending of the Mughal power structure in different regions, is a moot point.[40] In any case by the middle of the eighteenth century the empire was over and done with—only its semblance remained.

Widespread agrarian uprisings rocked much of north India during the late seventeenth and early eighteenth centuries, leaving a lasting impact on the polity, society, and economy, a factor which played a decisive role in limiting the fortunes of the Mughal empire. On the role of the Jats in the fall of the Mughal empire, Father Wendel, a contemporary observer, writing in 1768 had this to say, '. . . even one reflects cursorily upon the upheavals which have so violently agitated the empire in this century, one must acknowledge that the Jats have been if not the only, than at least the principal instigators'.[41] To unravel and analyse various facets and trajectory of the Jat rebellion in the Braj region[42] is the problem in this study. The extension of the Jat revolts into Mewat[43] and the formation of a broad-based coalition of zamindars against the Mughal empire, will form a part of this work. Reciprocal links between the rebels of Braj and Mewat and the refractory elements of Dundhar[44] will also be discussed.

The Jat state of Bharatpur was established in defiance of the Mughal centre. The economic and administrative tensions that impelled certain social classes to challenge the hold of the Mughal state in the neighbourhood of Agra and Delhi, is the central concern of my study. Following William Irvine and Jadunath Sarkar, K.R. Qanungo gave a narrative of events in 1925 in his *History of the Jats*. His researches merely reinforced the dominant theme in the historiography of his day, that the Jat revolt was a 'Hindu reaction' against Aurangzeb's policy of religious discrimination.[45] Since then this theme has been repeated time and again in various studies.[46] Even the well-crafted and readable biography of Maharaja Surajmal by Natwar Singh has not escaped the influence of Sarkar's biases.[47] Recently, Girish Chandra Dwivedi, basing himself on the evidence provided by M.C. Pradhan in *The Political System of the Jats of Northern India*, Oxford University Press, has come to the startling conclusion that the Jat uprising was a reaction to Aurangzeb's attempt to interfere with their 'traditional tribal and democratic ways'.[48] However, the documents used by Pradhan in support of his argument are not reliable.[49] Moreover, Pradhan is discussing the 'political system' of the Jats of Upper Doab which was not affected by the Jat uprising at all. Therefore, the causation attributed by Dwivedi to the Jat uprising in the Braj region falls apart.

W.C. Smith was the first scholar to seriously challenge the theory of 'Hindu reaction'. Following this Irfan Habib brought into light new dimensions of the Jat uprising in *The Agrarian System of Mughal India*. Here Habib gave a panoramic view derived from some foreign travellers' accounts, Indian chroniclers' statements, and a plethora of revenue-cum-administrative documents. If justification is needed for more a detailed examination of the problem on which Smith and Irfan Habib have initiated research, it is that history studied at a regional level often induces modifications of the panoramic view, even when such a view is its starting point. At the regional level, untouched dimensions of the global problem can enrich our understanding.

The focal point of this study is the circumstances leading to the emergence of Bharatpur state in the eighteenth century. Here, this has not been studied as an event but as a process with ramifications reaching several aspects of society. An attempt has been made to put the upheavals in the Braj-Mewat region in their socio-economic context: were these upheavals generated by catastrophic changes in the nature of the economy, or were they a manifestation of growing pressures exerted on an unchanging, unyielding economy? Can economic tensions alone explain major social and political developments? Where do culture, traditions and social institutions like caste and community assume crucial significance? Should we not also recognize the qualities of leadership displayed by individuals at various levels, qualities that enable them to grasp opportunities and turn them to advantage? It is all these aspects in mutual interaction which comprise for us the social background of the rise of Jat power and of the Bharatpur state. Apart from the background and the context of the rebellion I have also looked in detail at the actual actions of the rebels.

This study runs into six chapters. The first chapter provides the setting within which the villagers engaged in agricultural toil. The salient features of the village economy and rural class structure are explored to bring into relief the relations of subordination and super-ordination among the peasantry. In the second chapter, systems of agricultural production have been discussed. The soil, crops, and means of irrigation have been examined. The movement of the prices of cash and food crops have also been analysed. If the social distribution of resources like land and implements have been left out of consideration, it is not owing to lack of concern, but lack of adequate data in our sources. At any rate it is intended to examine whether the political developments had parallel changes in the economy, and we hope that this specific question has been answered, even if tentatively. In the third chapter we discuss the magnitude of land revenue demand and the total economic burden on different strata of the peasantry. An effort is made to establish concretely whether there was a constant increase in the revenue demand, or else a high level plateau with occasional transgressions by the *jagirdars* and others, which would provoke peasant resistance.

Chapter 4 is devoted to the study of changing position of the zamindars at every level. The flux in which the class of zamindars found itself and the consequent far-reaching disturbances forms a critical link in our argument, for it has appeared to us that the growing strength of zamindars at all levels and increasing impoverishment of the peasantry combined to register the agrarian uprisings of our region and period. The linkage between the growing economic strength of the zamindars and the pauperized peasantry is provided by caste and a shared historical experience. In Chapter 5 we have tried to trace the socio-cultural transformation of Jat society between the seventh and seventeenth centuries. The Jat tradition of resistance against all forms of cultural dominance is explored. The interplay of traditional cultural influences and immediate economic grievances located in the backstage of social life, were at the roots of the popular protest. The last chapter provides a detailed description of the actual locales of the uprisings. Various modalities of agrarian disturbance and the specific response of the Mughal state to the phenomenon are examined. Alignment between various groups and classes—between the peasants and the zamindars and among the zamindars themselves—are also studied. The nature of the zamindar leadership and the peasant following is discussed.

This study is largely based on original village level revenue records and a variety of reportage of the period. Most of these records are on loose sheets locally known as *tozih* and are written in the Dundhari language spoken in the Amber territories. As most of the parganas of the region were under the *jagir* or *ijara* of the Amber rulers at various intervals during Mughal rule, these records have been catalogued and preserved in the Jaipur Historical Section of the Rajasthan State Archives at Bikaner. The detailed village level records written in Dundhari provide an insight into the functioning of the Mughal system at the local level. A close scrutiny of these records shows that the principles of revenue administration and the structures of taxation conformed closely to the Mughal system. In the parganas of this study the Mughal principles and practices of governance were largely observed from the period of Mirza Raja Jai Singh (1622-67) to that of Sawai Jai Singh (1700-43). In the time of Mirza Raja Jai Singh the Mughal empire was at the peak of its power and stability, whereas during much of the reign of Sawai Jai Singh the empire was in the throes of its crisis. As successive Kachhwaha rulers from 1650 onwards had extensive *jagirs* between Agra and Ajmer, the records left by them are useful for an understanding of the working of the Mughal system. As such the Kachhwaha archive may be supposed to be an extension, if not a replica, of the Mughal archives though with the usual inputs of local customs and practices in a vernacular form.

I have used in this study *arsatthas, arzdashts, chithis, dastur amals, yaddashtis, vakil* reports, *Amber records, Takhmina, Taqsim Dahsala, Dastur Komwar, Mawazana kalan, Mawazana khurd, Khatoot ahalkaran, Siah huzur, Awariza and Nasukha-punya*. These records are available from roughly 1650 onwards. Although most of them pertain to those parganas which were held by the Amber rulers in *jagir* or otherwise, they do help us to establish some broad trends in the agrarian history of the region, as most of these parganas were frequently shuffled between the Amber rulers and other imperial *jagirdars*.

Of the village level revenue records, the *arsatthas* are of prime importance in terms of supplying information about crucial aspects of the economy of the region. The *arsatthas* provide comprehensive information about the total income and expenditure of the pargana of their origin. Basic data such as the total number of villages under sub-assignments and the Amber ruler's *khalisa* are given in them. The *arsatthas* also give the estimated income, arrears, returns, and expenditure incurred under different heads in the pargana. The area under the *zabti* and *batai jinsi* crops for the entire pargana (and also separately for each village) is given in the *arsatthas*. The amount of land revenue (*mal*) and the names and magnitude of numerous other cesses are also entered in the *arsatthas*. The income section of the *arsathas* has mostly been used in this study. The section showing the expenditures of the pargana is useful for determining the claims of the holders of superior rights in rural society. The *arsatthas* also provide abundant information about the seamy side of peasant life. Despite some irritating gaps, they are a mine of information on the system of agricultural production, prices, and the magnitude of the economic hardship faced by the peasantry. Moreover, from the *hasil-firohi* column of these *arsatthas* we can not only construct a narrative of everyday forms of peasant resistance but also get a graphic account of the nature and incidence of sundry other offences committed by the villagers.

The *arzdashts* were written by *amils*, *faujdars*, and other officials of Amber state, posted in various parganas. Their content would evoke the attention of any scholar working on peasant discontent. These *arzdashts* are addressed to the Raja of Amber in the form of supplications. Each mentions the prevailing political, social and economic conditions, and these documents are of enormous importance. These *arzdashts* also carry the Raja's directives to his officials. The actual course of political upheaval and the extent of peasant participation are widely covered by the *arzdashts*. They are thus an invaluable source of information on the political developments that were taking place on the ground. A vivid account of each encounter between the rebels and the authorities is the continuing refrain of these hitherto unused *arzdashts*.

The *vakil* reports were written by the *vakils* of the Amber rulers, posted in the imperial court. They are an important source for understanding the changing contours of imperial policies vis-à-vis the rebels.

The *chithis* were written by the *diwan* of Amber state to officials, particularly the *amils* and *faujdars*. Each *chithi* contains the substance of a complaint received by the *diwan,* and his instructions thereon. Complaints were lodged by the aggrieved persons of a *qasba* or a village and the *chithis* throw considerable light on the conflicts and emerging social tensions, as well as the customary practices operating at the village level. The structure of rural society can be reconstructed on the basis of information supplied by the *chithis*. We find a large number of *chithis* pertaining to the area of our study, but most of them belong to the eighteenth century. For the seventeenth century, only a negligible number are available.

Dastur amals are schedules of revenue rates. We come across many such for various parganas of our region. In each *dastur amal* the percentage of the shares of the government and the cultivators have been mentioned separately. The amount of other cesses and *zabti* rates have also been stated in some of the *dastur amals*. They are particularly helpful in establishing the differential rates of revenue on various sections of the cultivators. In the absence of these *dasturs* it would not have been possible to work out the magnitude of economic burden on peasants. The *dastur amals* were prepared by the local revenue officials in conformity with the rules laid down by the imperial authority.

The *yaddashtis* were a kind of memoranda or documents of remembrance. Written by the revenue officials like *chaudhuri, qanungo, patel,* and *patwari*, these *yaddashtis* give rich information about the land—cultivated and uncultivated—and livestock owned by the peasants of a village or a pargana. The availability of agricultural implements and other assets with various categories for the cultivators can be known from the *yaddashtis*. Unfortunately, such information for our parganas is extremely meagre. I have used whatever is available.

The *Khatoot-ahalkaran* contain useful information about the pargana administration. The *Siah-huzur* documents provide details about the knotty disputes directly settled by the Amber ruler. The *Nasukha-punya* papers contain detailed information about revenue-free land grants made for charitable and other purposes.

The *Amber records* contain letters written by the officials to the *diwan* of the Amber state. In these documents we get a lot of information about the day-to-day functioning of the administration at the pargana level. The economic and political dimensions of the local administration are a running theme of most of the letters. These documents are as important as the *arzdashts* for our study. Both categories also serve as some kind of corroborative evidence for each other. Occasionally this correspondence is expressed in few words otherwise most of the records are long and boring.

The other important source used in this work are the *Vartas* which according to Charlotte Vaudeville, should be viewed as 'some kind of *dharam-kathas* or *dharm-gathas* such as are found in Buddhist and Jaina literature'.[50] The *Chaurasi Vaishnavan ki Varta* (Accounts of the Eighty-four Vaishnavas), *Do So Bavan Vaishnavan ki Varta* (Account of Two Hundred and Fifty-two Vaishnavas) and the *Sri Nath Ji Prakatya ki Varta* (Account of the Manifestation of Sri Govardhan Nath Ji) are the three most important texts of the Vallabhi sect. These *Vartas* are written in the prose of the Braj dialect. They are a mid- or late-seventeenth-century hagiographic source.[51] If one can penetrate the Vaishnavite coating of these *Vartas*, one can discover the latent cultural tension between the high caste Vaishnavas and the Brajvasis. The recently published Vrindavan documents have also revealed the nature of the Mughal and Kachhwaha involvement in the Braj country.[52] They enable us to bring to the fore the latent tensions that existed between the Gaudias and local people (including the Jats). There is a small amount of supporting evidence from other sources, for instance the documents preserved by the Diggi *thikana*.[53] These *thikana* records supply information of varying worth for anyone writing about the life, condition and actions of the rebels. Various strategies of pacification devised by the rulers can be known from these documents. It is a matter of gratification that such multi-faceted evidence at the ground level is available for our study. This fact itself is a compelling justification for the present attempt, with all its numerous shortcomings.

NOTES

1. M. Athar Ali in his Presidential Address, *Proceedings of the Indian History Congress* (PIHC), 33rd Session, Muzaffarpur, 1972, pp. 175-88, emphasizes the significance of Akbar's reign for the evolution of these systems. See also Douglas

E. Streusand, *The Formation of the Mughal Empire*, Oxford University Press, Delhi, 1989, p. 14.

2. The degree of centralization and depth of the Mughal empire has been differently viewed by scholars. For an affirmative view see J.F. Richards, *The Mughal Empire* (The New Cambridge History of India 1.5), Cambridge University Press, 1993, pp. xv, 1-2. M. Athar Ali, *The Mughal Nobility Under Aurangzeb*, new revd. edn., Oxford University Press, Delhi, 1997, p. xxv and Irfan Habib, *The Economic History of Medieval India – A Survey*, Tulika, 2001, pp. 39-41. For an ambivalent position on this matter see C.A. Bayly, *Rulers, Townsmen and Bazaars*, Cambridge University Press, 1983, p. 10. For the opposite view on the Mughal empire's spread and depth see Frank Perlin, 'State Formation Reconsidered', *Modern Asian Studies*, vol. 19, pt. 3, 1985, pp. 415-80. Recently Muzaffar Alam and Sanjay Subramanyam, taking an extreme position on the issue, have likened the Mughal empire with a 'patchwork quilt'. See their *The Mughal State, 1526-1750*, Oxford University Press, 1998, p. 57.
3. Banarsi Das, *Ardhkathanak*, tr. Mukund Lath, Rajasthan Prakrit Bharati Sansthan, Jaipur, 1981, p. 38. Banarsi Das writes that the people of Jaunpur were so attached with the emperor that on hearing about the death of Akbar they felt 'orphaned'. Akbar is also fondly remembered in the Jain and Rajasthani traditions. See, for instance, Pushpa Prasad, 'Akbar and the Jains', in Irfan Habib (ed.), *Akbar and his India*, Oxford University Press, 1957, pp. 96-108 and B.L. Bhadani, 'The Profile of Akbar in Contemporary Rajasthani Literature', *Social Scientist*, vol. 20, no. 10, Sept.-Oct. 1992, pp. 46-53. These are but a few examples.
4. Irfan Habib, *The Agrarian System of Mughal India 1556-1707*, 2nd revd. edn., Oxford University Press, Delhi, 1999, p. 405; Irfan Habib, *Essays in Indian History: Towards a Marxist Perception*, Tulika, Delhi, 1997, pp. 231-2; Irfan Habib, 'The Eighteenth Century in Indian History', *PIHC*, Calcutta, 1995, pp. 360-2 and Ashin Das Gupta, *Indian Merchants and the Decline of Surat c.1700-1750*,Wiesbaden, Franz Steiner Verlag, 1979, p. 283.
5. Muzaffar Alam, *The Crisis of Empire in Mughal North India: Awadh and Punjab 1707-1748*, Oxford University Press, 1986, pp. 43-4; and John F. Richards, *The Mughal Empire*, Cambridge University Press, 1993, p. 261. Both Alam and Richards have noted an unprecedented annihilation of dozens of nobles during the reign of Jahandar Shah and Farukh Siyar.
6. Muzaffar Alam, *The Crisis of the Empire*, pp. 204-2.
7. P. Calkins, 'The Formation of a Regionally Oriented Group in Bengal 1700-40', *Journal of Asian Studies* (*JAS*), vol. 29, 1970, pp. 799-806.
8. K. Leonard, 'The Hyderabad Political System and its Participants', *JAS*, vol. 30, 1971, pp. 569-82.
9. S.P. Gupta, *The Agrarian System of Eastern Rajasthan*, Manohar, Delhi, 1986, pp. 5-17.
10. For example, the Marathas, the Jats, the Sikhs, and the Afghans.
11. Irfan Habib, *Essays in Indian History*, p. 252.
12. Ibid., pp. 244-55, brings out the ubiquity of the lower castes in the Sikh, Jat, Satnami, and Maratha revolts. Dirk H.A. Kolf, *Naukar, Rajput and Sepoy: The Ethnohistory of the Military Labour Market in Hindustan (1450-1850)*, Manohar, Delhi, 1990, discovers a strong urge among peripheral groups to acquire legitimacy via military service.

13. Iqtidar Alam Khan, 'Muskets in the Mawas: Instruments of Peasant Resistance', in K.N. Panikkar, Terence J. Byres, Utsa Patnaik (eds.), *The Making of History: Essays presented to Irfan Habib*, Tulika, Delhi, 2000, pp. 81-103.
14. William Irwin, *The Later Mughals* (ed.), Jadunath Sarkar, Oriental Books Reprint Corporation, New Delhi, 1971. Jadunath Sarkar, *History of Aurangzeb*, New Delhi (5 vols.) and *Fall of the Mughal Empire* (4 vols.), Hyderabad, Orient Longman Ltd., 1991.
15. Jadunath Sarkar, *History of Aurangzeb*, vol. III, 3rd edn., Calcutta, Orient Longman, 1952; rpt., Bombay, Orient Longman, 1974, Chapter XXXV.
16. M. Athar Ali, *The Mughal Nobility Under Aurangzeb*, Bombay, Asia Publishing House, 1966.
17. Satish Chandra, *Medieval India*, Delhi, Macmillan, 1982, pp. 61-75.
18. S.R. Sharma, *The Religious Policy of the Mughal Emperors*, Oxford University Press, Bombay, 1940 (3rd edn. 1962), pp. 178-80. Sharma's entire argument of religious discrimination against the Hindus rested on an assumed decrease in the number of Hindu nobles under Aurangzeb ; whereas M. Athar Ali in his *The Mughal Nobility under Aurangzeb*, pp. 30-1, has proved that the percentage of Hindu nobles rase from 21.6 per cent (1658-78) to 31.6 per cent in 1679-1707 when the emperor was at the height of religious orthodoxy.
19. Irfan Habib, *The Agrarian System*, pp. 364-405. Failure to understand this fundamental aspect of the Mughal state has been relatively common. Recent examples are: Muzaffar Alam, *The Crisis of Empire*, pp. 9 and 318; Chetan Singh, *Region and Empire: Punjab in the Seventeenth Century*, pp. 8, 271-5, and S.P. Gupta, *The Agrarian System of Eastern Rajasthan*, pp. 154-5. In all these works the magnitude of the land revenue demand and its impact on the peasantry has either been understated, rationalized, or overlooked.
20. Irfan Habib, *The Agrarian System*, p. 367.
21. Ibid. p. 369.
22. Ibid, p. 371.
23. Ibid, pp. 340-7.
24. Ibid, pp. 404-5.
25. Symposium: 'Decline of the Mughal Empire', *Journal of Asian Studies*, vol. XXXV. 2, 1976, pp. 221-63.
26. M.N. Pearson, 'Shivaji and the Decline of the Mughal Empire', *JAS*, vol. XXXV. 2, 1976, pp. 221-35.
27. J.F. Richards, 'The Imperial Crisis in the Deccan', *JAS*, Feb., 1976, pp. 237-56. Richards' contention that there was no *jagirdari* crisis has been contested. See, for instance, S.M. Azizuddin Hussain, 'Scarcity of *pai baqi* Lands During Aurangzeb's Reign in the Light of Inayat Jung Collection Documents', *PIHC*, 39th Session, 1978, pp. 426-30; M. Athar Ali, *The Mughal Nobility Under Aurangzeb*, 2nd edn. 1997, xxi-xxii and Satish Chandra, *Parties and Politics at the Mughal Court 1707-1740*, OUP, 2002, xii-xv.
28. P. Hardy, 'Commentary and Critique', *JAS*, vol. XXXV. 2, 1976, p. 263.
29. Karen Leonard, 'The "Great-Firm" Theory of the Decline of the Mughal Empire', *Comprehensive Studies in Society and History*, vol. 21, no. 2, 1979, pp. 161-7.
30. For example three Khatri traders and financiers, Raja Ayamal, Narayan Das, and Seth Govardhan Das and one Khandelwal *bania*, Mohan Ram, became the Diwan of the Jaipur state at different intervals during the eighteenth century.

Similarly, the working of the Jaipur state largely depended on the financial support of the Loonkaran Natani, Chaudhari Kushal Singh and Seth Dhanesar Das. See *Dastur Komwar*, bundles, 3 and 23. I owe this information to Kumar Ram Krishan.

31. M. Athar Ali, 'The Passing of Empire: The Mughal Case', *Modern Asian Studies*, vol. 9, no. 3, 1975, pp. 386-96.
32. C.A. Bayly, *Imperial meridian: The British Empire and the World 1780-1830*, Longman, London, 1989, p. 29.
33. J.F. Richards, *The Mughal Empire*, pp. 294-6.
34. Recently some suggestions have been made to divest Akbar's reign of structural significance in the agrarian and military fields. See, for instance, Sanjay Subrahmanyam, 'The Mughal State-Structure or Process? Reflections on Recent Western historiography", *The Indian Economic and Social History Review*, vol. XXIX, no. 3, July-September 1992, pp. 291-321.
35. M. Athar Ali, *The Mughal Nobility*, pp. 172-4.
36. However, Muzaffar Alam thinks that *ijara* was an act of creative statecraft contributing to growth. See his *The Crisis of Empire*, pp. 39-43 and 318.
37. Iqtidar Alam Khan, 'Muskets in the Mawas: Instruments of Peasant Resistance', pp. 81-103.
38. Satish Chandra, *Parties and Politics*, pp. 128-9; and M. Athar Ali, *The Mughal Nobility Under Aurangzeb*, revd. edn., pp. 93, 151-3.
39. Satish Chandra, *Parties and Politics*, p. 128.
40. Muzaffar Alam, *The Crisis of Empire*, pp. 176-203 and 204-42, provides an account of the contrasting processes of political collapse in two *subas*, Awadh and Punjab.
41. Jean Deloche (ed.), *Wendel's Memoirs on the Origin, Growth and Present State of Jat Power in Hindustan* (1768), Pondichery, 1991, p. 3.
42. The *Braj* country comprised of 18 parganas spread on both sides of the Jamuna river. These parganas are: Mathura, Sahar, Mangottah, Udai, Ao, Pahari, Khoh, Kama, Khoh (Mujahid), Noh, Khohri, Hodal, Baluchi?, Faridabad, Mahaban, Sadabad, Jalesar, Kol and Anup Nagar. See copy of the *parwana* of Mukhtiar Khan, the governor, of *suba* Akbarabad in A.D. 1704, in R.A. Alvi, 'The Temples of Vrindavan and their priests during the reign of Aurangzeb', *PIHC*, 49th Session, Dharwad, 1988. For various views about the territorial expanse of the Brajbhumi, see Charlotte Vaudeville, 'Braj Lost and Found', in her *Myths, Saints and Legends in Medieval India*, Oxford India Paperbacks, 1999, pp. 47-71 and Alan Entwistle, 'Rediscovery of Braj', papers published by the International Association of the Vrindavan Research Institute, School of Oriental and African Studies, University of London, Bulletin XIV, 1988.
43. The region of Mewat, situated in the triangle between Agra, Delhi and Jaipur is named after the Meos, the dominant inhabitants of the area. Mewat comprised the Mughal *sarkars* of Alwar (43 *mahals*) and Tijara (18 *mahals*) of *suba* Agra. See *Ain-i-Akbari*, tr. H.S. Jarrett, vol. II, third edn., 1978, pp. 202-4.
44. A cluster of 1,440 villages spread across Amber (360), Amarsar (360), Chatsu (360), Dausa (150), Mauzabad, Niwai and Lawain (50) was known as *Dundhar*. See *Muhta Nainsi ri Khyat*, part I, edited by Badriparsad Sakaria and published by Rajasthan Oriental Research Institute, Jodhpur, 1984, p. 273.
45. K.R. Qanungo, *History of the Jats*, 1925; rpt., 1987, p. 19.

46. P.C. Chundawat, *Maharaja Surajmal Aur Unka Yug*, Agra, 1982, p. 19.
47. K. Natwar Singh, *Maharaja Surajmal, 1707-1763, His Life and Times*, Vikas Paperback, 1983, p. xiii.
48. G.C. Dwivedi, *The Jats: Their Role in the Mughal Empire*, Arnold Publishers New Delhi, 1989, p. 21.
49. J.F. Richards, 'The Islamic Frontier in the East: Expansion into South Asia', *Journal of South Asian Studies*, no. 4, October 1974, pp. 91-109.
50. Charlotte Vaudeville, 'The Govardhan Myth in Northern India', in her *Myths, Saints and Legends in Medieval India*, Delhi, 1996, p. 92.
51. Harharinath Tandon, *Varta-Sahitya Ek Virhat Adhayan*, Vallabh Research Institute, Jatipura, Aligarh, 1960.
52. These documents have already been analysed by scholars. See, for instance, Tarapada Mukherji and Irfan Habib, 'Akbar and the Temples of Mathura and its Environs', *PIHC*, 48 (1987), pp. 234-50; 'The Mughal Administration and the Temples of Vrindavan during the Reign of Jahangir and Shahjahan', *PIHC*, 49 (1988, pp. 287-300 and 'Land Rights in the Reign of Akbar (The Evidence of the Sale-Deeds of Vrindavan and Aritha)', *PIHC*, 50(1989-90), pp. 236-55; R.A. Alvi, 'Persian Documents of the Reign of Aurangzeb', *PIHC*, 49 (1988). Most of these documents have been reproduced by Irfan Habib, 'A Documentary History of the Gosains (Goswamis) of the Caitanya Sect at Vrindavan', in Margaret H. Case (ed.), *Govinddeva: A Dialogue in Stone*, New Delhi, Indira Gandhi National Centre for the Arts, 1996, pp. 131-59.
53. All these records are preserved in the archives of the Diggi House, Jaipur. K.R. Qanungo's work, *History of the House of Diggi*, written in 1963, now edited by S.S. Ratnawat and published by the Centre for Rajasthan Studies, University of Rajasthan, Jaipur, 1997 is based on an extensive use of these documents.

1

The Rural Setting

Any study of the social and economic structure of a pre-modern region must begin with the village. It is indeed at this basic level that the dynamism of a society becomes operative; it is also at this level that imperial administration comes into contact with the mass of its subjects. Flowing from this, as in the past so often today, the organization of rural life has been a subject of interest to the social historian. Scholarly interest in village communities can be traced to the debates among early British administrators. As the main objective of the colonial officials was to find out whether it was more feasible to collect land revenue from the individual peasant or through a collective body, they focused their attention on the fiscal aspects of the village institutions.[1] In the last forty years or so there has been a considerable amount of writing on land ownership, revenue systems, and the structure of village societies. In these studies attention has been given to the relations which subsisted between social groups in village society. Irfan Habib's wide-ranging examination of various facets of medieval agrarian society made this complex subject comprehensible. He argued that the village society was economically stratified and internally beset with intricate contradictions. A small group of privileged village elite called the *panch muqaddam* dominated the social and economic life of each village. The 'village community' is a euphemism for this powerful body of village oligarchs. The village community was not only an instrument of agrarian exploitation at the disposal of the Mughal state, it itself constituted a class of exploiters at the local level.[2] Many fascinating studies have followed on the village societies of different regions of medieval India.[3] Notable among these are researches on the structure of the agrarian economy and rural society of medieval eastern Rajasthan.[4] Nevertheless some significant aspects of the rural society still remain unaddressed. In this chapter we shall discuss some hitherto untouched aspects of the rural landscape. Our focus will be on the nomenclature, typology, and pattern of rural settlements. The ongoing formation of new village settlements coupled with the desertion of existing ones are part of this study. We shall also examine the extent of caste conflict over land and village boundaries. We end our inquiry into rural life by assessing the relative position of the constituent segments of village society.

We learn a great deal about the village from revenue records. The records refer to the village, the primary unit of assessment and collection of revenue, by the term *mauza*. The boundary of each village was properly demarcated and meticulously entered in these records known as *taqsim-dahsala, raqba-bandi, muwazana-i-dahsala* and *yaddashti-gaon*. These records provide area and revenue statistics of the villages. The village land was divided into the habitation (*abadi*), lanes (*rah*), saline area (*sor*), pasture (*vihar*), forest (*jungle*), water-tank (*bahani-talaab*), drains and canals (*nal-khal*), waste land (*banjar*), land under endowments (*udik/inam*) and the arable (*laik-zaraat*). The cultivable land of the village was divided into two categories, namely, land under cultivation (*bahaat*) and uncultivated arable (*parat*). The *bahaat* was cultivated in two seasons, i.e. *rabi* (spring) and *kharif* (autumn).[5] The cultivable land of the village was also classified into categories like *polaj* (land under continuous cultivation) and *chachar* (land kept fallow for the past few years).[6] Landmarks such as, rivers, tanks, forests, pastures, and *inam* or *udik* lands not only provide insights into rural geography but also give us an idea about the constituent elements of the villages.

New villages were settled on the *parat* land of existing settlements, often in the face of resistance by inhabitants of the latter.[7] In fact, struggles over the timing and method of the utilization of the *parat* land between the villagers and the revenue officials was quite common. The administration could press for the immediate cultivation of the *parat* land when the peasants wanted to preserve it for a future contingency. However, the administration ultimately succeeded in pressurizing villagers to accept new settlements on their *parat* land.[8] Strife amongst the peasants gave the administration an opportunity to so intervene. For instance, peasants of the Jat and Thathera castes had been living together in village Vasani of pargana Mandawar. At some stage the Jats decided to leave Vasani and settle a new village to be named Kalyanpur. The Thatheras protested about this, threatening to desert their own village. However, the Jats refused to go back to Vasani on the plea that 'there is no tradition among Jats to live in a village dominated by other caste'.[9] Ultimately the local officials managed somehow to persuade both castes to live in separate settlements.

Boundary disputes (*kankar ki khenchal*) between two or more neighbouring villages were quite frequent.[10] Such disputes were either settled by the local officials or arbitrated by the *bhomias* or the *panch-patels* of adjacent villages.[11] A boundary dispute between two adjacent villages could involve many other villages of the locality. In course of time, if the disputants happened to belong to different castes, such disputes were transformed into veritable caste wars. In such circumstances the initial cause of the dispute would well be forgotten and the administration's sole concern would be somehow to contain the spread of the accumulating tension. Two such villages, namely, Dhawani-bujurg of pargana Hindaun and Kemari of pargana Udai had a border dispute since the beginning of the eighteenth century. The cultivators of these villages belonged to the Mina and Gujar castes respectively. By 1733 the conflict had spread to many neighbouring villages. Both parties got the backing of their respective castes in a large number of villages. In all, 19 villages of pargana Hindaun, 6 of Bhusawar, 4 of Toda Bhim, 2 of Abhaneri and many villages of pargana Bayana and Udai participated in this tussle. The immediate fall-out of such disputes was the considerable loss of cultivation in the affected villages.[12] Our evidence shows that such caste/village conflicts tended to subside in the event of natural calamities and strict official action. If left unresolved, the dormant tensions resurfaced with the return of normalcy. However, to portray the relationship between castes and villages as one of perpetual conflict would be untrue to the social temper of the times. On the contrary, the sentiments of lasting brotherhood with occasional rivalry were the twin features of the rural landscape inhabited by many different castes

The villages were mostly named after rulers or officials or the original colonizers.[13] It is interesting to note that caste had a bearing on many place names. A caste suffix could be tagged on to the name of a village after its dominant agriculturist caste. This, however, seems to have been the practice with only peasant communities as is evident from the villages listed in Table 1.1.[14]

TABLE 1.1: VILLAGE NAMES IN FIVE PARGANAS

Name of the village	*Pargana*
1. Pali Mina	Bayana
2. Virbhan Gujar	Bayana
3. Malai Jat	Bayana
4. Malai Gujar	Bayana
5. Khalilpur Meo	Ao
6. Fatehpur Meo	Ao
7. Sahipur Meo	Ao
8. Norangwas Gujar	Toda Bhim
9. Norangwas Mina	Toda Bhim
10. Chalai Mina	Toda Bhim
11. Chalai Gujar	Toda Bhim
12. Ranapara Mina	Toda Bhim
13. Ranapara Gujar	Toda Bhim
14. Kaluhar Jat	Hindaun
15. Kaluhar Gujar	Hindaun
16. Kaluhar Mina	Hindaun
17. Kheri Gujar	Hindaun
18. Gawra Mina	Hindaun
19. Nagla Mina	Hindaun
20. Nagla Jat	Hindaun
21. Vai Jat	Hindaun
22. Raipur Jat	Hindaun
23. Singhan Jat	Hindaun
24. Sikroda Jat	Hindaun
25. Sikroda Mina	Hindaun
26. Sikroda Gujar	Hindaun
27. Khohra Mula	Bhusawar
28. Dehni Mina	Bhusawar
29. Dehni Gujar	Bhusawar

There is an obvious caste imprint on the nomenclature of these villages. It may be stressed here that such villages were usually named after the dominant peasant caste. But we also come across villages which were inhabited by more than one peasant caste. Such villages consisted of habitats called *pattis* with clear lines of demarcation. Each *patti* was known either by the caste of its inhabitants or the name of its founder. For example, village Lohsil of pargana Bahatri was divided into *patti* Brahman and *patti* Gujar. Village Rajpur Khara of the same pargana consisted of *patti* Brahman and *patti* Mina.[15] The *qasba* settlement was also bifurcated on similar lines. For instance *qasba* Hindaun consisted of *patti* Jat and *patti* Kayasth.[16] Similarly, *qasba* Wazirpur was bifurcated into *patti* Jat and *patti* Khaildar.[17] *Qasba* Mandawer was divided into *patti* Sukhram and *patti* Pahlad.[18] Many villages had *pattis* bearing the names of their original founders. Thus village Brahmanvas of pargana Udai was divided into *patti* Jodha and *patti* Tarachand, both of whom had jointly founded this village.[19] Another village known as Kishorepur was bifurcated into *patti* Narad and *patti* Kirparam.[20]

The existence of multi-caste villages divided into *pattis* are too numerous to be mentioned here. However, it may be emphasized that there are many instances when some *pattis* broke away from the parental village and morphed into independent settlements. This trend is apparent in pargana Naharkhoh, where eight villages, though known as *pattis*, had attained the status of independent settlements.[21] The separation of these *pattis* and their subsequent upgradation into villages could not have been a smooth affair, if we go by the case of village Vasani, discussed above.

With the diminishing allegiance of the Kachhwaha ruler to the Mughal emperor, a new pattern in the system of naming of villages can be discerned in the Jaipur territories. This change coincided with the growing influence of the militant Ramanandis in the Kachhwaha court and its rituals.[22] From the reign of Sawai Jai Singh onwards, new village settlements tended to be named after some Vaishnava deity. For instance in pargana Fagi, 5 out of 32 villages had names showing Vaishnava affiliations.[23] When two new villages were settled in pargana Jalalpur in 1735, one of them was named Nandgaon, the other Barsana.[24] Another settlement, founded in 1737 in pargana Lalsot was named Govindpura.[25] The extent of change in nomenclature needs to be further investigated, but it appears to be part of a broader shift in the political culture of the Jaipur State.

In the *arsatthas* the villages have been classified as *raiyati* and *taalluqa*. The peasants of the *raiyati* villages could pay their land revenue directly to the pargana officials, whereas the peasants of the *taalluqa* villages paid their revenue through a contracting *bhomia* known as *taalluqdar*.[26] Thus the position of the *taalluqdar* in our region differed significantly from his counterparts in Awadh and Bengal.[27] *Taalluqa* villages were not ubiquitous. The proportion of the *raiyati* and *taalluqa* villages also varied from pargana to pargana and from year to year.

Pargana Toda Bhim was divided between the *raiyati* and *taalluqa* villages. All the *taalluqdars* were of the Kalyanot lineage of the Kachhwaha Rajputs. From 1712 to 1720 the number of the *taalluqa* villages fluctuated, between 82 and 176.[28] The largest *taalluqa* of Chhattar Singh Kalyanot comprised 43 villages while the smallest consisted of just one village.

In 1729 the *taalluqa* villages were detached from Toda Bhim and a new pargana – Paota – was created.[29] The new pargana was largely inhabited by peasants of the Gujar caste. The remainder that stayed in Toda Bhim were *raiyati* villagers, preponderantly Mina by caste. Apparently such a division of a pargana located at the border of Braj and Dundhar, was meant to check recurring boundary feuds between Gujars and Minas. The bifurcation of Toda Bhim could also have been done to pre-empt the extension of Kalyanot control over the *raiyati* villages. In pargana Chatsu where the Rajawats had extensive zamindaris, Sangram Singh Rajawat had emerged as a *taalluqdar* of 32 villages.[30] In pargana Kol (Aligarh) Amar Singh Chauhan's *taalluqa* comprised 250 villages out of a total of 449.[31] Kishan Singh Naruka was the sole *taalluqdar* of the entire pargana of Banawar.[32] The Jats, Kalyanots, and Narukas had their respective *taalluqas* in pargana Sonkhar etc.[33] In pargana Bhusawar there were 5 *taalluqa* and 56 *raiyati* villages in 1733.[34] In Hindaun Raja Kanwar Pal Jadon of Karoli was the *taalluqdar* of 12 villages.[35] The area around Thoon has been mentioned as *taalluqa-i-zamindari* of Churaman Jat.[36] Thus it is clear that *taalluqa* villages were not confined to a few parganas. These were extensive units and widely spread. The conversion of a *raiyati* village into a *taalluqa* was opposed by the peasants and *patels*. It seems that the local officials too did not favour an increase in the number of *taalluqa* villages. The *amil* of Udai expressed his reservations when many erstwhile *raiyati* villages were transferred to the Panchanot *taalluqdars*.[37] On the other hand some villages were also taken away from the *taalluqdars* and declared *raiyati* under continuous peasant and *patel* pressure.[38]

The territorial boundaries of the parganas as delineated by the imperial administration had come under various kinds of stress. First, the Amber rulers began to acquire multiple rights such as *jagir, ijara, bhom,* and *faujdari* in the proximity of their hereditary dominion (*watan*), as a direct spin-off of the Jat and other revolts. These developments gave them a free hand to alter the pargana boundaries and fortify their hold over vast territories. Second, the increasing incidence of *shirkat* (mixed) as opposed to *darobast* (complete) assignments of the parganas also enabled the Amber rulers to tamper with the original boundaries. A comparative study of some of these parganas shows that the number of villages in them kept changing largely as a result of administrative decisions at the local level. Their number as recorded in the *arsatthas* and *arzdashts* would help us to throw some light on this subject. The numerical variation of villages in seven parganas, over a period of more than half a century, is given below to examine if any trends are visible.

TABLE 1.2: CHANGING NUMERS OF VILLAGES IN SEVEN PARGANAS

Pargana	*Year*	*Number of villages*[39]
Khohri	1663 to 1753	+ 9
Toda Bhim	1693 to 1756	–22
Bahatri	1665 to 1755	+73
Hindaun	1712 to 1755	–30
Wazirpur	1712 to 1748	constant
Udai	1712 to 1750	constant
Pahari	1716 to 1743	constant

These figures clearly show the existence of three conflicting tendencies. Whereas in three parganas the number of villages was constant, the remaining four parganas show both increase and decrease. Before a separate year-wise break-up of villages for each of these parganas is given, the causes responsible for the rise or fall in the number of village settlements need to be addressed.

New villages were settled by bringing in peasants from different areas, a slow and desultory process. As soon as a new village was settled, it was immediately entered in the village list of the *arsatthas*.[40] A new village was founded but rarely, and not all villages thus settled could endure for long, owing perhaps to lack of economic viability. Very often a small village would be tagged on to a larger one for the revenue assessment. Such villages have been entered as *dakhali* in the *arsatthas*. In the course of time they were either absorbed by the original ones, or collapsed, being unsustainable. A *dakhali* village seldom morphed into an *asli* village. The revenue figures of such villages do not show much increase on account of the addition of the *dakhali* to the *asli* villages, and their disappearance was phenomenal. Such were the *dakhali* villages of parganas Hindaun and Toda Bhim, which collapsed after a few years. Thus in 1693 pargana Toda Bhim comprised 245 villages, 224 *asli* and 21 *dakhali*. By the end of 1712 the *dakhali* villages had disappeared and there remained only the 224 *asli* villages in the pargana.[41] Similarly, in 1712 pargana Hindaun also contained 36 *dakhali* villages in its total of 279. By the end of 1717 the *dakhali* villages had given way and there remained the 243 original villages in the pargana.[42] Both the parganas were rocked by massive uprisings during this period.

Apart from the founding of new villages, the number of villages in a pargana increased as a result of the transfer of villages from another pargana. Thus the total number of villages of pargana Hindaun went up from 244 to 247 in 1739 as three villages of pargana Machilpur were incorporated into it.[43] The phenomenal increase in the size of pargana Bahatri was also due to such administrative reshuffling. This pargana had 261 villages in 1665.[44] After twenty years the number went up to 317.[45] This impressive increase of 56 villages is not due to the settling of new villages but because; most of these villages were detached from adjacent parganas and added to Bahatri. For example 8 villages of pargana Umarni and 5 villages of pargana Harsana were merged with Bahatri in 1690 and 1701 respectively.[46] This shows that the real cause in the increase of villages of Bahatri was due to its territorial expansion and not the rise of new settlements. Between 1685 and 1708 the number of *dakhali* villages of Bahatri increased from 23 to 25 villages.[47] In the remaining three parganas, Udai, Pahari, and Wazirpur, the total number of villages remained constant and the ratio between the *asli* and *dakhali* also continued to be the same. The continuity of the *dakhali* villages in these parganas also suggests their comparative viability, contrary to the trend in the other two parganas discussed above. This could be the result of the restoration of partial peace in these parganas. A separate year-wise break-up of the villages of seven parganas is given in Table 1.3 to bring into relief the emergent pattern.

Clearly, in most of the parganas the number of deserted villages was large. In fact it was always much larger than the new settlements in any of these parganas. In each pargana there were more currently deserted (*viran*) as compared to previously deserted (*sanwat-viran*) villages.[48] Every year crops failed in many parganas due to natural or man-made causes. Most of the currently deserted villages remained uncultivated, despite the endeavour of administrators to

TABLE 1.3: NUMBERS OF VILLAGES IN DIFFERENT YEARS IN SEVEN PARGANAS

(a) PARGANA KHOHRI

Year	*Total no. of villages*	*Asli*	*Dakhali*	*Deserted*	*Wadh**
1666	333	276	57	6	Not known
1711	342	262	80	27	Not known
1724	342	263	79	27	Not known
1735	342	264	78	27	1
1753	342	264	78	1	10

* *Wadh* means the village allotted to a trooper.

(b) PARGANA WAZIRPUR

Year	*Total no. of villages*	*Asli*	*Dakhali*	*Deserted*	*Rebel*
1712	19	–	–	3	2
1721	19	18	1	2	–
1745	19	17	2	–	–
1748	19	17	2	1	–

(c) PARGANA BAHATRI

Year	*Total no. of villages*	*Asli*	*Dakhali*	*Deserted*	*Udiki**
1665	261	238	23	–	–
1685	317	290	26	–	–
1686	226	202	24	–	–
1689	319	–	26	–	–
1690	327	–	–	–	–
1696	321	294	26	–	–
1697	321	294	26	9	2
1701	325	–	–	–	–
1702	327	–	–	–	–
1703	331	–	–	–	–
1705	334	309	25	–	–
1706	331	–	–	–	–
1708	334	308	25	–	4

*Villages assigned in revenue-free grants.

(d) PARGANA PAHARI

Year	Total no. of villages	Asli	Dakhali	Deserted	Rebel	Wadh
1716	209	194	15	7	–	–
1724	209	194	15	22	3	–
1726	209	194	15	30	–	–
1736	209	194	15	29	18	–
1741	209	194	15	21	–	1
1743	209	194	15	41	–	1
1747	209	194	15	–	–	–

(e) PARGANA HINDAUN

Year	Total no. of villages	Asli	Dakhali	Deserted	Rebel	Udiki	Wadh
1712	279	243	36	18	17	12	–
1717	–	243	–	10	–	20	–
1718	–	243	–	16	–	24	–
1720	–	243	–	11	–	24	–
1725	–	243	–	13	–	24	–
1733	–	243	–	19	–	24	–
1739	271	244	–	11	–	23	4
1746	250	247	–	13	–	26	8
1747	250	247	–	15	–	26	10
1755	250	247	–	3	–	26	12

(f) PARGANA TODA BHIM

Year	Total no. of villages	Asli	Dakhali	Udiki	Deserted	Wadh
1693	245	224	21	1	29	–
1712	224	–	–	1	3	–
1721	223	–	–	4	3	–
1728	223	–	–	3	4	–
1729	223	–	–	3	6	–
1730	223	–	–	3	3	–
1731	223	–	–	3	4	–
1732	223	–	–	3	2	–
1733	223	–	–	3	9	–
1735	223	–	–	3	3	4
1756	223	–	–	3	6	6

(g) PARGANA UDAI

Year	*Total no. of villages*	Asli	Dakhali	*Deserted*	Udiki	*Rebelious*	Wadh
1712 (*rabi*)	153	131	20	16	1	–	–
1712 (*kharif*)	153	131	20	18	1	9	–
1713	153	131	20	18	1	24	–
1714	153	131	20	16	1	–	–
1716	153	131	20	15	2	–	–
1718	153	131	20	7	2	–	–
1736	151	131	20	13	2	–	2
1738	151	131	20	2	2	–	–
1744	153	131	20	5	3	–	3
1750	–	–	–	2	–	–	–

settle *pahis* or *wadhdars* in some of them to carry on the cycle of agricultural production. This period witnessed a phenomenal increase in the ranks of the *pahis* and *wadhdars*. This was due perhaps to the desertion of villages on some scale. In the absence of original inhabitants of a village, its land was earmarked to such *pahis* who were willing to cultivate the deserted lands. In 1664, the entire land of 32 villages of pargana Khohri were cultivated by the *pahis*.[49] Out of the 63 deserted villages of pargana Malarna, 19 were cultivated by the *pahis*.[50] Similarly in pargana Kotla, *pahis* cultivated the lands of the 64 villages that had been abandoned by the original cultivators.[51] When pargana Pahari was assigned to the Amber ruler in 1689 it was totally deserted. For its rehabilitation, he ordered the *amils* of Pahari to bring peasants from Khohri. While some settlers originally belonged to Pahari, a large number were brought from Khohri in the capacity of *pahis*.[52] Some villages remained deserted for about a decade in pargana Tonk. During this decade most of these village lands were cultivated by the *pahi* peasants.[53] Thus the temporary arrangements made to cultivate the land of deserted villages during the intervening period is actually illustrative of large-scale abandonment of cultivation by the original peasants.

We thus conclude that the information contained in the *arsatthas* does not show a real increase in the number of new villages during our period. New settlements were not only insignificant but more than off-set by the cyclic occurrence of yearly desertions in most of the parganas. The size of a pargana contracted or expanded largely due to the changing boundaries of that pargana. It was perhaps owing to the growing prevalence of the *ijara* (revenue-farming) system that the boundaries of a pargana fixed by the central administration and those reorganized by the Amber rulers began to overlap.[54] On the other hand wherever there was a decrease in the number of villages it was either due to the complete collapse of the *dakhali* villages or peasant migration.

That the number of villages diminished considerably is evident from the *arsatthas* of various parganas. Other evidence also corroborates the unending phenomenon of desertion of villages and declining cultivation, a definite setback to agricultural production. Thus the *jama* of parganas Nainwai,[55] Dausa[56] and Sanganer[57] declined substantially. While the annual *hasil* of pargana Malarna declined somewhat, that of Mehmdabad came down to 42 per cent of its *kamil* (optimum) year's production.[58] The *amil* of pargana Malarna reported in 1694 that 'three to four peasants were absconding each day from every village'.[59] This trend continued upto 1703 when only 50 villages of the pargana were left populated and the remainder were completely ruined.[60] Large-scale peasant migrations took place from almost every pargana. A large number of peasants abandoned their fields in parganas Kiroli, Sironj, Kalibhit, and Handia and migrated to the Ganga-Yamuna *Doab*.[61] Peasant migrations from many other parganas such as Toda Bhim, Bahatri, Tonk, Pahari, Salawad, Chatsu, Boli, Jalalpur, and Khohri were reported very frequently.[62] The following report written in 1694 by the *amil* of pargana Bahatri sums up the general condition in the countryside:

> Owing to the failure of rain the peasantry is miserable (*dudli*) throughout the country. There is no *bohra* (moneylender) to be seen in the villages to advance loans to the needy peasants. The *bohras* who are present in some places are refusing to advance agricultural loans to the indigent (*nadar*) peasants. Hence peasants are migrating from those villages daily due to an acute shortage of foodgrain. Unless the *rahdari* cess is fully abolished for the time being, grain from other regions cannot be expected. [63]

The result was that village after village became depopulated. This is clearly evident from the fact that 62 out of 321 villages of pargana Bahatri were totally deserted in 1697.[64] Many villages of pargana Tonk remained deserted for about 8 to 10 years.[65] The desertion of villages by the peasants of Chatsu continued upto 1718.[66] The reports of such considerable migration of the peasants started pouring in from around 1660 and continued upto 1730 without any let-up. The causes of these migrations leading to desertions of villages were deep and varied and will be discussed in a subsequent chapter. Here it would suffice to say that the causes were both natural and man-made, though heavily weighted in favour of the latter.

The net result of these migrations/desertions was a depletion of the peasant labour force in many parganas. Fields that were under the plough were overrun by weeds. The *jama* declined, so naturally did the *hasil*. Such a situation eventually alarmed the rulers. Face to face with diminishing revenue, the administration launched a vigorous programme of resettling the abandoned villages through various inducements, one of which was providing of immediate financial help from the *bohras* or the state treasury. Assurances were given to the migrant peasants. Errands were sent to *chaudhuris* and *qanungos* to bring back the scattered peasants of their respective areas. In 1665 *qanungos* and *patels* of four parganas were sent to *suba* Malwa province to bring back the migrant peasants.[67] An year earlier 2279 peasants with a total number of 8142 bullocks were settled in pargana Nainwai.[68] It may be noted here that these peasants had to depend largely on external financial assistance for resettling. About 45.30 per cent of them obtained loans from the *bohras*; the state *taqavi* of Rs 7,000 enabled 29.00 per cent peasants to resettle. Only 25.70 per cent peasants could mobilize their own resources to start afresh.[69] and institutional support was crucial for any recovery. Similarly a *taqavi* loan of Rs 7,000 was provided by the administration in pargana Malpura to enable the peasants to resettle.[70] In parganas Amber and Fagi the administration spent a considerable amount of money in sinking 400 and 150 wells respectively, to enable the poverty stricken peasants to tide over the ravages of drought.[71] In all the three parganas namely, Dausa, Amber, and Fagi, the land of the deserted villages was temporarily allotted to the *pahi* peasants for cultivation. In 1694, the *amils* of pargana Toda Bhim launched a massive programme of rehabilitation.[72] The *amils* of Bahatri specially sought the help of the *chaudhuris* and *qanungos* to rehabilitate the pargana.[73] Many peasants and *mahajans* were brought to *qasba* Sanganer and settled there. In 1697 about 633 families were settled in the *qasba*, of nearly 369 families came from other parganas and here settled afresh.[74] The Amber officials undertook to rehabilitate 25 partially deserted villages of pargana Dausa after taking them on *ijara* from the imperial *jagirdars*.[75] Similarly the *patels* and *paltis* of pargana Tonk who had earlier migrated were brought back. Thus about 7 villages that were previously cultivated by the *pahis* were now made *chhapparband* (permanently settled).[76]

Speedy desertion and gradual recovery are evident in pargana Pahari. When this pargana was assigned to the Amber Raja, only 14 villages were populated. His *amils* succeeded in resettling 100 villages immediately thereafter, and fixed a target of repopulating the remaining 90 villages by bringing over peasants of the Ahir caste from pargana Khohri, contiguous to Pahari.[77] It appears that the peasants of Pahari had earlier migrated to Khohri.

This process of desertion/resettlement was an ongoing feature of social and economic life of the peasantry. Moreover, if the administration succeeded in resettling some deserted villages, others elsewhere would be abandoned. This unending cycle of desertion and resettlement was to continue so long as the underlying causes leading to desertion persisted. The speed with which the migrant peasants were brought back to their original places shows that the range of mobility of such peasants was within the not-too-distant countryside. They normally moved from one pargana to another irrespective of whether the latter was a *jagir*, or *khalisa* land, or a zamindari, or a *raiyati* village. Only in the eventuality of a severe and prolonged famine did people move much beyond their immediate locale. The aggravation of various resource crises forced the exodus of the peasant communities to lands and climes to which they could not adapt; hence the inclination to return home. Nonetheless such large scale movements of people widened the network of their linkages with other agrarian regions.

It needs to be said that there are some documents which show an increase (*ijafa*) in the number of peasants, ploughs, and oxen. For example, in pargana Chatsu the number of peasants and oxen increased from 193 to 200 and 405 to 422 respectively in two consecutive years, i.e. 1665 and 1666.[78] Similarly in pargana Kotla the number of ploughs increased from 1,078 to 1,142 in 1666.[79] In yet another pargana, Chal Kalana, the number of ploughs owned by the *gavetis* went up from 103 to 114 in the year 1665.[80] A facile reading of these and such other documents may suggest a progressive trend of increase in the number of peasants and their assets. But placed in their context, these documents simply suggest a post-drought drive of resettling the parganas.

Most 'additions' were achieved in 1665-6. These years were

preceded by the severe drought of 1660-4.[81] This calamity caused large-scale peasant migrations from various parganas. When the severity of the drought eased, the peasants started coming back home along with their ploughs which naturally 'enhanced' the total number of peasants and their assets.

VILLAGE SOCIETY

Those who participated in agricultural production and paid revenue to the state or its nominees were known by the generic term of *raiyat*. *Raiyat* actually means 'subject', so that any subject of the empire would be a *raiyat*. However, its usage in Mughal literature and documents suggests that it denoted revenue paying cultivators including the zamindars. The peasantry comprised various sections demarcated by economic strength and social status. At the bottom of the hierarchy were low-caste landless agricultural workers who sold their labour for wages. This vast body of the rural poor fulfilled the labour requirements of the entire land-owning peasantry. Except for a few isolated cases, the landless rural poor were not allowed to own land for their own subsistence.[82] It is possible that the higher and middle caste peasants used the institution of caste as an instrument to bar the landless poor from acquiring land. Their labour was not in demand throughout the year, but it peaked at the time of sowing and harvesting, and so a reserve labour force had to be maintained. This was, perhaps, the basic reason for not allowing landless agricultural workers to own land even in the context of a favourable land–man ratio. Here it is significant to note that the Mughal state preferred not to disturb the caste system as it helped it 'generate larger revenues from the village and lower the wage cost in the cities'.[83] To enable all to acquire land for the subsistence of their family would imply a drastic change in the very system of production: extra, seasonal, labour would be expensive. A relatively egalitarian distribution of land corresponding to the labour potential of each peasant family in turn would necessitate a major social transformation. Besides, apart from seasonal employment in agriculture these low castes had their own ancestral occupations such as curing leather and scavenging.[84] In the village a large section engaged in the manufacture of a variety of agricultural implements and rendered other domestic services.[85] Their income was too meagre to figure prominently in the fiscal calculations of the state. Often enough it was their services and sometimes their products, rather than a contribution to taxes, that the dominant groups of the villages and state officials extracted *gratis*.[86] For all that, the economic condition of the great body of artisans and menials was miserable. Yet in our region their plight did not translate into anger against the Mughal State.

A rung above the landless wage earners there were the non-resident or migrant cultivators. As their holdings were constantly changing, they did not have security of tenure. They sold part of their labour to *chhapparband* (resident) cultivators with superior rights or those with large chunks of lands. They also rented draught animals and a significant amount of agricultural equipment from the rural rich and the village usurers.[87] They wandered from village to village and pargana to pargana in search of better leases. These peripatetic cultivators were known as *pahis*.[88] The *pahis* were mainly born of the depressed peasants of the third category, to which we shall return. The revenue officials invariably used these wandering peasants as a temporary substitute for runaway permanent peasantry.[89] They were offered slightly favourable or attractive terms of revenue rates but their connection with the land remained tenuous.[90] In these decades of economic downward slide and relative uncertainty in agricultural production, the number of *pahi* peasants was increasing, as has already been discussed. The *pahis* belonged to various castes. But on close scrutiny the documents tell us that a majority of the *pahis* came from the intermediate castes. In pargana Khohri out of 35 villages, 19 were cultivated by the Ahir *pahis* while 3 villages were cultivated by the *pahis* of Mina caste. The remaining 13 villages were under the plough of either Jat or Meo *pahis*.[91] All the *pahis* who were supposed to be brought to cultivate the land of the hundred villages of pargana Pahari belonged to the Ahir caste.[92] Though there were villages which were entirely cultivated by the *pahis*, their total number seldom exceeded that of the *gavetis*. A *yaddashti* of pargana Pindayan gives a total of 391 cultivators in 20 villages, of which 315 were *gavetis* and 76 *pahis*. Of these 20 villages, 5 had no *pahis*, and in the remaining 15 their number varied from 1 to 22. Thus the strength of the *pahis* in Pindayan was 19 per cent of the total number of cultivators.[93] And this is far from being an atypical example. The availability of *pahi* cultivators normally helped the village elite to maintain its hold over the original peasantry of the village. Their presence also enabled the administration to overcome its own predicament caused by the recurrent absconding of the *gaveti-paltis*. As the desolation of land proceeded on an increasing scale, and production plummetted, with which the state's revenue too declined, the role of the *pahis* became more crucial for recovery. The resort taken to the employment of *pahis* could never redeem the situation fully, and therefore was itself suggestive of the administration's desperation. Born of the ranks of a distressed peasantry, the *pahis* had to be offered concessions in the revenue rates, which was invariably 33 per cent as compared to the 40 to 50 per cent charged from the *gavetis*.[94] The mushrooming growth in the ranks of *pahis* could be the result of a gradual *pahi*-ization of the *gaveti-paltis*, specially those who belonged to the middle castes.

Above the *pahis* were those petty producers who were more or less self-sufficient as much as they did not hire out or hire in labour, and who lived at the subsistence level, though occasionally they contracted loans for purchasing agricultural equipment.[95] They formed the single largest stratum of the peasantry. Known as *gaveti-palti*, most of them belonged to the intermediate castes (Jats, Gujars, Ahirs, Minas and Malis).[96] In pargana Wazirpur out of a total number of 249 households in 4 big villages, the number of peasants belonging to this stratum was 186, i.e. 76 per cent.[97] In *qasba* Chatsu they constituted about 50 per cent of the total peasant population.[98] It is this section of peasantry that was the pivot of the production process, and it bore the main brunt of the fiscal pressure of the state. It formed the fulcrum of the Mughal economy. Unable to bear the growing economic pressure of the state, a large number of its members became migrants, forced to join the ranks of the *pahis*, or else the army of a rebellious zamindar.

At the apex of the rural hierarchy were the owners of large holdings. This group was characterized by a regular hiring of labour and leasing out of livestock and equipment that yielded a relatively large income. Known as *gharuhalas*, they either belonged to the higher castes (Brahmans, Rajputs, Mahajans), or occupied a pivotal position in the revenue administration and village society. They were assessed at relatively concessional rates.[99] It is essential to mention here that only those Rajputs who were armed and rendered services to the state on demand enjoyed revenue concessions. Similarly, only those Brahmans were entitled to revenue concessions who used to recite the *Gayatri mantra*.[100] This appears to be an exceptionally local custom. The *gharuhala* cultivation could not be carried on with the help of family labour alone. The extensive nature of the *gharuhala* holdings entailed large scale employment of wage labour. For example in pargana Hindaun a *qanungo* named Jhamraj had 178 *bighas* of *gharujot* spread over 12 villages. Obviously members of his family could not go to each village to cultivate their fields.[101] Instances of this kind are too numerous to be enumerated.

The dominant section of rural society were those large-scale producers who depended entirely on hired labour. The zamindars, *qanungos*, *chaudhuris* and *patels* termed *gharuhala* cultivators largely belonged to this section of the peasantry.[102] Their holdings were assessed at the lowest current rates of revenue demand.[103] Whenever some peasants abandoned their fields under conditions of economic depression, the *gharuhala* tended to convert the former's land into their *gharujot,* for which they claimed revenue concessions.[104] The state therefore put curbs on the expansion of privileged land-holdings, apprehending a decline in total revenue.[105] Thus the conversion of high revenue-yielding landholdings (*gaveti-palti*) into low revenue-yielding holdings (*gharuhala*) was strictly forbidden. Given the rationale, it is unlikely that this had been permitted earlier. On the other hand such holdings were encouraged as largely depended for cultivation on family labour.

The *gharuhala* peasants were socially and economically the most dominant class in the villages. Since they had the maximum say in the day-to-day management of village affairs, they controlled all the sinews of political power in the village society.[106] Historically this class was attuned to the working of the Mughal land revenue administration. The *gaveti-paltis* who largely belonged to the intermediate castes may be termed a middle class peasantry. Being the principle source of revenue extraction in the countryside, this stratum frequently attracted the attention of the medieval rulers. Whenever an *amin, amil* or *faujdar* was appointed, he was clearly instructed to work with a view to '*kifayat sarkar* and *rifayat raiyati*' (financial interest of the state and welfare of the peasantry.[107] It is a different matter that such directives seldom alleviated the problems of the peasantry and remained a charade. The *pahis* about whom much has been said in the preceding pages, constitute a distinct group of peasants. Buffeted by the uncertainties of the times, theirs was a proliferating class. They were used by the revenue officials as a source of labour when there was a dearth of cultivators in the villages. At the lowest rung of rural society were the *kamins* or *naniponis* who constituted the class of agricultural labourers.

Dilbagh Singh has grouped the entire peasantry into two broad categories, privileged (*riyayati*) and unprivileged (*raiyati*).[108] His categorization largely follows caste lines which, in his view, corresponded to the class status of the respective sections also. But our evidence suggests that only a micro-section of the upper caste cultivators were treated as *riyayatis*. The largest number of *gharuhala riyayatis* belonged to a heterogeneity of castes. Together they constituted the class of the rural rich, with considerable influence and affluence in the countryside.

The land that was cultivated by the *wadhars*[109] and *vasidars* needs separate treatment because these cultivators existed at the margins of village society. The holdings of wadhdars and *vasidars* could not remain under continuously cultivation as they were transferred frequently. The official policy was to allot the *parat* land of a village to *wadhdars* for cultivation.[110] Local administration frequently resorted to the settling of *wadhdars* in the deserted villages. In pargana Nainwai many *wadhdars* were recruited and each one of them was allotted 500 *bighas* of land for cultivation.[111] In another year 200 *wadhdars* were allotted 500 *bighas* of land each in various parganas. They had to pay an annual *peshkash* of Rs 10 on each 100 *bighas* of land.[112] As 500 *bighas* were far too big a field for one peasant family, the *wadhars* usually hired labour to cultivate it. It is not clear from the documents whether the entire allotted area was cultivated, or a part of it. Many villages were entirely allotted to the *wadhars* as has already been shown in Table 1.3. As already stated, land was also allotted to *wadhdars* in those villages which were disobedient. When a refractory *bhomia* of village Paharya of Chatsu was evicted in 1683, its 9,550 *bighas* of land was allotted to 25 *wadhdars*. Land allotted to the *wadhdars* was treated as their *gharujot*.[113] The actual peasants of the villages where *wadhdars* were allotted *parat* or *banjar* land did not welcome it, if we go by the report of the *amil* of pargana Chatsu.[114] In fact the function of the *wadhdars* was to maintain law and order in the area and cultivate the *parat* land of the village. They were expected to establish *thanas* and work under the charge of the local *faujdar* and *kotwal*. Functionally, they acted as soldiers-cum-loyal cultivators.

Most of the parganas under discussion were either under the *jagir* or the *ijara* of the Amber rulers. The latter would allot villages to their troopers, as is evident from the *arsattha*' list of *alufajagirs* (salary assignments). These assignees were also allowed to settle their own tenants on the *parat* land and have it cultivated. Such allotments were known as *vasi,* and those who cultivated this *vasi* were called *vasidars.* The cases of these *vasis* are too numerous to be mentioned here. It may, however, be noted that the status of the *vasi* was equal to *gharujot,* and its cultivators were by and large wage earners.[115] Like the *wadhdars*, the *jagirdars* were also officially allowed to settle their *vasidars* on *parat* land and not on peasants' land.[116] A considerable amount of money had to be spent in organizing a *vasi.*[117] The assignees were permitted to settle *vasidars* on *parat* land to make up for their dwindling income. When the allotted village was fully repopulated, the *vasi* could be disbanded. Besides, with the lapse of *jagir*, the *vasi* also ceased to exist. There is not much evidence to suggest that the land cultivated by the *vasidars* was a growing phenomenon. However, there is plentiful evidence showing more and more land being allotted to the *wadhdars*, necessitated by the rising number of *thanas* in the countryside. For example in 7 villages of pargana Sonkhar, out of 6,926 *bighas* of land the peasants cultivated 2,530 *bighas*, the remaining 4,396 being cultivated by the *wadhdars.*[118] The state frequently sent instructions to pargana officials to allot the uncultivated land of villages to the *wadhdars*, but such allotments did not lead to a permanent acquisition of land by *wadhdars*.

This broad vista of the rural landscape sketched here shows that the countryside was inhabited by miscellaneous castes, each competing for more space. In the seventeenth century no uniform pattern of founding and naming of village settlements was followed. But during the eighteenth century a new trend, naming villages after Vaishnava religious deities, can be detected. The local administration, expressly concerned with revenue collection, classified the villages into binary combinations of *asli* vs *dakhali* and *raiyati* vs *taalluqa.* Life in the villages was rife with friction and tension, arising out of caste and class differences. However, the domineering presence of an intrusive administration had a mitigating impact on rural conflict. Recurring famine and increasing fiscal pressure experienced from the state invariably forced large-scale movements of peasant communities. In such circumstances individual peasants and peasant groups exhibited considerable solidarity, thereby reinforcing the ambience of amity in the villages.

NOTES

1. Louis Dumont, 'The village community from Munro to Maine', *Contributions to Indian Sociology*, 1966, pp. 67-89; and S.N. Mukherjee, 'The Idea of Village Community and British Administrators', *Enquiry*, n.s. III(3), 1971, pp. 56-67.
2. Irfan Habib, *Agrarian System*, pp. 123-60. Only the revised version of Habib's thesis on the Indian village community is given here.
3. N.A. Siddiqi, *Land Revenue Administration under the Mughals (1700-1750)*, Asia Publishing House, Bombay, 1970; Indu Banga, *Agrarian System of the Sikhs: Late Eighteenth Century and Early Nineteenth Century*, Manohar, Delhi, 1978; H. Fukazawa, *The Medieval Deccan: Peasants, Social Systems and States, Sixteenth to Eighteenth Centuries*, Oxford University Press, Delhi, 1991 and A.R. Kulkarni, 'The Indian Village with special reference to medieval Deccan (Maratha country)', General Presidential Address, *Indian History Congress*, Delhi, 1992.
4. Satish Chandra, *Medieval India, Society, the Jagirdari Crisis and the Village*, Delhi, 1982; S.P. Gupta, *The Agrarian System of Eastern Rajasthan (c. 1650-1750)*, Manohar, Delhi, 1986; and Dilbagh Singh, *The State, Landlords and Peasants: Rajasthan in the Eighteenth Century*, Delhi, Manohar, 1990. All three scholars had published papers on village society much earlier. As those papers are reproduced in these books, earlier references are not given here.
5. *Taqsim pandrehsala*, pargana Antela Bhabhra, vs 1706-20 (1649-63); *Taqsim dahsala*, pargana Antela Bhabhra, vs 1756-65 (1699-1708); *Taqsim dahsala*, pargana Bahatri, vs 1761-70 (1704-13); *Taqsim dahsala*, pargana Punkhar, vs 1787-98 (1730-41); *Taqsim dahsala*, pargana Udai, vs 1791-1800 (1734-43) and *Muwazana dahsala*, pargana Hindaun, vs 1790-99 (1733-42).
6. *Amber Record* dt. Kati Sudi 5, vs 1722/1665.
7. For instance a new village called Kalyanpur was carved out of the *parat* land of five villages (Muhammadpur, Jasore, Khohra, Khidrava, and Gahlavata) of pargana Sonkhar. When 20 Mina peasants of village Virdodh of pargana Toda Bhim came to settle in the new village, they were attacked by about 300 Jat peasants led by the *patels* of Muhammadpur. See Amber Record dt. Vaisakh Vadi 11, vs 1723/1666.
8. *Arzdashts* dt. Vaisakh Sudi 12, vs 1702/1645 and Vaisakh Sudi 8, vs 1722/1665. A new village named Kalyanpur was settled on 2,360 *bighas* of land of which 900 *bighas* were etached from Dewalda, 1,460 from Kadlodha. Bihari Mina brought a group of peasants with 41 ploughs from pargana Lalsot and settled in the new village without any opposition.
9. *Auzdasht* dt. Chet Sudi 1, vs 1721/1664 and Amber Record dt. Asadh Sudi 9, vs 1722/1665.
10. *Amber Records* dt. Chet Vadi 8, vs 1723/1666, Sawan Vadi 4, and 11, vs 1723/1666 and *Daftar Muwazana-Khurd* pargana Toda Bhim, vs 1791/1734.
11. Thus the border dispute between the villages of pargana Khohri and Ao was settled by the *Shiqdar*. It was the *Bhomias* who arbitrated the border dispute between the villages of pargana Lahsana and Fatehabad. See Amber Records dated Chet Vadi 8, vs 1723/1666 and Falgun Sudi 14, vs 1723/1666.
12. *Arsattha* pargana Hindaun, vs 1790/1733, *arsattha* pargana Bhusawar, etc. vs 1790/1733 and *arsattha* pargana Abhaneri, vs 1790/1733. Because of this

Mina-Gujar *fisad* (riot), the peasants of many villages ran away, leaving their fields uncultivated. In 6 villages of pargana Bhusawar alone, the state lost revenues to the extent of Rs 5,396.

13. There were villages called Akbarpur, Jahangirpur, Bishanpur, Jaisinghpur, Ramchandpur, Kalyanpur, and so on.
14. The names of these villages occur in the *arsatthas* of respective parganas.
15. *Arsattha* pargana Bahatri, VS 1783/1726.
16. *Arsattha* pargana Hindaun, VS 1778/1721.
17. *Arsattha* pargana Wazirpur, VS 1779/1722.
18. *Arsattha* pargana Pindayan, etc. VS 1772/1718.
19. *Arsattha* pargana Udai, VS 1769/1712.
20. *Arsattha* pargana Bahatri, VS 1783/1726.
21. *Arsattha* pargana Banawar, etc. VS 1748/1691. These villages were *pattis* Ratnu, Bihari, Dharbn, Ladbhan, Rawat, Sial, Sarang and Gujar.
22. According to Monika Horstmann the Kachhwaha rulers stopped expressing allegiance to the Mughal emperor around 1716. She has also given evidence showing the growing influence of the Ramanandis after 1730. See her 'Religious Dignitaries in the Court Protocol of Jaipur (mid-eighteenth to early nineteenth century)' in *Explorations in the History of South Asia*, pp. 139-55, ed. George Berbemer, Hermann Kulke, Tilman Frasch and Jurgen Lutt, Delhi, Manohar, 2001.
23. *Arsattha* pargana Fagi, VS 1778/1721. These villages were Mohanpur, Rampur, Kishanpur, Gokulpur, and Biharipur.
24. *Arsattha* pargana Jalalpur, VS 1792/1735.
25. *Arsattha* pargana Lalsot, VS 1794/1737.
26. S.P. Gupta, *Agrarian System of Eastern Rajasthan*, p. 117 and Dilbagh Singh, *State, Landlords and Peasants*, p. 36n.
27. For the position of *taalluqdar* in Awadh and Bengal see Irfan Habib, *Agrarian System*, pp. 211-12 and N.A. Siddiqi, *Land Revenue Administration under the Mughals (1700-1750)*, Bombay, 1970, pp. 26-28.
28. *Arsattha* pargana Toda Bhim (*kharif*), VS 1769/1712 and (*rabi*), VS 1776/1720. The total number of villages in Toda Bhim were 224.
29. *Arsattha* pargana Toda Bhim (*kharif*), VS 1786/1729.
30. *Arzdasht* dt. Asoj Vadi 7, VS 1751/1694.
31. *Arzdasht* dt. Chet Sudi 7, VS. 1751/1694.
32. *Arzdasht* dt. Asadh Sudi 14, VS *1760/1703*.
33. Ibid.
34. *Arsattha* pargana Bhusawar (*rabi*), VS 1790/1733.
35. *Arsattha* pargana Hindaun (*kharif*), VS 1770/1713.
36. Shiv Das Lakhnawi, *Shahnama Munawwar Kalam* (tr. S.H. Askari), Janaki Prakashan, Patna, 1980, p. 19.
37. *Arzdasht* dt. Asadh Sudi 13, VS 1740/1683.
38. For example three villages of Kanhi Ram *taalluqdar* were taken away from him and brought under *raiyati amal*. See *arsattha* pargana Toda Bhim (*rabi*), VS 1782/1725. The Mina-Gujar *fisad* of 1733-4 also forced many *taalluqdars* to give up their *taalluqas*. For example in four villages of Toda Bhim and three villages of pargana Sonkhar the *taalluqdars* gave up their claim. See *arsattha* pargana Bhusawar, etc. (*unhalu*), VS 1791/1734.

39. These figures have been culled from the *arsatthas* of the respective parganas.
40. *Arsatthas* pargana Bahatri, vs 1746/1689 and 1759/1702 specifically mention the names of newly settled villages. In other parganas too this practice was followed.
41. *Arsatthas* pargana Toda Bhim, vs 1750/1693 and 1769/1712.
42. *Arsatthas* pargana Hindaun, vs 1769/1712 and 1779/1717.
43. *Arsattha* pargana Hindaun, vs 1796/1739.
44. *Arsattha* pargana Bahatri, vs 1722/1665.
45. *Arsattha* pargana Bahatri, vs. 1742/1685.
46. *Arsatthas* pargana Bahatri, vs 1747/1690 and 1758/1701.
47. *Arsatthas* pargana Bahatri, vs 1742/1685 and 1765/1708.
48. In pargana Wazirpur 3 out of 19 villages were *sanwat-viran* while in pargana Malarna 50 out of 152 villages were *viran* in 1695. Out of a large number of deserted villages of pargana Udai, two were *sanvat-viran* for about 40 years.
49. *Arsattha* pargana Khohri, vs 1721/1664.
50. *Arsattha* pargana Malarna, vs 1754/1697.
51. *Arsattha* pargana Kotla, vs 1722/1665.
52. *Arzdasht* dt. Falgun Sudi 12, vs 1746/1689.
53. Amber Records dt. Asadh Sudi 13, vs 1740/1683.
54. In 1665 pargana Bahatri had 261 villages in it. By 1783 this number went upto 564. It is most unlikely that 303 new villages were settled in this pargana even during the long stretch of time between the two dates, for nearly 3 new villages every year is something our evidence otherwise does not support. Similarly pargana Chatsu had 266 villages in 1708. After an interval of 80 years this number went up to 415—an increase of 149 villages in 80 years, once again leaving one in considerable doubt. Both these parganas were with the Amber rulers for a long time. See also Gupta, *Agrarian System of Eastern Rajasthan*, pp. 11-12.
55. *Arzdasht* dt. Asadh Sudi 2, vs 1721/1664.
56. *Arzdasht* dt. Jeth Sudi 10, vs 1740/1683.
57. *Arzdasht* dt. Asadh Sudi 5, vs 1755/1698.
58. *Arzdasht* dt. Bhadwa Sudi 13, vs 1749/1692.
59. *Arzdasht* dt. Bhadwa Sudi 11, vs 1751/1694.
60. *Arzdasht* dt. Kati Sudi 14, vs 1760/1703.
61. *Arzdasht* dt. Vaisakh Sudi 14, vs 1722/1665.
62. *Arzdashts* dt. Falgun Sudi 3, vs 1740/1683; Asadh Sudi 13, vs 1749/1683; Falgun Vadi 9, vs 1749/1692; Sawan Vadi 13, vs 1650/1693; Asoj Vadi 7, vs 1751/1694; Falgun Sudi 15, vs 1752/1695 and Asadh Sudi 2, vs 1760/1703.
63. *Arzdasht* dt. Asoj Sudi 2, vs 1751/1694.
64. *Arzdasht* dt. Asadh Vadi 1, vs 1754/1697.
65. *Arzdasht* dt. Asadh Sudi 2, vs 1760/1703.
66. *Arzdasht* dt. Jeth Vadi 11, vs 1775/1718.
67. *Arzdasht* dt. Vaisakh Sudi 14, vs 1722/1665.
68. *Arzdasht* dt. Asadh Sudi 9, vs 1721/1664.
69. *Arzdasht* dt. Sawan Vadi 2, vs 1721/1664.
70. *Arzdasht* dt. Bhadwa Vadi 11, vs 1721/1664.
71. *Arzdasht* dt. Sawan Sudi 3, vs 1741/1684.
72. *Arzdasht* dt. Kati Sudi 10, vs 1751/1694.

73. *Arzdasht* dt. Asadh Vadi 1, vs 1754/1697 and Asadh Sudi 5, vs 1755/1698.
74. *Arzdasht* dt. Bhadwa Sudi 5, vs 1754/1697.
75. Ibid.
76. *Arzdasht* dt. Asadh Sudi 2, vs 1761/1704.
77. *Arzdasht* dt. Falgun Sudi 12, vs 1746/1689.
78. *Haqiqati Yaddashti Hal Bail* pargana Chatsu, vs 1723/1666.
79. *Yaddashti Raqba Hal*, pargana Kotla, *sarkar* Tijara, *suba* Shahjahanabad, vs 1723/1666.
80. *Yaddashti Haqiqati Hal,* pargana Chal Kalana, vs 1722/1665.
81. *Arzdasht* dt. Vaisakh Sudi 14, vs 1722/1665.
82. Out of 2,448 cultivators of pargana Chatsu only 2 were Chamars. Both Dunga Chamar of village Thali and Naraina Chamar of village Dahar owned 2 bullocks each. Similarly in pargana Kuthumbari one Chamar cultivated 7 *bighas* of land. The evidence suggests they were tenants, not proprietors. See *Yaddashti Haqiqati Hal Bail Jubani patel patwari,* pargana Chatsu, vs 1723/1666 and *arsattha* pargana Kuthumbari, vs 1774/1717. In these documents the cultivators have been written about as *asamis.*
83. Irfan Habib, 'Caste in Indian History', pp. 172-3.
84. Irfan Habib, *Agrarian System*, pp. 141-5. And Tapan Raychaudhury, 'The Agrarian System of Mughal India', *Enquiry*, Spring, 1965, pp. 92-121.
85. About 15 such castes have been mentioned in a list of persons fined in Kama: Mewati potters, barbers, and carpenters along with Deswali potters, barbers, and carpenters *arsattha* pargana Kama, vs 1826/1769.
86. Harbans Mukhia, 'Illegal Extortions from Peasants, Artisans and Menials in Eighteenth Century Eastern Rajasthan', *IESHR*, vol. XIV, no. 2, April-June 1977, pp. 231-45.
87. *Arzdashts* dt. Asoj Sudi 9 and 13, vs 1751/1694 and Kati Vadi 6, vs 1751/1694.
88. Satish Chandra, 'Some Aspects of the Indian Village Society in Northern India during the 18th Century', *The Indian Historical Review*, I(1), 1974, pp. 51-64; Dilbagh Singh, 'Caste and Structure of Village Society in Eastern Rajasthan during the Eighteenth Century', *IHR*, vol. 2, 1976, pp. 299-311.
89. Amber Records dt. Jeth Sudi 4, vs 1723/1666 and Asadh Sudi 1, vs 1784/1731.
90. *Chithis* dt. Asadh Vadi Amavasya, vs 1781/1724 and Vaisakh Sudi 13, vs 1798/1741.
91. *Arsattha* pargana Khohri, vs 1721/1664.
92. *Arzasht* dt. Falgun Sudi 12, vs 1746/1689.
93. *Yaddashti Hal Bail* pargana Pindayan, vs 1786/1726.
94. *Dastur amal* pargana Khohri, AM 1049-50/1642-43, Maujpur vs 1770/1713 and Udai, undated.
95. Dilbagh Singh, 'Role of Mahajans in the Rural Economy of Eastern Rajasthan during the Eighteenth Century', *Social Scientist*, May 1974.
96. *Yaddashti Hal Bail Jubani patel-patwari* pargana Chatsu, vs 1723/1666 and *Yaddashti Ghar* pargana Wazirpur, dt. vs 1786/1726.
97. *Yaddashti Ghar* pargana Wazirpur, dt. vs 1783/1726.
98. *Yaddashti Hal Bail Jubani patel-patwari* pargana Chatsu, dt. vs 1723/1666.

99. They paid land revenue at the rate of 25 to 33 per cent of the gross produce.
100. *Arzdasht* dt. Asoj Sudi 15, vs 1783/1726 and *Chithi* dt. Posh Vadi 6, vs 1784/1727. According to a *Chithi* written to the *amil* of pargana Tonk, dt. Vaisakh Vadi vs 1784/1711, one Keso Ram Sultanot had his *gharujot* in villages Karhami and Karhara. He was to keep one gun for each plough and serve at the fort of the *qasba* without any payment for 10 days. Similarly one Devi Ram Brahman had his *gharujot* in *qasba* Ajabgarh. He was entitled to revenue concessions so long as he continued reciting *Gayatri mantras*. See *Chithi* dt. Sawan Vadi 9, vs 1796/1739.
101. *Arsattha* pargana Hindaun (*kharif*) dt. vs 1770/1713. There are about 20 more such *qanungos* who had their *gharuhala* landholdings scattered in many villages.
102. *Jagirdars* were not cultivators by virtue of being *jagirdars*; if they cultivated land (and mostly sub-assignees did so), it was incidental to their *jagirdari* rights.
103. They had to pay 25 per cent of the gross produce.
104. Copy of *Parwanas* dt. Bhadwa Sudi 10 and Sawan Vadi 9, vs 1783/1726.
105. Copy of *Parwana* dt. Bhadwa Sudi 10, vs 1783/1726. See also Irfan Habib, *Agrarian System*, pp. 128 and 137.
106. Irfan Habib, *Agrarian System*, pp. 144-60. According to Habib the *panch-muqaddams* constituted the 'village community', an instrument of agrarian exploitation by the ruling class. Moreover, this oligarchy itself was a class of 'sub-exploiters'.
107. *Clilhis* dt. Asadh Vadi 7, vs 1782/1725 and Kati Vadi 9, vs 1786/1729. There are many more such *chithis* in the Rajasthan State Archives at Bikaner. The language of these 'directives' has a striking similarity with clause 3 of Aurangzeb's *farman* to Rasikdas. See Shireen Moosvi, 'Aurangzeb's *Farman* to Rasikdas on Problems of Revenue Administration, 1665', in Irfan Habib (ed.), *Medieval India I*, OUP, 1992, p. 203.
108. Dilbagh Singh, 'Caste and the Structure of Village Society in Eastern Rajasthan during the Eighteenth Century', pp. 299-311. Irfan Habib has doubted the use of the term *riyayati* (concessional rate-holders)in medieval revenue records. See his *Agrarian System*, p. 137n. But large number of *parwanas* putting curbs on the expansion of *riyayati* holdings are extant in the Rajasthan State Archives at Bikaner..
109. *Wadhar* appears to be a Rajasthani version of *wajhdars* i.e. officers holding *wajh* or territorial assignments in lieu of salary. See Irfan Habib, *Agrarian System*, p. 298-9n.
110. *Chithi* to the *amil*, pargana Pindayan, dt. Mah Sudi 12, vs 1795/1742.
111. *Arzdasht* dt. Bhadwa Vadi 11, vs 1721/1664.
112. Ibid.
113. Ibid.
114. *Chithi* to the *amil*, pargana Tonk, dt. Jeth Sudi 14, vs 1792/1735.
115. *Chithi* to the *faujdar*, pargana Ghazi-ka-Thana, dt. Posh Sudi 4, vs 1818/1761. In the *vasi* of one Brij Singh Rajawat, Kolis and Chamars were employed.

116. *Chithi* to the *amil* pargana Tonk, dt. Jeth Sudi 12, vs 1784/1727.
117. *Arzdasht*, dt. Sawan Vadi 9, vs 1783/1726. Kishan Singh Naruka spent 5,000 *mans* of grain and settled his *vasidars* in village Kaithwar of Khohri. After some *vasidars* had left his village, the remaining number was still 200.
118. *Arsattha* pargana Bhusawar, etc. (*Sayalu*), vs. 1784/1727.

2

Agricultural Production

The system of agricultural production tells us about the dynamics of rural society. No meaningful work on agrarian societies can be undertaken without research in archives where the lived experience of the people making up those societies is generally documented. The prime concern of the historian must be to scrutinize such documents. Though this is an immense task, I have made an attempt. This chapter investigates the question of whether or not in the region of our study, the late seventeenth and early eighteenth century was a period of great strides in terms of the spread of irrigation facilities, the increasing cultivation of cash crops, and the expansion of the cultivated area.[1] We shall also consider whether agricultural production was hampered by the ratchet effect of the revenue demand[2] and the bruising impact of famines and other natural calamities.[3]

We have referred above to village level records in the form of *arsatthas, arzdashts, yaddashtis* and *chithis*.[4] These records are not available in continuous series and at times the gaps become quite irritating. A large number of the parganas under study were held by the rulers of Amber under their *jagir* or on *ijara* from other imperial *mansabdars*. Four parganas, Khohri Rana, Toda Bhim, Hindaun, and Pahari, have been chosen for an analysis of the nature and pattern of agricultural production. For the purpose of discerning trends in the prices of foodgrains three parganas, Bahatri, Khohri Rana, and Jalalpur have been selected largely because these were in the centre of agrarian revolts, and because the kind of data that we need are available only for these parganas. Further, certain neighbouring parganas, for which the data are rich, have been studied by S. Nurul Hasan et al.[5] Since the period studied by them is the same as mine I draw on their work for purposes of comparison and it has on the whole been possible to bring into relief certain salient features of the agrarian economy of the region.

The *arsatthas* provide information about the total revenue

demand and the proportion of demand from the *rabi* and *kharif* seasons. The area under the *zabti* system and the amount realized according to the *batai jinsi* system are also given, So too the distribution of different crops over the area and revenue rates per *bigha*. But all this information is about those villages which were held by the Amber rulers under their own *khalisa*. No details are available about the villages given in *ijara* or *jagir* to the soldiers. Moreover, the number of villages under *khalisa* kept fluctuating. Hence it has been assumed that the trends that were visible in the *khalisa* villages represent the picture of the allotted tracts. As the figures of revenue in the *arsatthas* are given in two non-comparable sets, these have been converted into one form by adopting the method suggested by S. Nurul Hasan, K.N. Hasan and S.P. Gupta.[6] To study the relative position of different crops two variables have been taken into consideration, the area under each crop and the percentage of value realized therefrom.

As there is not enough information in the contemporary sources on the soil and climatic ecology, we have to rely on the modern works. There are two distinct soil zones in our region of study. The soils in the areas near Bayana and Hindaun are sandy, sandy-loam, clay, clay-loam (*chiknot*) and loam (*matiyar*). Roughly speaking, about half the total soil in present Bharatpur district is sandy-loam, found mostly in the south-west, and about a third is clay-loam lying in the north-east, whereas loam in the central region forms about one-sixth.[7] The soil retains moisture for several weeks and is capable of producing a variety of crops. The annual rainfall is about 24 inches on an average. In the rainy season most of the land becomes water-logged. In the bordering two parganas – Hindaun and Toda Bhim – the land is mostly plain and partly undulating hilly. The soil is light and sandy in the plains; and very fertile. The water level lies between 5 metres to 18 metres below surface.[8]

The parganas of Mewat straddle the Aravalli range. Here the soils near the hills are very shallow. At a distance from the hills, the soil is slightly better, approaching a light loam in character. Some parts are dotted with high sand dunes and present a desolate appearance. Between Palwal and Ferozepur Jhirka there is a stretch of country, 30 to 35 miles, which is of a level good loam. Between this plain and the range of hills dividing Gurgaon and Alwar, there is the low-lying country (in Nuh) where the soil is clay. The land around Ferozepur is generally good.[9] In a rare document the land has been classified as *awwal* (first class), *dom* (second class) and *som* (third class), on the basis of productivity, the areas covered being 6.53, 14.87 and 78.59 per cent respectively.[10] The share of the first two, fairly good and good soil types is small in comparison to the third (poor quality) category, which would be crucial for agricultural production. Similarly in pargana Khohri about 40 villages out of 333 have been mentioned as *bagar* (arid) where *rabi* crops did not grow.[11] The land in pargana Toda Bhim is called as *naram* or soft,[12] while the land of pargana Mauzabad is *kathor*, hard.[13] The water found in this region is mostly brackish. It is used for crops grown on sandy soil. Towards Rewari and Bawal, we get hard brackish/saline (*matwala*) water also. In some parts of the sandy region, sweet water is also found. A notable feature of the region is the existence of two layers of water, an upper layer of sweet water, with only salty water below.[14]

The unirrigated lands are given one or two ploughings before the monsoon begins in order to prepare the fields for the *kharif* crops. These ploughings are essential so that the soil is upturned and rain water may be quickly absorbed. It also helps soft sand that has strengthening properties, to be caught in the furrows. The land on which sugarcane is sown is subjected to six or seven ploughings before the ground is actually planted. Other important *kharif* crops such as *bajra* and pulses are sown after two ploughings while the land under jowar is given three ploughings. Among the *rabi* crops wheat requires five and barley four ploughings.[15]

Agricultural production in our region was largely dependent on the bounty of the monsoon, supplemented by irrigation. Irrigated lands have been referred as *chahi*, *kyari*, and *seka*. Non-irrigated lands were called either *vor* or *birani*. There is mention of the use of non-masonry as well as masonry wells for irrigation purposes.[16] Water from the non-masonry wells was drawn with the help of *dhenkli* working on the lever system. Wherever the water-table was high and the soil was conducive to the digging of a non-masonry well, the *dhenkli* was generally used to draw water. The *dhenkli* was in vogue in some parganas.[17] The second method was that of *laav-charas*, in which water from deep masonry wells was lifted in a leather bucket attached to a rope drawn over a pulley by a yoke of oxen. Three to four *laav-charas* could be working at a well at a time. In village Udhranpur in the *rabi* season of 1665, about 14 *charas* were deployed on 9 wells to irrigate 140 *bighas* of wheat. The remaining 260 *bighas* of land on which gram was cropped, depended on rain.[18] According to a *taqmina*, paper of 73 villages of pargana Udai for the *rabi* of 1720, the total cultivated land was 4,673 *bighas*, of which 1,548 *bighas* (1232 under barley, 316 under wheat) were irrigated. The remaining 3,125 *bighas* (under barley, wheat, and gram) were unirrigated.[19] Similarly in 13 villages of pargana Bhusawar 6,845 *bigha* land was cultivated in the *rabi* of 1,726. About 2,140 *bighas* (wheat: 1246, barley: 894 *bighas*) were irrigated. The remaining 4,705 *bighas* were unirrigated. On the unirrigated land, gram occupied 4,306 *bighas*.[20] From these instances it is evident that 30 to 35 per cent of the land was irrigated in our region. In pargana Toda Bhim the *laav-charas* was used on a large scale.[21] As it was very costly to construct a masonry well, only very well-to-do peasants or groups of villagers might have gone for it.[22] The life of non-masonry wells is short, depending on the character of the soil and intensity of rainfall. If the low cost of their construction enabled individual peasants to dig them, their frequent dilapidation might have caused the creation of a professional class of well-diggers.[23] Other sources of irrigation were the lakes, springs and seasonal rivers in this region. Babur had noticed the Kotla lake and other springs in some parts of Mewat.[24] Some canals might have been cut from these lakes and springs, channellized into the neighbouring parganas. In two parganas, Khohri and Pahari, a tax on irrigation termed as *hasil-pani* was actually levied in those villages which made use of such canals.[25] This tax was levied at the rate of 4 per cent of the land revenue (*mal*) on the *patels* and 5 per cent on ordinary peasants.[26] Besides these, there were rainfed rivers – the Sabi, the Banganga and the Indori – which passed through some parts of Mewat. But these were more a cause of destruction of crops than of any irrigational utility. There is no mention of the use of the Persian-wheel in our region and period. Because of these ecological conditions, there had always been a precarious balance between agricultural production and the pattern of investment.

A prominent feature of agriculture in the region was the production of a multiplicity of food crops along with some cash crops. The *arsatthas* mention 32 crops for *kharif* and 34 crops for *rabi* in pargana Khohri.[27] In pargana Toda Bhim, 21 crops were grown in the *kharif* and 19 in the *rabi* seasons. In pargana Hindaun as many as 48 crops were produced in *kharif* and 33 in the *rabi* harvest. Thus in two parganas, Khohri and Hindaun, not less than 60 crops were being cultivated within a year. The number of crops mentioned in the *Ain-i-Akbari* for *suba* Agra as a whole is 41 in a year.[28] The production of such a rich variety of crops, clearly suggests that the peasantry of the region was well informed and open-minded.

If the number of crops varied from pargana to pargana and season to season, the area occupied by each of them also had regional and seasonal variations. The tables given at the end of this chapter clearly suggest that in both seasons a high percentage of the arable was under food crops. On an average the area under wheat, barley, gram, and mixed cross (gojara, bejhari) in pargana Toda Bhim was 89.07 per cent of the total cropped area (Table 2.12). In pargana Hindaun these crops occupied 96.98 per cent area on an average (Table 2.14). In pargana Khohri the food-crops of the *rabi* season (excluding its *banjar* zone) occupied 88.84 per cent in 1713 and it declined to 62.51 per cent in 1733. In 1743 their share rose to 75.59 per cent (Table 2.16). In pargana Pahari the food-crops of *rabi* occupied 99.11 in 1722 and 80.74 per cent of the area in 1743 (Table 2.18). In Toda Bhim various kinds of vegetables were grown on more than one per cent area. The share of the vegetables in terms of area was somewhat on the rise (Table 2.12). Cash crops like tobacco, opium, and mustard were grown but on an insignificant scale in this pargana. In Hindaun, the area under cash crops of *rabi* remained insignificant and almost steady (Table 2.14). In Khohri the production of vegetables in *rabi* was considerably on the rise. Its share of the total area increased from 7.34 in 1713 to 15.17 per cent in 1743 (Table 2.16). The percentage of area under tobacco also tended to increase. Similarly in Pahari, if the area under vegetables was on the increase, tobacco also had its impressive share of 7.67 per cent in 1743 (Table 2.18). The general pattern of mixed food-crops is obviously erratic, but their adoption was largely meant to spread the risk of crop-failure on a wider area.

During the *kharif* season *bajra* and *jowar* occupied an area ranging between 50 and 60 per cent of the total in Toda Bhim and Hindaun (Tables 2.13, 2.15). In Khohri and Pahari their share ranged between 20 and 35 per cent up to 1733 after which it tended to increase (Tables 2.17, 2.2). In Toda Bhim and Hindaun the production of cash crops such as sugarcane, cotton, and indigo was impressive while in Khohri and Pahari the production of pulses was significant. If the share of sugarcane increased from 2.84 in 1693 to 11.87 per cent in 1730, the area under cotton also registered an increase from 21.65 per cent in 1693 to 33.17 per cent in 1730 in Toda Bhim

(Table 2.13). A high percentage of area went under *masina* (opium) after 1720 in this pargana. It seems to have done so at the cost of pulses such as *moong* and *moth*. *Til*, sesame vegetables, and tobacco each had a share of less than one per cent of the area. The cultivation of cash crops like sugarcane, and cotton was on the increase in pargana Hindaun. Among the pulses *moth* (Dew pea) was mostly grown, followed by *urd* (black gram) and *moong* (green gram). Lesser cash crops like sun-hemp, tobacco and vegetables accounted for an area of less than one per cent each in this pargana, and they seem to have been cultivated for local consumption rather than for distant markets. The most interesting feature in the crop-pattern of Hindaun is the steady decline in the cultivation of *bajra* and indigo and the rise in the cultivation of cotton and sugarcane up to the 1730s (Table 2.15). In 1713 indigo was cultivated in 83 villages and sugarcane in 69 villages.[29] By 1728, the trend was reversed and the cultivation of indigo fell to 59 villages whereas that of sugarcane extended to 93 villages.[30] We shall return to this later.

The value realized from various crops of both seasons shows a common pattern for all the parganas under study (figures in brackets in Tables 2.12 to 2.19). It has already been noted that the percentage of area under food-crops was higher in *rabi* than in *kharif*. On the other hand the cultivation of cotton, cash crop par excellence, was much in practice during the *kharif* season. Among the *rabi* crops wheat demanded more inputs as compared to barley and gram, and understandably therefore wheat was rated at a higher value in the market. Moreover, wheat found an easy market in the two capital cities, Agra and Delhi.[31] There seems to be a parity between the area cultivated and value realized from barley (Tables 2.12, 2.14, 2.16). In terms of value, the contribution of coarse crops was as meagre as the area occupied by them. Was it due to their utility for local consumption by the poor segments of society?

During the *kharif* harvest the percentage of fibre crops like cotton and *san* or sun-hemp and the famous dye-yielding indigo, was high in terms of their value. Sugarcane was another high value-yielding crop (Tables 2.13, 2.15, 2.17, 2.19). In Toda Bhim and Hindaun the percentage of value from sugarcane was much higher than the area under this crop. In 1693, about 2.84 per cent of the area under sugarcane yielded about 9.02 per cent of the total value from Toda Bhim (Table 2.13). In Hindaun also it yielded 8.56 per cent of the total value from 1.82 per cent of the total cultivated area during 1713 (Table 2.15). Indigo produced in our region formed a segment of India's overseas trade. This partly explains why its production tended to decline sharply around 1730 when the process of Surat's decline began.[32] In 1724 it was reported that indigo buyers were not coming to Hindaun.[33] With the decline in demand elsewhere, only the inferior variety indigo remained to be cultivated. Although tobacco and maize had been introduced in our region, it seems from the meagre amount of land under them that their commercial value had not been discovered by the peasants during our period. Perhaps the quality of these crops grown in the region was also somewhat inferior going by the low cash returns on them. A large number of vegetables were grown,[34] but in terms of value their contribution was far from impressive. Perhaps demand for them seldom crossed the precincts of the *qasba* markets. Local officials, given their standard of living, might have found in melons etc. a substitute for fruits, which were less grown in our region.

Information on the yield of crops per unit of land is limited. One document pertaining to pargana Bawal gives per *bigha* yield of various crops. The per *bigha* yield has been given for good, middling and bad lands. Table 2.1 gives a comparison of the average yield of 1540-5[35] with the yields estimated for pargana Bawal in 1664.[36]

TABLE 2.1: AVERAGE YIELDS PER CROP IN PARGANA PAWAL

	(man-i-Akbari per bigha-i-Ilahi)	
	(a) *1540-5*	*(b)* *1664*
Wheat	12.95	8.50
Barley	12.93	10.83
Gram	10.93	–
Bajra	7.62	2.00
Jowar	10.30	5.00
Moth	5.16	1.41
Mash	7.77	–

The Mughal administration regularly undertook the measurement of land for the purposes of revenue assessment. The measured area has been elaborately recorded in the *taqsim* papers. These papers contain records of area and revenue of years past. Luckily some of these *taqsim* papers of the late seventeenth and early eighteenth century have survived. For the region of this study the available documents of this kind are meagre in number but precise in information. In the *taqsim* papers the total measured area (*raqba*) is divided into uncultivable and cultivable (*laik zarait*) land. The arable land has been further divided into cultivated (*zaraiti*) and uncultivated (*parat*).[37] The cultivated land was separately measured for the *kharif* and *rabi* seasons. In some villages a part of the land was cultivated during both seasons and such lands were designated *dufasli* and twice counted.[38] The area of the actually cultivated land during both seasons in relation to the available arable will help us to determine the extent of cultivation. The area figures of four parganas are discussed here to shed some light on the extent and nature of cultivation (Table 2.3, 2.4, 2.5, 2.6, 2.7).

In pargana Hindaun the area of arable was 61.89 per cent of the total measured area, that actually cultivated land being 65.97 per cent of the total arable. From 1733 to 1739 an impressive expansion of cultivation is recorded, though the entire cultivable land was never ploughed. From 1740 onwards a contraction of the actually cultivated area can be observed (see Table 2.3). The area figures of pargana Punkhar show that the area of the arable land was 74.40 per cent of the total measured area. When we compare the figures for 1730 and 1741, we notice a contraction of about ten per cent. The average extent of cultivation in this pargana bordered around 52.16 per cent of the arable. Thus a large amount of arable land was still waiting to be brought under the plough. Was it because of the peasants' inability to bring more arable under cultivation? An avid reader of the area figures for pargana Hindaun might see in them an extension of cultivation. But when we compare the measured area of pargana Hindaun as given in the *Ain-i-Akbari* and the *taqsim* papers, we find a considerable contraction (see Table 2.7).[39] A similar trend of decrease in the measured area emerges for pargana Udai. Even if we take into consideration the transfer of seven villages (with an area of 9,139 *bighas*) from Udai to pargana Malarna,[40] we still have a difference of 19,418 *bighas* between the *Ain* and *taqsim* year's figures. It may be noted that the area figures for Hindaun and Punkhar pertain to that period of the eighteenth century when Jaipur State was at its zenith of political power and peace prevailed in the countryside. This might partly explain a temporary flash in the agricultural sector of pargana Hindaun.

When we analyse the area figures of some parganas pertaining to the period 1670 to 1730, a different picture of agriculture emerges. The area figures for pargana Antela Bhabhra are available for almost a period of 60 years. The first *taqsim* document of Antela Bhabhra covers a period of 15 years (1649-63)[41] and the second paper covers a period of ten years (1699-1708).[42] Out of the total measured area of this pargana, 65.05 per cent land was arable. But the extent of actually cultivated land never crossed 46 per cent of its arable. On an average 54 per cent of the arable remained uncultivated. The extent of cultivated acreage in this pargana during the last two years of Aurangzeb's reign was abysmally low as compared to the first two years of his rule. Though the number of villages and the size of the arable during these 60 years remained constant, the extent of cultivated acreage was contracting. The average cultivated area during 1649-63 was 33.24 per cent of its arable. In the next phase (1699-1708) the percentage of cultivated land contracted to 25.03 per cent of the arable.

A similar trend of shrinkage of cultivation is observable in *tappa* Rini of pargana Bahatri (Table 2.6). The area figures of this *tappa* covered the last years of Aurangzeb's reign and the full span of Bahadur Shah's rule. In this *tappa,* 85.41 per cent of the total measured area, was arable and the extent of cultivation remained less than 50 per cent of the arable. Thus extensive lands remained uncultivated. Moreover, the *taqsim* papers clearly show a considerable contraction of cultivation from 1704 to 1713 in *tappa* Rini. In pargana Bahatri, *tappa* Rini was the only area affected by peasant unrest.

The revenue figures (*hasil*) of two villages for a decade (1735-45) given in Table 2.2 also reflect a trend of declining cultivation.[43] Village Pali was situated in pargana Sonkhar and Balupura belonged to pargana Kuthumber. Both parganas were in the centre of peasant revolts. Evidently, the parganas in and around the region of the agrarian revolts witnessed declining levels of agricultural production in 1675-1730. In certain parganas the downward trend persisted for a longer period.

TABLE 2.2: REVENUE FIGURES OF TWO VILLAGES BETWEEN 1735 AND 1745

Year	*Amount of collected revenue in Rupees*	
	Village: Pali	*Village: Balupura*
1735	1701	–
1736	885	800
1737	1901	800
1738	1210	500
1739	683	500
1740	1901	500
1741	401	500
1742	801	376
1743	513	376
1744	825	191
1745	1025*	225*

Note: * Given on *ijara*.

TABLE 2.3: CULTIVATED AREA IN HINDUAN 1733-42

Pargana: Hindaun, *sarkar* Agra. No. of villages: 245.
Total area (*raqba*): 699,527 *bighas*
Total cultivable area: 433,000 *bighas* (61.89 per cent of the total area)

Year	*Yearly cultivated area in* bighas	*percentage of cultivable*	Kharif bighas *(in percentages)*	Rabi bighas
1733	258620	59.73	179417 (69.37)	79203 (30.62)
1734	331191	76.43	219005 (66.12)	112186 (33.87)
1735	378487	87.41	219679 (58.04)	158808 (41.95)
1736	344986	79.63	221116 (64.09)	123870 (35.90)
1737	371917	85.89	244795 (65.81)	127122 (34.18)
1738	406039	93.77	265121 (65.29)	140908 (34.70)
1739	408647	94.38	277503 (67.90)	131144 (32.09)
1740	316470	73.08	208757 (65.95)	107713 (34.03)
1741	260888	60.02	191408 (73.36)	69480 (26.63)
1742	217732	50.28	138991 (63.83)	78741 (36.16)

Source: *Muwazana dahsala, pargana* Hindaun, VS 1790-9 (1733-42)

TABLE 2.4: CULTIVATED AREA IN PUNKHAR, 1730-41

Pargana: Punkhar, *sarkar* Alwar. No. of villages: 36.
Total area (*raqba*): 59,047 *bighas*
Total cultivable area: 43,936 *bighas* (74.40 per cent of the total area)

Year	*Yearly cultivated area in* bighas	*percentage of cultivable*	Kharif bighas *(in percentages)*	Rabi bighas
1730	29789	67.80	15200 (51.25)	14589 (48.97)
1731	26077	59.35	10142 (38.89)	15335 (58.80)
1732	23660	53.85	16156 (68.28)	7485 (31.63)
1733	18509	42.13	10523 (56.85)	7986 (43.14)
1734	24496	55.64	13034 (53.20)	11462 (46.79)
1735	28424	64.69	14067 (49.48)	13557 (47.69)
1736	23038	52.44	10035 (43.55)	13003 (56.44)
1737	27757	63.18	14142 (50.94)	13615 (49.05)
1738	33292	75.77	15802 (47.46)	17490 (52.53
1739	24634	56.07	14244 (57.82)	10590 (42.18)
1740	25313	57.61	13253 (52.35)	12060 (47.64)
1741	25589	58.24	14304 (55.89)	11285 (44.10)

Source: Taqsim dahsala, pargana, Punkhar, VS 1787-98 (1730-41).

TABLE 2.5: CULTIVATED AREA IN ANTELA BHABHRA, 1657-1707

Pargana: Antela Bhabhra, *sarkar* Alwar. No. of villages: 17.
Total area (*raqba*): 61,180 *bighas*
Total cultivable area: 39,800 *bighas* (65.05% of the total area)

Year	*Yearly cultivated area in* bighas	*percentage of the cultivable*
1657	13550	34.04
1658	13944	35.03
1659	18501	46.48
1706	5547	13.94
1707	7964	20.01

Source: Taqsim pandrehsala, pargana, Antela Bhabhra, VS 1706-1720 (1649-63) and *taqsim dahsala,* pargana Antela Bhabhra, VS 1756-65 (1699-1708).

TABLE 2.6: CULTIVATED AREA IN BHATRI, 1704-13

Pargana: Bhatri (*tappa* Rini), *sarkar* Alwar. No. of villages: 67.
Total area (*raqba*): 152,021 *bighas*
Cultivable area: 129,854 *bighas* (85.41 per cent of the total area)

Year	*Yearly cultivated area in* bighas	*percentage of the cultivable*
1704	53087	40.88
1705	33712	25.96
1706	33931	26.13
1707	46601	35.88
1708	17376	13.38
1709	13135	10.11
1710	22515	17.33
1711	19753	15.21
1712	15160	11.67
1713	22708	17.48

Source: Taqsim dahsala, pargana Bahatri, VS 1761-70 (1704-13).

TABLE 2.7: MEASURED AREA (IN *BIGHA-I-DAFTARI*)

Pargana	Ain *area*	Taqsim *area and year*
Hindaun	724395	699527 (AD 1733-42)
Udai	411100	382543 (AD 1734-43)

The prices of the principal food crops have been taken from the *arsatthas* of three parganas, Jalalpur, Khohri, and Bahatri. The *arsatthas* are not available for the entire period continuously, and there are considerable gaps. These prices are based on the actual sale price of grain collected as revenue. In order to make comparison possible, prices of all commodities have been converted into rupees per *man*. (In the *arsattha* the figures are given in terms of quantity per rupee.) Keeping in view the variations in the weight of a *man* in different parganas, the prices have been calculated in terms of the *man* of 40 *sers*. The prices of the principal crops of the three parganas are given in the Tables 2.20, 2.22 given in the end of this chapter.

The movement of prices for various crops shows a remarkable similarity. In 1664-5 food grain prices were abysmally low. This is not only evident from the tables 2.20, 2.22 but is corroborated by other sources too. This pattern of the price movement was reported from a large number of parganas. For example, in the six adjoining parganas of our region, the prices of grain were particularly low during 1665-6.[44] Our evidence clearly shows that grain traders from outside were not coming to buy grain from these parganas and there was a glut in the *qasbas*, which had caused such low prices. In 1666, when the emperor moved his camp from Agra to Delhi, it raised the hopes of the officials of our parganas. They thought that the demand for grain from the region would increase due to the arrival of the imperial camp.[45] After this prices tended to stabilize up to 1690,[46] only to rise a bit in the 1690s (Tables 2.20 and 2.22). There is a remarkable rise in prices in the 1710s. Prices of almost all commodities more than doubled during this decade, 1710-20.

The marginal rise in the 1690s was due to a shortage of grain.[47] This scarcity might have been caused by the drought of 1694-8,[48] and agrarian dislocation caused by the revolts. Irfan Habib has attributed the relative stability of prices between 1665 and 1710 to the decline in currency supply, and the subsequent rise in the years after 1710 to cumulative effect of the increasing currency supply. A brisk movement of grain from pargana Khohri, Maujpur, Pindayan and Punkhar caused by enhanced demand in Agra, Delhi and Thoon (stronghold of Churaman Jat), might have contributed to the rise of prices.[49] Moreover the intensification of the *bhomia* revolts during this decade perhaps caused a dislocation in agricultural production in the region, while the demand for grain increased in the area owing to successive campaigns organized against Churaman and others. Thus various interrelated factors appear to have contributed to a steep rise in the grain prices during this decade. The successful campaigns of Sawai Jai Singh, leading ultimately to the death of Churaman in 1723, brought comparative peace to the region. There is a remarkable coincidence from that year onwards between political stability and the stabilization of agricultural prices down to 1743.

Some aspects of agricultural production in the adjoining parganas of eastern Rajasthan have been studied by S. Nurul Hasan and others. In a nutshell their findings are as follows.[50] The period 1650-1750 registered an advance both in terms of agricultural production as well as of an upward price mobility. The production of cash crops in the *kharif* season increased and the proportion of crops of the *rabi* harvest grew as compared to the *kharif* harvest as a whole. The *rabi* crop in eastern Rajasthan requires a considerable degree of investment. The availability of additional surplus for investment in agriculture would thus be indicated by these. The price rise similarly might have benefited the peasantry, though the benefits would be shared unequally by its different sections.

The validity of these conclusions need to be considered more closely. First of all the argument that *zabti* rates were not revised in tandem with the rise in prices is based on a selective reading of the evidence. The apparent stability of *zabti* rates in the *arsatthas* can mislead the researcher unless he takes cognizance of some taxes specially levied in 'pursuit' of the price rise. A special tax stated in numbers, which denoted its value, was invariably imposed on the *zabti* crops on account of price rise (*sabab girani*). The incidence of this tax has been clearly recorded in the *arsatthas* of the parganas of eastern Rajasthan. For instance, the amount of this tax was 8.5 per cent (*sadh atthotra*) in pargana Wazirpur[51] and 9.5 per cent (*sadh-nirotra*) in pargana Hindaun.[52] In both parganas this tax was imposed on all *zabti* crops on account of the price rise. The imposition of this numerical tax on the *zabti* crops grown in the parganas covered by the study of Hasan and Gupta, has also been recorded in the *arsatthas*.[53] Though Gupta is aware of the incidence of this special levy,[54] he has somehow missed its link with the *zabti* crops and price rise. Hence his claim that extra benefit accrued to the peasants under the *zabt* system on account of price rise, is highly questionable. Had it been so the peasants would have pressed for the extension of the *zabt* system to cover all crops, but the peasantry made no such demand even in the context of rise in prices. On the other hand a predominance of the crop-sharing (*jinsi*) system in the *rabi* harvest and its application to all non-cash crops of the *kharif* season, continued to be a notable feature of the system of agricultural production in eastern Rajasthan.[55] It has also been argued by Hasan and Gupta that the production of cash crops in the *kharif* season increased, and the proportion of the *rabi* harvest grew as compared to the *kharif* harvest as a whole. In our view, such a simultaneous expansion could not have taken place because of the prevalent cropping pattern. In this region cotton (*van*) and sugar cane (*var*) were the two major cash crops sown in *kharif*. As both continued to occupy the same land even during the ensuing *rabi* season, their expansion would have led to a corresponding contraction of the area under *rabi*. The occurrence of such a phenomenon has also been recorded in the *arsatthas*. For example, and such examples are many, the *amil* of pargana Jalalpur reported in 1692 that less land was left for the *rabi* season because of an increase in the cultivation of cotton and sugar cane.[56] Had Hasan and Gupta been aware of such an overlap perhaps their verdict on the pattern of agricultural productivity would have been different. Moreover, when we compare the revenue figures of *kharif* and *rabi* for parganas Hindaun, Toda Bhim, Udai, and Maujpur, we do not find any shift in the respective shares. In fact the figures for Hindaun and Maujpur show some decline in the share of the *rabi* season. Needless to say, we cannot hazard any generalization on this issue. A seasonwise break-up of revenue collected from all the four parganas is given in Table 2.8 for a better understanding of the situation.

TABLE 2.8: PARGANA HINDAUN: PERCENTAGE OF COLLECTED REVENUE

Year	Kharif	Rabi
1713	56.55	43.45
1720	62.14	37.86
1723	72.85	27.15
1726	64.07	35.93
1728	63.41	36.59
1730	55.21	44.79
1734	66.24	33.76
1746	62.39	37.61

We see that the cultivation of some cash crops, sugarcane and cotton, was increasing in parganas Toda Bhim and Hindaun (2.14, 2.16) during the *kharif* harvest. In Hindaun, increase in sugar cane and cotton cultivation was at the cost of indigo, whereas in Toda Bhim the cultivation of both cotton and sugarcane was at the cost of *bajra* and *jowar*. The period of this trend almost coincides with the period of intensive disturbances. It is true that disturbed conditions should have discouraged the peasants from investing in high value cash crops. The rise in the percentage of area under cash-crops at the cost of food crops in the context of peasant desertion of land, suggests that the poor peasants were affected by the disturbances more than were the well-to-do sections of the peasantry. First, the *qasbas* being less disturbed, normal agricultural production was seldom disrupted there. Not a single revolt originated from the

TABLE 2.9: PARGANA TODA BHIM: PERCENTAGE OF COLLECTED REVENUE

Year	Kharif	Rabi
1693	51.26	48.74
1717	52.14	47.86
1718	48.14	51.86
1720	56.67	43.33
1724	53.93	46.07
1726	51.36	48.64
1728	58.48	41.52
1729	54.89	45.11
1730	55.12	44.88
1731	56.07	43.93
1732	59.22	40.78
1733	60.05	39.95
1734	62.18	37.82
1735	51.84	48.16
1736	58.41	41.54
1737	58.07	41.93
1741	63.49	36.51
1742	57.40	42.60
1743	55.29	44.71

TABLE 2.10: PARGANA MAUJPUR: PERCENTAGE OF COLLECTED REVENUE

Year	Kharif	Rabi
1716	38.86	61.13
1717	38.35	61.64
1718	50.42	49.57
1719	28.32	71.67
1720	37.54	62.44
1721	41.81	58.18
1722	–	–
1723	55.50	44.49
1724	41.61	58.38
1725	47.06	52.93

TABLE 2.11: PARGANA UDAI: PERCENTAGE OF COLLECTED REVENUE

Year	Kharif	Rabi
1734	51.04	48.95
1735	36.21	63.79
1736	53.85	46.15
1737	50.73	49.27
1738	55.34	44.66
1739	57.96	42.03
1740	54.82	45.18
1741	55.11	44.89
1742	51.47	49.53
1743	48.87	51.13

TABLE 2.12: PARGANA TODA BHIM
(YEAR-WISE PERCENTAGE OF AREA UNDER VARIOUS CROPS)

Rabi Crops	*1693*	*1713*	*1720*	*1730*	*1743*
Wheat	29.52	23.37	50.07	14.40	24.77
	(48.93)	(38.39)	(62.63)	(36.10)	(40.70)
Barley	33.42	19.86	27.08	11.91	31.55
	(30.34)	(26.87)	(28.85)	(20.76)	(41.75)
Gram	13.30	51.46	11.47	56.18	29.89
	(4.51)	(29.40)	(2.55)	(27.97)	(8.68)
Gojara	3.34	1.79	2.00	0.29	–
	(5.35)	(2.49)	(2.46)	(0.79)	–
Bejhari	3.67	1.46	3.69	14.36	11.76
	(2.12)	(1.75)	(1.43)	(11.90)	(6.73)
Vegetables	1.06	1.36	2.23	1.35	1.69
	(1.49)	(0.94)	(1.73)	(1.33)	(1.35)
Cheena	15.44	0.26	3.10	1.30	0.90
	(6.91)	(0.10)	(0.72)	(0.63)	–
Mustard	0.04	–	–	0.20	0.06
	(0.02)	–	–	(0.17)	(0.34)
Tobacco	0.01	0.04	0.10	–	0.19
Opium	0.14	0.02	0.03	0.07	–
	(0.21)	(0.05)	–	–	–
Misc.	0.06	0.38	–	–	–

Note: The figures in brackets indicate the percentage of value realised from each crop. This has been estimated for both the harvests of each *pargana*.

TABLE 2.13: PARGANA TODA BHIM
(YEAR-WISE PERCENTAGE OF AREA UNDER VARIOUS CROPS)

Kharif Crops	*1693*	*1713*	*1720*	*1730*	*1743*
Bajra	31.52	40.38	26.79	20.71	42.25
	(21.09)	(32.96)	(23.38)	(13.33)	(34.05)
Jowar	37.63	20.34	16.38	10.58	36.82
	(27.62)	(23.00)	(16.74)	(8.68)	(42.52)
Sugar cane	2.84	2.70	2.68	11.87	3.15
	(9.02)	(9.04)	(4.77)	(19.91)	(7.16)
Cotton	21.65	9.23	20.19	33.17	4.69
	(31.92)	(15.22)	(29.17)	(36.70)	(7.11)
Rice	1.50	1.33	–	–	–
	(1.77)	(1.63)			
Moong & Moth	2.28	22.53	–	0.33	–
	(6.67)	(13.71)			
Masina	–	–	28.41	16.92	10.33
			(19.39)	(8.50)	(7.44)
Til	1.44	0.63	0.22	0.29	0.25
	(1.50)	(0.89)	0.25	–	(0.25)
Vegetables	0.20	0.56	0.89	2.27	0.39
	(0.36)	(0.67)	(1.70)	(2.23)	(0.16)
Tobacco	–	–	–	–	–
	(0.09)	(1.60)	(0.59)	(0.57)	(0.16)

TABLE 2.14: PARGANA HINDAUN
(YEAR-WISE PERCENTAGE OF AREA UNDER VARIOUS CROPS)

Rabi Crops	*1713*	*1720*	*1730*	*1734*	*1746*
Wheat	30.04	46.17	42.94	51.27	32.29
	(40.00)	(50.22)	(53.57)	(59.01)	36.11)
Barley	27.77	50.48	30.73	39.17	65.04
	(29.67)	(45.81)	(31.29)	(37.25)	(62.65)
Gram	36.11	1.46	20.59	4.50	0.10
	(25.87)	(0.78)	(12.24)	(2.40)	(0.04)
Mixed grain	3.44	0.02	0.01	–	0.51
	(2.63)	–	(0.02)	–	(0.04)
Cheena	0.66	0.50	4.91	4.24	1.03
	(0.31)	(1.90)	(2.08)	(1.60)	–

Vegetables	1.31 (0.87)	0.73 (0.69)	0.80 (0.76)	0.62 (0.62)	0.89 (0.96)
Tobacco	0.06 (0.04)	0.10 (0.12)	– –	– –	0.01 (0.06)
Opium	0.01	0.03	–	0.01	0.10
Mustard	– –	0.06 (0.35)	0.03 (0.02)	0.11 (0.08)	0.02 (0.01)

TABLE 2.15: PARGANA HINDAUN
(YEAR-WISE PERCENTAGE OF AREA UNDER VARIOUS CROPS)

Kharif Crops	*1713*	*1720*	*1730*	*1734*	*1746*
Bajra	53.05 (44.41)	35.29 (29.33)	31.82 (19.36)	30.66 (17.62)	42.46 (35.38)
Jowar	7.53 (9.48)	17.19 (20.04)	14.68 (13.09)	24.53 (24.56)	19.72 –
Moth	15.98 (11.52)	17.95 (12.60)	10.43 (5.64)	6.44 (5.24)	4.21 (4.37)
Til	4.03 (5.20)	0.84 (1.00)	1.24 (1.19)	1.32 (3.12)	0.57 (1.90)
Urd	2.54 (3.19)	0.07 (0.08)	2.24 (2.03)	0.78 (0.96)	0.08 (0.53)
Moong	0.85 (0.96)	0.01 (0.01)	1.33 (1.14)	1.46 (1.26)	0.02 (0.06)
Sugar cane	1.82 (8.56)	4.76 (8.22)	10.68 (22.95)	4.09 (14.88)	3.47 (18.48)
Cotton	2.25 (4.65)	7.50 (14.66)	16.93 (26.16)	16.72 (25.54)	19.23 (30.31)
Indigo	4.80 (5.64)	11.76 (11.97)	4.40 (3.95)	5.83 (5.00)	6.29 (6.70)
Sanhemp	0.08 (0.16)	0.06 (0.10)	0.19 (0.36)	0.08 (0.12)	0.09 (0.22)
Kuri-varti	3.70 (1.11)	1.55 (0.67)	1.12 (0.39)	4.20 (1.42)	0.61 (0.30)
Vegetables	0.44 (0.41)	0.72 (0.39)	0.56 (0.76)	0.39 (0.59)	0.27 (0.77)
Tobacco	0.16 (0.40)	0.30 (0.21)	0.15 (0.28)	0.16 (0.29)	0.11 (0.28)

Mandwa	1.77	1.00	–	1.00	1.00
	(2.05)	(0.21)	(0.59)	(0.27)	(0.5)
Rice	1.00	1.00	–	2.34	1.96
	(2.06)	(0.36)	(1.99)	(1.13)	(0.20)

TABLE 2.16: PARGANA *KHOHRI*
(YEAR-WISE PERCENTAGE OF AREA UNDER VARIOUS CROPS)

Rabi Crops	*1713*	*1733*	*1743*
Wheat	34.08	19.59	19.79
	(57.62)	(64.45)	(46.61)
Barley	22.84	8.59	28.98
	(15.10)	(3.80)	(23.75)
Gram	31.82	31.59	20.65
	(20.98)	(16.33)	(11.49)
Rice	3.97	10.25	–
	(1.08)	(6.59)	
Vegetables	7.34	9.47	15.17
	(3.10)	(3.21)	(7.98)
Tobacco	0.01	0.32	5.46
	(0.10)	(0.15)	(3.66)
Bẹjhari	–	1.82	1.08
		(0.79)	(0.99)
Gochạni	–	0.77	0.46
		(0.53)	(1.02)
Gojara	–	0.15	4.63
Mustard	–	0.92	1.64
	(2.07)	(1.57)	(2.84)
Masur	–	16.48	1.27
		(0.53)	(1.62)

TABLE 2.17: PARGANA *KHOHRI*
(YEAR-WISE PERCENTAGE OF AREA UNDER VARIOUS CROPS)

Kharif Crops	*1666*	*1713*	*1733*	*1743*
Bajra	24.10	9.27	13.36	40.19
	(30.27)	(22.10)	(11.31)	(5.78)

Jowar	4.80	11.37	7.97	24.83
	(7.09)	(17.43)	(9.70)	(50.19)
Moth	61.68	15.49	26.71	15.30
	(35.63)	(14.71)	(14.78)	(14.30)
Moong	3.59	0.52	–	0.70
	(3.56)	(0.43)	–	–
Urd	2.37	12.20	4.28	–
	(4.38)	(15.96)	(4.30)	(1.21)
Chola	0.14	6.14	20.82	10.38
	(0.39)	–	–	–
Sugar cane	0.01	–	1.35	0.37
	(0.01)	–	(2.71)	(1.42)
Indigo	0.18	–	2.67	1.60
	(0.77)	–	(2.89)	(4.05)
Cotton	1.12	9.78	0.94	1.13
	(1.42)	(6.28)	(1.06)	(2.27)
Rice	1.04	0.38	4.68	0.11
	(7.39)	(2.79)	(23.83)	–
Kuri-varti	0.29	17.42	1.84	3.28
	(0.70)	(7.85)	(1.18)	(3.74)
Modu-Mandwa	0.36	15.82	13.09	1.94
	(1.21)	(8.37)	(11.36)	(3.02)
Vegetables	0.03	0.56	0.10	0.07
	(0.01)	(0.36)	(0.11)	(0.14)
Chari	0.33	1.00	–	–
	(0.84)	(2.37)	(14.84)	(13.35)
Til	–	–	0.07	0.02
	(6.18)	(1.27)	(1.61)	(0.04)

TABLE 2.18: PARGANA PAHARI
(YEAR-WISE PERCENTAGE OF AREA UNDER VARIOUS CROPS)

Rabi Crops	*1733*	*1743*
Wheat	1.77	0.29
	(3.77)	(1.54)
Barley	9.53	34.15
	(10.3)	(34.02)

Gram	56.89 (45.84)	26.98 (23.89)
Gojara	21.77 (29.98)	16.75 (27.78)
Bejhari	6.14 (7.65)	2.97 (3.48)
Vegetables	4.32 (2.69)	8.48 (3.02)
Tobacco	–	7.67 (4.83)
Ghano	–	2.02 (1.00)
Mustard	–	0.55 (0.40)

TABLE 2.19: PARGANA PAHARI
(YEAR-WISE PERCENTAGE OF AREA UNDER VARIOUS CROPS)

Kharif Crops	*1716*	*1733*	*1743*
Bajra	18.99 (27.32)	3.79 (4.81)	31.69 (31.88)
Jowar	17.93 (16.39)	12.73 (16.17)	40.61 (45.43)
Moth	8.29 (9.51)	– (3.75)	5.43
Urd	49.47 (42.61)	51.67 (61.48)	1.98 (1.57)
Rice	1.05 (1.15)	– (0.18)	1.83 (2.66)
Moong	0.12 (0.20)	–	–
Cotton	2.02 (1.28)	1.17 (1.17)	3.23 (3.87)
Kodu	1.59 (1.0)	–	0.29 (0.30)
Kuri-varti	0.6 (0.02)	2.07 (1.41)	4.48 (2.24)
Chari	0.43 (0.20)	14.18	4.25

Onion	–	14.36 (14.75)	3.30 (3.44)
Chola	– (0.02)	–	0.29 (0.30)
Til	– (0.25)	– –	5.72 (6.17)
Sugar cane	–	–	0.07 (0.12)
Indigo	–	–	0.07 (0.06)

TABLE 2.20: PARGANA JALALPUR
(YEAR-WISE COMPARISON OF PRICES (IN RUPEES PER *MAN*)

RABI

Year	*Wheat*	*Barley*	*Gram*	*Mustard*	*Arhar*
1666	0.90	0.53	(0.52)	–	–
1689	0.86	0.53	0.53	1.05	0.44
1690	–	0.66	0.66	1.08	0.45
1691	1.00	0.76	0.56	0.75	0.54
1692	1.05	0.80	0.70	0.88	0.66
1709	0.97	0.58	0.60	1.33	–
1711	1.60	1.08	0.85	2.00	1.08
1712	2.85	2.66	2.66	2.66	2.50
1713	1.66	1.08	1.08	1.66	0.95
1718	2.50	1.73	2.00	2.50	1.81
1720	2.35	1.90	2.10	1.81	1.81
1735	1.73	1.33	1.29	2.35	1.25
1739	1.11	0.65	0.93	1.81	0.67

KHARIF

Year	*Jowar*	*Bajra*	*Moth*	*Urd*	*Mong*	*Til*	*Rice*
1666	0.47	0 52	0.40	0.51	0.55	1.11	0.90
1689	0.48	0.66	0.48	0.53	0.66	1.73	–
1690	0.56	0.72	0.53	0.57	0.62	1.48	–
1691	0.56	0.88	0.61	0.65	0.70	1.14	–
1692	0.57	0.75	0.54	0.57	0.59	1.25	–
1711	0.75	0.76	0.58	0.70	0.76	2.22	1.14
1716	1.53	1.66	–	1.66	1.73	4.44	3.33

1718	1.73	2.00	2.10	2.10	2.35	4.44	–
1719	1.00	1.29	1.08	1.14	1.33	2.35	–
1720	1.73	1.90	1.90	1.90	2.00	2.85	–
1723	1.33	1.42	1.37	1.66	1.81	2.66	2.00
1735	–	–	1.25	1.53	–	2.85	–
1736	2.00	2.35	2.50	2.50	1.05	5.71	–
1739	0.74	0.80	0.75	0.75	1.08	1.73	1.81

TABLE 2.21: PARGANA KHOHRI
COMPARISON OF PRICES (IN RUPEES PER MAN)

KHARIF

Year	*Bajra*	*Jowar*	*Til*	*Moth*	*Urd*	*Moong*	*Gochani*	*Gojra*	*Bejhari*
1664	0.57	0.56	2.16	0.70	0.86	0.66	–	–	–
1666	0.57	0.56	1.29	0.54	0.66	2.50	–	–	–
1716	2.42	2.42	5.71	2.50	2.85	–	–	–	–
1717	1.14	1.08	4.00	1.33	1.42	–	–	–	–
1733	–	–	–	–	–	–	1.29	1.33	1.29
1735	–	–	–	–	–	–	1.48	–	1.33
1741	–	–	–	–	–	–	1.21	1.21	1.05
1743	–	–	–	–	–	–	1.66	1.29	1.29
1744	–	–	–	–	–	–	1.08	1.02	0.95
1747	–	–	–	–	–	–	1.21	1.02	1.08
1751	0.88	0.70	1.52	0.56	0.71	0.72	1.00	0.93	0.88

RABI

Year	*Wheat*	*Barley*	*Gram*	*Mustard*	*Sathi Rice*	*Arhar*
1713	1.60	1.14	1.14	1.08	2.35	1.00
1715	1.90	1.17	1.33	–	–	–
1716	2.10	1.37	1.25	2.22	–	–
1733	1.81	1.05	1.21	2.66	1.42	1.08
1735	1.81	1.60	1.29	2.10	1.66	1.60
1741	1.37	1.08	1.08	1.73	–	1.02
1743	1.90	1.14	1.06	1.48	2.10	1.60
1744	1.14	0.90	1.02	1.81	1.81	1.00
1747	1.42	1.05	1.11	1.29	1.42	–
1751	1.17	0.81	–	1.21	1.05	0.66

TABLE 2.22: PARGANA KHOHRI
COMPARISON OF PRICES (IN RUPEES PER MAN)

Year	Wheat	Barley	Gram	Bajra	Jowar	Moth	Urd	Moong
1665	0.99	0.65	0.69	0.61	0.55	0.58	0.71	0.58
1669	0.94	0.60	0.63	0.72	0.63	0.62	0.76	1.03
1684	0.75	0.55	–	0.85	0.55	0.45	0.48	0.59
1686	1.10	0.76	0.81	0.79	0.76	0.77	–	0.88
1688	1.01	0.76	0.56	0.87	0.81	0.74	0.79	0.81
1689	0.79	0.55	–	0.65	0.53	0.51	0.57	0.69
1696	1.32	1.03	–	1.87	1.70	2.12	2.14	–
1697	0.87	0.60	0.73	–	–	–	–	–
1706	0.95	0.64	0.69	0.53	0.45	0.53	0.86	0.72
1708	1.67	1.13	1.36	–	0.89	1.03	1.45	1.39
1710	–	0.72	0.66	0.74	0.64	0.68	0.95	0.90
1711	1.83	1.41	1.13	–	–	–	–	–
1716	1.78	1.22	1.23	2.06	1.70	1.55	1.61	1.98
1717	3.68	2.82	3.77	4.19	4.10	4.37	–	–
1718	2.65	1.91	2.98	2.30	2.08	2.36	2.67	2.80
1720	2.56	1.27	2.47	1.96	1.70	1.76	1.35	2.01
1721	2.58	1.96	1.88	1.35	1.23	1.26	–	1.32
1723	1.66	1.15	1.30	1.37	1.22	1.22	1.44	1.43
1724	1.38	1.08	0.99	1.25	1.17	0.94	1.10	1.11
1725	1.69	1.21	1.13	1.27	1.23	0.94	1.06	1.12

qasbas. In fact, all kinds of cultivators with superior rights tended to concentrate in *qasbas*. For instance in *qasba* Maujpur the *chaudharis* and *qanungos* alone cultivated 19 per cent of its land.[57] In *qasba* Bhusawar the *qanungos* and *patels* had their *gharujot* on 87.34 per cent of its cultivated land.[58] In *qasba* Pahari the *chaudharis* and *qanungos* had 60 per cent of its total land as their *gharujot*.[59] Thus cultivators with superior rights in land had large holdings in the *qasbas*. Their holdings were exempted from various tax obligations. For instance in pargana Tonk, when a tax levied on various pretexts, *virar* was imposed on the peasants of all the villages at the rate of 14 per cent of the *mal*, the Rajputs were spared from its payment.[60] The *qanungos*, *ashraf* and indigo cultivators (*neel-ka-karinda*) of *qasba* Hindaun were exempted from the payment of *virar* (12 per cent) and *partal* (5 per cent) taxes.[61] The *chaudharis* of village Sherpur Harauli in Hindaun also enjoyed similar immunities.[62] Apart from the standard land revenue demand (*mal*), many other cesses termed *jihat* were imposed on the peasants to meet expenditures involved in the process of the assessment and collection of revenue. The Brahmans, Mahajans, bards, *qanungos,* and *patels* of *qasba* Udai were exempt from all *jihat* taxes.[63]

All the *chaudharis,* and *qanungos* of *qasba* Chatsu, were free from the payment of a tax called *serina.* This was collected from the peasants of the pargana at the rate of 2 *ser* per *man.*[64] Chaudhari Das, who had village Kalhar of pargana Sonkhar as his *watan*, was completely exempted from the payment of revenue for the entire *rabi* harvest.[65] The Amber ruler used to collect the *bhom* tax at the rate of 3 per cent of the *mal* from the villages of various parganas. In this case also all the cultivators of many *qasbas* were exempted from the payment of the *bhom* tax.[66] *Sadir* tax, which amounted to one to two per cent of the *mal,* was not levied on the *qasbas.*[67] When a special tax at the rate of 7 per cent of the *mal* was imposed on the villagers of pargana Salawad, the cultivators of *qasba* Salawad were exempted.[68] Thus there is plentiful evidence to suggest that all cultivators of the *qasbas* and the entire class of superior right holders in the villages enjoyed substantial tax concessions. This enabled this minority of producers to maintain a flow of investments into agriculture. There are strong indications that the steady level of the production of cash crops was confined to the holdings of these privileged producers. On the other hand the weight of the various tax obligations being heavy on the mass of the peasantry in the villages, agricultural progress was impeded. Large-scale desertions of villages by impoverished peasants had left vast stretches of land uncultivated for years.[69] Somehow, the so called proponent of 'growth in eastern Rajasthan' have completely ignored the well documented phenomena of village desertions.[70]

Indigo and cotton merchants continued to do business in the region as long as the demand for these commodities remained steady in distant markets.[71] Interestingly, the local grain merchants were more frightened by the rural disturbances than the traders of high value crops, perhaps because the *bhomias* would target the grain traders every now and then.[72] As long as the demand for indigo and cotton remained steady, merchants from distant places continued to buy them. Even the fear (*vahda*) of the rebels, called *fisadis*, had not yet deterred these traders from visiting the region. Nonetheless the impact of the disturbances began to be felt during the third decade of the eighteenth century, as is evident from the break down of communications between the upcountry markets and the port of Surat.[73] This loss of distant markets was partly compensated by the rise of Jaipur as an important trading mart. An increase in sugarcane and cotton cultivation at the cost of indigo in some parganas, as discussed earlier, could have been due to the enhanced demand for these products in Jaipur.[74]

In short, a close examination of a variety of revenue records of some parganas of *sarkar* Agra, Sahar, and Alwar shows the existence of an uneven pace in agricultural production. There are unmistakable signs overall sluggishness in agriculture during the late seventeenth and early eighteenth century. Only the brief period between 1730 and 1740 witnessed some progress in a few parganas because of the coincidence of a bunch of contributory factors. The discriminatory revenue policy of the state encouraged a small section of the producers, specially in the *qasbas*, to produce high value crops, but the vast majority of ordinary peasants was compelled to grow mostly food crops. The size of the available arable remained constant, but a large part of it could not be cultivated. The quality of agricultural implements and irrigation facilities remained what they were. Surprisingly, there is no evidence of the introduction of the Persian wheel, despite the high water table in some parganas. As a large number of peasants were engaged in a grim struggle against nature and the state's fiscal pressure, a steady improvement in agriculture was not possible.

The poor peasants could manage to survive only because of their vast experience of the arrangement of crops and the management of land.

NOTES

1. This is the general purport of researches done by S. Nurul Hasan, Satish Chandra and S.P. Gupta on eastern Rajasthan. See S. Nurul Hasan, K.N. Hasan and S.P. Gupta, 'The Pattern of Agricultural Production in the territories of Amber (*c*. 1650/1750)', *PIHC*, 28th Session, Mysore, 1966, pp. 244-64. Satish Chandra, 'Role of the Local Community, the Zamindars and the State in Providing Capital Inputs for the Improvement and Expansion of Cultivation', *IHR*, vol. 3. 1, 1976, pp. 83-98 and S.P. Gupta, *Agrarian System of Eastern Rajasthan*, pp. 38-74.
2. Irfan Habib in his *Agrarian System*, pp. 366-78 has argued that the increasing exploitation of the peasantry proved ruinous for agricultural production in the long run.

3. Moreland considered weather as the most important fact in determining the contours of medieval Indian agriculture. See his *The Agrarian System of Moslem India*, 2nd edn., Delhi, 1968, p. xii. Shireen Moosvi also underlined the vulnerability of agriculture to climatic fluctuations. See her, 'Scarcities, Prices and Exploitation: The Agrarian Crisis, 1658-70', *Studies in History*, I, 1, n.s. (1985), p. 53.
4. These records are available in the Jaipur Historical Section of the Rajasthan State Archives, Bikaner.
5. S. Nurul Hasan, K.N. Hasan and S.P. Gupta, 'The Pattern of Agricultural Production in the Territories of Amber (*c.* 1650-1750)', *PIHC*, 28th Session at Mysore, 1966, pp. 244-64; S. Nurul Hasan and S.P. Gupta, 'Prices of Foodgrains in the Territories of Amber (*c.* 1650-1750)', *PIHC*, 29th Session at Patiala, 1968, pp. 345-68.
6. S. Nurul Hasan, K.N. Hasan and S.P. Gupta, 'Pattern of Agricultural Production', pp. 246-7.
7. *The Imperial Gazetteer of India*, vol. VIII, New Edition, Oxford, Clarendon Press, 1908, pp. 72-4 and *Rajasthan District Gazetteers*, Bharatpur, 1971, p. 143.
8. *Rajasthan District Gazetteers, Sawai Madhopur*, 1981, p. 4.
9. *Land Revenue Settlement of the Gurgaon District* by F.C. Channing, Lahore, 1877, pp. 5-8 and *District Gazetteers, Alwar* by P.W. Powlet, London, 1872, pp. 90-1.
10. *Arsattha, Ro Naj ki*, pargana Bawal, vs 1721/1664.
11. *Arsattha,* pargana Khohri, vs 1781/1724.
12. *Arzdasht*, dt. Asoj Vadi 12, vs 1751/1694.
13. *Amber Record*, dt. Sawan Sudi 15, vs 1722/1665.
14. Ibid.
15. *District Gazetteers*, Alwar, op. cit., p. 88.
16. *Haqiqati* of village Run-Devati in *Amber Record* dt. Asoj Vadi 6, vs 1760/1703. In this village there were 5 *pucca* and 5 *kacha* wells to irrigate 200 *bighas* of land.
17. The *arsatthas* of Hindaun, Toda Bhim, Khohri, Pahari, Kotla and Jalalpur mention use of *dhenkli* for the *rabi* season.
18. *Amber Record*, dt. Sawan Sudi 2, vs 1722/1665. *Taqmina* of village Udhranpur, *tappa* Khohri.
19. *Arsattha*, pargana Udai (Unhalu), vs 1777/1790.
20. *Arsattha*, pargana Bhusawar (Unhalu), vs 1783/1726.
21. *Arzdasht*, dt. Asoj Vadi 12, vs 1751/1694.
22. In *qasba* Biwan (between Ferozepur and Pahari) there is an old masonry well. Till recently 12 *charas* were put to use at this well at a time.
23. *Muntakhabut-Tawarikh*, tr. W.H. Lowe (rpt. 1973), vol. II, p. 250. This reference is to Bhusawar.
24. *Baburnama*, tr. A.S. Beveridge (rpt. 1979), vol. II, pp. 580-1.
25. *Arsatthas*, pargana Khohri, vs 1722/1666 and 1770/1713; Pahari vs 1773/1716 and 1800/1743.
26. Ibid.
27. In the tables, insignificant and infrequently grown crops have been omitted. Also all kinds of vegetables have been placed in one column.

28. Tapan Raychaudhuri and Irfan Habib (eds.), *The Cambridge Economic History of India*, vol. I, *c.* 1200-1750, Cambridge University Press, 1982, p. 217.
29. *Arsattha*, pargana Hindaun (Syalu), vs 1770/1713.
30. *Arsattha*, pargana Hindaun (Syalu), vs 1785/1728.
31. *Amber Records*, dt. Asoj Sudi 6, vs 1722/1663, Chet Vadi 6, vs 1722/1665 and Mangsir Vadi 12, vs 1723/1666.
32. Ashin Das Gupta, *Indian Merchants and the Decline of Surat, c. 1700-1750*, p. 110.
33. *Arsattha*, pargana Hindaun, vs 1781/1724.
34. These were *bengan, muli, arya, kharbuja, torai*, onion, *karela, kakari*, etc. *Henna, arhar, ajwain*, etc., were also grown here and there. In Toda Bhim *varejapaan* was grown too.
35. Tapan Raychaudhuri and Irfan Habib (eds.), *The Cambridge Economic History*, p. 219.
36. *Arsattha Ro Naajki*, pargana Bawal, vs 1721/1664.
37. *Taqsim dahsala*, pargana Punkhar vs 1787-98 (1730-41) and *Muwazana dahsala*, pargana Hindaun, vs. 1790-99/1733-42.
38. For instance, in village Jagner of pargana Khohri the total land (*raqba*) was 575 *bighas*. Of this, only 500 *bighas* were under cultivation (*chalat*). The seasonwise division was as under. Land under cultivation in *rabi*: 500 *bighas* (which included *rabi* land of 350 *bighas* plus *kharif's dufasli* land of 150 bighas. The remainder 150 *bighas* was only *kharif* land. Thus the total cultivated land (including *dufasli*) came to 650 *bighas*. See *arsattha*, pargana Khohri, vs 1783/1726 and vs 1784/1727, for more details.
39. *Ain-i-Akbari*.
40. *Taqsim dahsala*, pargana Udai, vs 1791-1800/1734-43.
41. *Taqsim pand'rehsala*, pargana Antela Bhabhra, vs 1706-1720/1649-63.
42. *Taqsim dahsala*, pargana Antela Bhabhra, vs 1756-65/1699-1708.
43. *Haqiqati Gaon* Pali, pargana Sonkhar, vs 1792-1802/1735-45 and *Haqiqati* Gaon Balupura, pargana Kuthumber, vs 1743-1802/173-45.
44. *Amber Records*, dt. Asadh Sudi 4, Asadh Vadi 6, Asoj Sudi 6, Chet Vadi 6, Mah Sudi 6, vs 1722/1665 and Mangsir Vadi 12, Vaisakh Sudi 12, Kati Vadi 5, Mah Vadi 1, Asoj Sudi 9, Jeth Sudi 3, Mangsir Sudi 15, Bhadwa Sudi 15, Asoj Vadi 10-11, vs 1723/1666. These parganas were: Kotla, Sakras, Khohri, Punkhar, Mandawar and Sonkhar.
45. *Amber Records*, dt. Mangsir Vadi 12, vs 1723/1666.
46. *Arzdasht*, dt. Kati Vadi 13, vs 1741/1684.
47. *Arzdasht*, dt. Asoj Vadi 2, vs 1751/1694.
48. *Arzdashts*, dt. Kati Vadi 2, vs 1753/1696 and Asadh Sudi 7, vs 1755/1698.
49. Tapan Raychaudhuri and Irfan (eds.), *The Cambridge Economic History*, p. 376.
50. *Amber Records*, dt. Bhadwa Sudi 8, vs 1769/1712. The Amber ruler instructed his officials not to divert grain from parganas Khohri, Maujpur, Pindayan, and Punkhar to Agra, Delhi and Thoon.
S. Nurul Hasan, K.N. Hasan and S.P. Gupta, 'The Pattern of Agricultural Production', pp. 244-64; and S. Nurul Hasan and S.P. Gupta, 'Prices of Foodgrains', pp. 345-68.
51. *Arsattha*, pargana Wazirpur, vs 1769/1712.

52. *Arsattha*, pargana Hindaun, VS 1777/1720.
53. *Arsatthas*, pargana Malarna, VS 1722/1665 (9 per cent); Niwai, VS 1721/1664 (8.5 per cent); Chatsu, VS 1771/1714 and Toda Raisinghpur, VS 1774/1717 (10 per cent).
54. S.P. Gupta, *Agrarian System of Eastern Rajasthan*, p. 151. It seems that Gupta has misunderstood the nature of this tax. For instance, in the *arsattha* of pargana Chatsu the amount of this tax is clearly recorded as 8.5 per cent (*sadh-atthotra*) of the *mal*. One fails to understand on what basis Gupta has converted it into 1 per cent to 4 per cent. Similarly in the *arsattha* of pargana Malarna the tax is stated to be 9 per cent (*norotra*), but the range given by Gupta is between 4 per cent and 36 per cent.
55. S.P. Gupta, *Agrarian System*, pp. 60-2.
56. *Arsattha*, pargana Jalalpur, VS 1749/1692.
57. *Arsattha*, pargana Maujpur, VS 1771/1714.
58. *Arsattha*, pargana Bhusawar, VS 1773/1716.
59. *Arsattha*, pargana Pahari, VS 1791/1732.
60. *Arsattha*, pargana Tonk, VS 1765/1708.
61. *Arsattha*, pargana Hindaun, VS 1770/1713.
62. *Arsattha*, pargana Hindaun, VS 1775/1718.
63. *Dastur amal*, pargana Udai, VS 1771/1714.
64. *Dastur amal*, pargana Chatsu, VS 1769/1712.
65. *Dastur amal*, pargana Sonkhar-Sonkhari, VS 1773/1716.
66. The *arsattha* of parganas Pahari, Maujpur, Khohri, Wazirpur and Udai for different years clearly show the cultivators of these *qasbas* either totally exempted from the *bhom* tax or nominally subjected to it.
67. *Arsattha*, pargana Salawad, VS 1768/1711 and Pahari, VS 1788/1731.
68. *Arsattha*, pargana Salawad, VS 1768/1711.
69. For instance pargana Pahari consisted of 209 villages, out of which about 80 to 90 villages were kept under the *khalisa amal*. A large number of these *khalisa* villages are reported as deserted year after year.

Year	*No. of villages*	*Description*
1724	21	Deserted due to poverty (*nadari*)
1731	21	Drought year (*kahatsal*)
1734	16	No cultivation (*zarait nahi*)
1737	29	Uncultivated (*ajot*)
1743	41	Deserted due to poverty (*nadari*)

See Chapter 1 for further details of village desertions in other parganas.

70. A large number of villages are reported as deserted (*viran* or *ujar*) in the parganas covered by the study of Gupta etc. For example pargana Malarna consisted of 132 villages of which the number of deserted villages was 52 in 1695; 63 in 1697, and 50 in 1699. In another pargana, Chatsu, the number of deserted villages was 41 in 1696. The phenomenon of village desertion persisted. Had Gupta taken cognizance of this phenomenon, his conclusions would have been more realistic.
71. *Auzdashts*, dt. Asadh vadi 8, VS 1744/1687 and Mah vadi 4, VS 1775/1718.
72. *Auzdashts*, dt. Jeth sudi 8, VS 1752/1695 and dt. Mah vadi 4Vs 1761/1704.

73. Ashin Das Gupta, *Indian Merchants and the Decline of Surat*. In the *arsattha* of Hindaun, the non-arrival of indigo merchants in 1724 is clearly recorded.
74. Kumar Ram Krishna, 'Internal Trade System of Eastern Rajasthan (1720-1780) Ph.D. thesis submitted to the University of Delhi, 2006. The centrality of Jaipur in providing market to some cash crops, is indicated in this work.

3

Magnitude of the Land Revenue Demand

The Mughal land revenue administration functioned in two distinct phases, assessment (*tashkhish*) followed by collection (*tahsil*). The term *jama* denoted the amount assessed while *hasil* was the amount collected. The assessment was separately made for *kharif* and *rabi*. In our region it was made in two ways. The first was crop-sharing, known as *batai jinsi*, and the other was *zabt* or the cash system. The extent of the actual application of these systems varied from pargana to pargana and from season to season.[1] Both methods had their merits and demerits; hence the notion of their utility was different for rulers and peasants. Change from one form to the other, on demand or otherwise, was not frequent but was never completely ruled out. There are instances of such shifts in the method of assessment.[2] At times fixed collections (*bil-muqta*) were also made. *Bil-muqta* actually meant 'in a lumpsum' or 'on the whole'.[3] From our evidence it appears that the *bil-muqta* was resorted to in those areas prone to defiance (z*ortalab*).[4]

Under the *zabt* system, revenue was assessed and realized in cash.[5] Under the crop-sharing system, the revenue was stated in kind but collected in cash.[6] Whenever the revenue was realized in kind it was at once stored in the granaries (*Khasas*) and subsequently sold in the market.[7] Irfan Habib says:

> . . . Since the demand under *zabt* was based, first, on an unvaried crop rate and then, finally, on unvaried cash rates, the peasant was left to bear practically all the risks from the inconsistency of the harvests. Manifestly, then the proportion under *zabt* could not have been set as high as under, say, crop-sharing, where the risks were evenly shared between the peasant and the state.[8]

This of course is a plausible explanation of the difference in the proportion of revenue demand which the peasants had to meet under the two systems. The actual magnitude of revenue burden on the peasantry can be worked out from information provided by the *arsatthas* and *dastur amals* of various parganas. The *arsattha* was a register of income and expenditure of the pargana. Its form might have varied from pargana to pargana but the content was always uniform. It is divided into three parts, total collection (*muqarar jama*) the expenditure (*kharach* or *minzalik*) and the arrears (*baqaya*). The income is recorded according to assessment (*muafiq jamabandi*) and unassessed (*siwai jamabandi*). While *mal-o-jihat* (land revenue) constituted the bulk of the total income, it was followed by *sair-jihat* (other cesses).[9]

The *dasturs* are administrative manuals of revenue rates. The percentage of land revenue demand on each section of the peasantry is mentioned separately. Revenue-collectors were guided by these *dasturs* at the time of collection. While there is a near uniformity in the percentage of land revenue paid by the peasants out of their total produce, the number and percentage of other cesses varied from time to time and pargana to pargana.[10] This chapter is basically concerned with the working out of the total tax burden to which peasants were subjected.

The operation of the Mughal revenue system at uniform rates for all peasants irrespective of their resources was regressive by itself, imposing a higher burden on those with least resources. Added to this was further discriminatory tax rate much to the benefit of the higher strata of peasantry as Table 3.1 would show.

Thus the *gaveti-palti raiyat* had to part with 50 per cent of the total produce under the crop-sharing system to meet the land revenue

TABLE 3.1: REVENUE RATES UNDER THE BATAI SYSTEM[11]
(IN PERCENTAGES)

Pargana	*Raiyat*	*Pahis*	*Kamins*	*Patels*	*Qanungo/ Chaudhuri/ Rajputs*	*Brahmins*
Antela	50	33	40	40	25	33
Gijgarh	50	33	33-40	33	25	30
Niwai	40-50	25-33	33-40	40-50	– 25-33	
Chatsu	50	–	40	40	25	45
Sonkhar	40-50	–	40	–	33	–
Khohri	50	50	–	–	–	–

demand of the state. They were immediately followed by the *patels* and the *kamins*. The least burdened were the *chaudhuris, qanungos* and the *bhomias*. Between the *raiyat* on the one hand and *chaudhuri* on the other, there were the *pahis* and Brahmans. Same *dastur* was applied whether the pargana was under *khalisa* or *jagir*.[12] For reasons already stated, the land revenue demand on the peasants under *zabt* was 40 per cent of the gross produce.[13] A large army of officials was recruited to accomplish the task of regular assessment. Similarly a fleet of watchmen had to be maintained to guard the crops under the crop-sharing system. The entire expenditure spent on the assessment of land and the collection of revenue was charged from the peasants in the form of various cesses which were locally called *vav* (which seems to be a local version of the Persian word *abwab*). The more important of these cesses are mentioned here along with their quantum which had minor variations from pargana to pargana.

In the *zabti* region *jaribana* (expense on account of the measuring rope) was charged at the rate of 28 *dams* per *bigha*.[14] The rate of *zabitana* (daily expenses of the measuring party) was 15 *dams* per *bigha*.[15] *Rozina zabti* (daily expenses on assessment) was charged at the rate of Rs 2 on each 100 *bighas* of land under cultivation.[16] The rate of *dahnimi* (lit. a half of ten) was one *taka* on each *zabti* rupee.[17] Half a *taka* on each 100 *zabti* rupees was taken as *sarhi* (a cess related to the assessment of *zabti* crops).[18]

Similarly the crop-sharing system also involved huge expenses which were charged from the peasants. Therefore, the total burden of the cesses under the crop-sharing system was enormous. *Farah-serina* (from *faruat*) was the heaviest cess under crop-sharing. It ranged between 2 and 5 *sers* per *man*.[19] *Tankina*[20] (exaction collected in *takas*) and *bhara*[21] (expenses on the transportation of grain) were respectively charged at the rate of one *taka* per *man*.[22] Last but not least was the *lata-kharach* (expense on crop division) cess which was charged at the rate of one *ser* per *man*.[23]

Apart from these cesses, the perquisites paid to the rural potentates who functioned as semi-officials in various capacities, were also charged from the peasants. The list begins with the *bhom*. In most of the parganas the *bhom* cess formed 3 per cent of the land revenue.[24] In pargana Antela the rate of the *bhom* was as high as 6.25 per cent of the *mal*.[25] A separate cess, ranging from 1.25 to 2.50 per cent, was charged from the peasants in order to pay the remuneration of the *chaudhuris* and *qanungos*.[26] It was called *dastur chaudhurai* and *qanungoi*. Similarly, *dastur patwara* at the rate of one per cent of the land revenue was levied to make up for payment to the *patwaris*.[27] To organize the payment of the *diwan* a cess called *diwan-dasturi* at the rate of 2 per cent was charged.[28] The *waqai-nawis* (news-writer) also claimed one per cent of the revenue as his share.[29] The *fotadars* (treasurers) were paid out of a separate cess which amounted to one per cent of the land revenue.[30] A *sadir* cess (short form of *kharaj-i-sadir-o-warid* (expenses to meet the needs of the officials during their visits) was also realized at the uniform rate of one per cent from peasants of all the parganas.[31]

The land revenue and other cesses mentioned above were not the only taxes collected from the peasants. They also had to pay up for their cattle and agricultural equipment. Thus they had to pay one *taka* as tax on each bullock, cow, buffalo, and goat separately.[32] Those who owned axes had to pay one rupee for each axe.[33] There was no floor level exemption allowed in case of the ordinary peasants. Yet the oxen of the rural potentates were exempted up to a limit from the tax on cattle.[34] The peasants had to pay taxes for grazing their cattle on pasture lands. The peasants were also subjected to various *salamis* (salutation fee) and *bhents* (presentations) regularly paid to the pargana officials. The peasants were not asked to pay such taxes individually; the village as a unit appears to have paid them. Their number and volume varied from pargana to pargana as the number of *amils* and *amins* also varied. Invariably one rupee each for the *diwan*, *faujdar*, *amils* (whose number varied from 2 to 4 in a pargana) and *amins* was charged as *bhent* or *salami* from every village.[35] This also added to the financial burden of the middle and poor peasants as the *gharuhala* cultivators were exempted from contributing their share to the *malba* (the common financial pool) of the village.[36]

Apart from these cesses there were others which were not realized uniformly from all parganas but with a specific incidence in some. In pargana Malpura two such cesses were *hasil muharrirana*—the scribe's dues at the rate of Rs 4 per village—and *hasil lawazma* (for making payment to various servants in the *amil's* court) at the rate of Rs 6 per village.[37] In two parganas a tax on ploughs was levied. In Bahatri it was termed *halkati* and charged at the rate of Re 1 for every Rs 500 of *mal*,[38] while in another pargana it was called *halsari* and its rate was six *annas* per plough.[39] Each village was subjected to a regular tax, the amount of which obviously varied from pargana to pargana, to make up 4 per cent of the land revenue for meeting the expenses incurred in the *amil*'s court on ink, paper thread, ropes, etc.[40] As already stated, a large number of watchmen (*sehnas*) were needed to look after the crops assessed under the crop-sharing system. The salaries of these watchmen were also collected from the peasants under two special levies, namely, *chak-sehna*[41] and *ghughari-sehna*.[42] A letter allowing the peasants to start harvesting was issued by the *amils* in some parganas. This also occasioned the levy of a cess which was termed *hasil chithawan* or *hasil balkati* or *hasil faslana*.[43] A kind of house tax on the permanent residents of the village was charged in most parganas.[44] In all those parganas where the Amber ruler claimed his zamindari right, a special cess was frequently levied. On the occasion of the marriage of any member of the royal house, the peasants had to pay the *nyota* tax.[45] The quantity of this levy was doubled between 1665 (8 *annas* per plough) and 1697 (Re. 1 per plough), yet another irritant for the peasants. Wherever land was irrigated with water from the canals, it was also taxed by the state. In pargana Pahari the peasants and *bhomias* who used canal water had to pay 5 per cent and 4 per cent of the *mal* respectively.[46] In some parganas the *patels* had to pay a regular tax called *ghiwai* at the rate of 2 per cent.[47]

This period is marked by an upward price mobility.[48] The price rise should have normally benefited the peasantry. The preference of the cultivators during our period (1650-1750) to shift to *zabti* crops, the revenue from which was collected in cash, is a testimony in the view of some scholars for an additional surplus left with the peasants by the price rise.[49] On the other hand Irfan Habib has argued that the cultivators could not benefit from any rise in food grain prices because the *zabti* rates, a fixed proportion of the total produce, were also enhanced in tandem.[50] Our evidence shows that, with minor exceptions, the *zabti* rates were neither increased nor decreased in proportion to the rise or fall in agricultural prices.

The *zabti* rates on various crops in different parganas remained constant even when there were fluctuations in the prices of the same commodities. The rates in two parganas on various crops are given here to illustrate the point. The tables are based on documents extending over large periods of time, yet revenue rates remained constant over these periods.

TABLE 3.2: *ZABTI* RATES ON DIFFERENT CROPS
PARGANA HINDAUN[51] (AD 1713-42)

Kharif crops	*Zabti rates per bigha*	
	Rs	*Annas*
a. Cheena, Bajra, *Marwa*, *Kaguni*, *Rodu*, *Chola* and *Guwar*	1	05
b. Arhar, Kachra, Torai, Tarbuj, Bhagi, Ariya, Til, Urd, *Moong*, *Maka* and *Karela*	1	15
c. Neel (*Jari*)	2	00
d. Neel (*Noti*, *Teesala* and *Chausala*)	1	08
e. *Vaar* (*Noti*)	7	09
f. Van, San, Patsan, Gajar, Muli, Kali mirach and Chari	3	03
g. *Bengan*, Tobacco, *Singhara*, *Methi*, *Mehandi*, *Kanda* and Sakargandi	3	13
h. *Vaar* (*Peri*)	5	01
i. *Dhan*	2	09
Rabi crops		
a. Wheat (irrigated), Tobacco, Post, *Kanda*, *Ajwain*, Vegetables, *Bengan*, *Methi*, *Asala*, *Kharbuja*, *Alsi*, *Palej* and *Afu*	3	13
b. *Gojra*	3	08
b. Wheat (irrigated by *Dhenkli*), Barley (irr.), *Gajar*, *Muli*, *Kasuma*	3	13
d. Wheat (non-irri.), Barley (irr. *Dhekli*)	2	09
e. Barley (non-irr.), Gram, *Bejhari*, *Masur*, *Rai*, *Kakri*, *Sarson*, *Matar*, *Tarbuj*, *Lahalra* and *Bhagi*	1	15
f. Cheena	1	05

TABLE 3.3: *ZABTI* RATES ON DIFFERENT CROPS
PARGANA KHOHRI[52] (AD 1712-53)

Kharif crops	*Zabti rates per bigha*	
	Rs	*Annas*
a. Rice		
sathi	5	00
dhani	6	00
sukhdas	8	00
b. *Barti*, *Kuri* and *Kaguni*	1	02
c. Van, San, *Torai*, *Bengan*, *Maka*, *Arya* and Jawar	2	00
d. *Kodon*, *Marwa*, Bajra and Til	1	08
e. *Chola* and *Chari*	1	04

f. Indigo	2	08
g. Tobacco, *Sakargandi* and *Vaar*	3	08
h. *Urd* .	1	12
Rabi crops		
a. Cheena	1	04
b. *Muli* and *Barti*	1	08
c. *Bengan, Kakri, Tarbuj, Vari* and Rice	2	00
d. Barley, *Bejhar* and *Sarson*	3	00
e. *Pyaj, Bhagi, Karar,* Somp, *Ghana, Ajwain, Methi, Kasuma* and *Sakargandi*	3	08
f. *Gajar*	3	04
g. Gram and Wheat	4	00
h. Rice (*sathi* and *kor*)	5, 7	00

It is fairly certain that no benefit accrued to the cultivators as a result of the rise in food grain prices. The state invented an ingenious method whereby the peasants were deprived of any benefit resulting from a rise in agricultural prices. A tax with a wide range of incidence and named after the digits it denoted was imposed on almost all the *zabti* crops. The digits were from *Ikotra*[53] (1 per cent) to *Pandrehotra*[54] (15 per cent). The varying percentage of this tax in various parganas is given below.

TABLE 3.4: SPECIAL TAX ON *ZABTI* CROPS DUE TO PRICE RISE

Pargana	*Percentage of the*[55] *digit tax in relation to the mal*	*Year*
Chatsu	8.25	1664
Niwai	8.25	1664
Khohri	7	1664
Bahatri	5	1665
Malarna	9	1665
Jalalpur	5	1666
Hindaun	12	1712
Punkhar	5	1740
Wazirpur	8.25	–
Kakrala	12	–
Salawad	7	–

In the case of pargana Hindaun this tax was 12 per cent in the *rabi* season. But during the *kharif* season the same tax was 9.50 per cent of the *mal* and has been termed *hasil girani* (lit. dearness levy)[56] which is obviously a tax on account of dearness of the *zabti* crops. The variations in the range of this tax were perhaps the result of uneven prices.

Peshkash was realized from territories of almost every form of administration in the territories that formed the *watan* of the Amber rulers, those given in *jagir* to them and those taken by them from the imperial jagirdars on *ijara*. In the territories of Amber the system of paying *peshkash* was also twisted to the disadvantage of the peasantry. The amount of money paid as *peshkash* to the *subadar* and the *faujdars* by the Amber rulers had customarily to be drawn from their own treasury. But now attempts were made to transfer this fiscal demand on to the peasants, who strongly protested against this imposition.[57] The Amber rulers collected this amount from the peasants under a special head called *virar*.[58]

TABLE 3.5: AMOUNT OF (*VIRAR*) TAX ABOVE THE *DASTUR*

Pargana	*Percentage of virar*[59] *(in rupees)*	*Year*
Chatsu	10	1664
Tonk	14.5	1708
Hindaun	11	1718
Bhusawar	25	1731
Khohri	15	1741

If the magnitude of land revenue demand was as high as 50 per cent under crop-sharing and 40 per cent under the *zabt* system,[60] the total fiscal burden borne by individual peasant, other than the land revenue, was not much lighter. In the case of some parganas it was as follows:

TABLE 3.6: NO AND QUANTITY OF *DASTUR* TAXES
PARGANA KHOHRI, 1642[61]

S. No.	*Name of the cess*	*Percentage of mal (in rupees)*
1.	*Jihat* (cesses other than the *mal*)	15
2.	*Tapdari* (Tapdar's dues)	2.5

(*contd.*)

TABLE 3.6 (*contd.*)

3.	*Tehsildari* (Tahsildar's dues)	4
4.	*Alri* (?)	1
5.	*Chirotra* (digit cess in the genre of Ikotra)	4
6.	*Tafawat* Shahjahani	2
7.	*Shiqdari Karkuni* (Karkun's dues)	1.75
	Total	30.25

TABLE 3.7: PARGANA BHUSAWAR: 1714[62]

S. No.	*Name of the cess*	*Percentage of mal (in rupees)*
1.	*Mapa Mal* (expenses on the assessment of *mal*)	2
2.	*Sarah mal* (cess related to the assessment of *zabti* crops	2
3.	*Sadar mal* (expenses to meet the needs of the officials during the visits to the villages)	1
4.	*Bhara mal* (expenses on transportation)	1
5.	*Peshkash mal* (to pay for the tribute to the officials of the *subah*	25
	Total	31

TABLE 3.8: TOTAL AMOUNT OF COLLECTED TAXES PARGANA HINDAUN, AD 1734[63]

S.No.	*Village*	*Mal (in rupees)*	*Cesses (in rupees)*	*Percentage of mal*
1.	Jatwara	3,000	512	17.06
2.	Jewar	900	188	20.88
3.	Jagar	3,950	688	17.41
4.	Qutubpur	2,200	387	17.59
5.	Kalohari Jat	1,650	306	18.54

Thus the total surplus realized from the peasants, leaving aside irregular exactions, was above 52 per cent under *zabt* and nearly 65 per cent under the *batai* system. The exact rates set for most of these cesses can be further gleaned from a wide variety of documents. They could hardly have been uniform. Though separately these cesses appear to be negligible, together they amounted to large sums, as is evident from the figures of three parganas mentioned above.

All kinds of village revenue records bear witness to the

deteriorating economic condition of the peasantry from the middle of the seventeenth century. Several factors combined to contribute to this: the rate of revenue demand was already high enough; there were, in addition new imposts that will be discussed presently. Besides, the *bhomias* would terrorize the peasants and subject them to irregular and illegal extortions. The highhandedness of the officials often led to the confiscation of their belongings. Then there was the periodic drought. It is possible that all these factors were operative even under the regime of the early Mughals; also by themselves, none of them would suggest a deterioration of the peasants' conditions in the late seventeenth century. But there are specific instances of new imposts being introduced which inevitably provoked peasant protest. In fact the recurring theme of a variety of reportage unmistakably suggests an increasing economic depression of the peasantry.

In 1645 the peasants of pargana Chatsu, when asked to pay the newly imposed *patwara* cess at the rate of 10 *annas* per Rs 100, told the *amil* that they were already under the burden of a number of taxes. Thereupon the *amil* reminded the peasants of Chatsu that the people of pargana Amber were paying the *patwara* cess and they might as well accept similar obligations. The peasants of Chatsu retorted that they were already paying more taxes than those in Amber. In the same document, the *amil* writes that the peasantry of Chatsu was indigent (*asami nadar chhe*).[64] Yet the *arsattha* of pargana Chatsu for the year 1664 shows that the *patwara* tax at the rate of one per cent of the land revenue was actually being realized.[65] Obviously the peasants had, during the intervening period, lost out to the administration. This may be further illustrated by the complaint of the peasants of pargana Rinsi. In order to highlight the general plight of the peasantry of eight parganas, they gave the example of one village, Akahera. The peasants bemoaned the fact that of the 16,000 *man* grain produced in Akahera in the *kharif* season, 8,000 *mans* had been taken by the *jagirdar* as land revenue. From the remaining 8,000 *mans* they had to pay *dastur qanungoi; sehngi, tankina* and *sehngi-dihangi* which totalled 4,500 *mans*. So they were left with a bare 3,500 *mans*.[66] Paying out 78 per cent out of their gross produce as revenue, they could hardly be accused of being obstructive. This was indeed a joint complaint of the peasants of the eight parganas and therefore suggests a general condition prevailing in those parganas. These parganas were Rinsi, Mundawar,

Behror, and Dadri in the *jagir* of Raja Bishan Singh; Faridabad and Sohna in the *jagir* of Nawab Zafar Khan, Pilgawa in the *jagir* of Murtaza Khan and two parganas in the *jagir* of Raja Jaswant Singh. It may be noted that most of these parganas were either those that later became the cradle of the Jat uprising, or parganas, continuous to the latter.

The peasants of pargana Niwai were subjected to a double *bhom* tax in 1683. When the *amil* asked them to pay one *taka* on each *zabti bigha* and one *ser* on each *batai man* as *bhom* cess, they replied that they were already paying this bhom cess to Gaj Singh Rajawat, the traditional *bhomia* of Niwai. The *amil* of Niwai not only ignored this protest but further imposed a new *patwara* cess at the rate of one *ser* per *batai man*.[67] It may be noted here that the *arsattha* for the year 1664 of pargana Niwai does not include the collection of any *patwara* and *bhom* cesses.[68] Thus the relevant revenue records of both these parganas leave one in no doubt about the addition of the *patwara* and *bhom* cesses. As if this were not enough, collectors came from Ajmer and demanded the *jizya* at the rate of 4 per cent of the *mal* from the peasants.[69] This invited a uniform reaction from the peasants who refused to pay all the three additional cesses, (double *bhom*, *patwara* and *jizya*). The watchmen (*sehnas*) posted in the villages of pargana Nainwai conventionally used to get *ghughari* as a reward for their work. But in 1664, an additional cess, namely, *sehngi* at the rate of one *ser* per *man* was levied on the peasants.[70] The peasantry protested against this imposition. Similarly, peasants of pargana Mauzabad refused to pay the *bhom* cess and *hasil-kawarya* on the ground that these were fresh exactions.[71] In 1684, the peasants of Kuvava, Saner, and Gijgarh, pargana demanded the conversion of *zabti amal* into *batai* so that they could 'clear their tax arrears'.[72] Though it was not normally allowed, the peasants wrested a concession of four annas per *bigha* under the existing *amal* to enable them to clear all their arrears. In pargana Salawad a new tax (*nava sire se lena kiya*) called *sadar-kharach* at the rate of two rupees of the *mal* was imposed in 1691. This provoked the peasants of 12 villages to abandon cultivation.[73] In 1693, the peasants of 40 villages of an unspecified pargana, when asked to pay a general *virar* levy for the campaigns organized against the Jats, refused to pay on the ground that there was no such custom in the pargana.[74] Peasants of some villages of Toda Bhim complained in 1693 that in the *dastur* of the pargana excessive revenue (*vih*) was 'charged' from them.[75] Hence they refused *en bloc* to pay revenue according to the rates mentioned in the *dastur.* The *amil* as usual allowed some concessions to the *pahis*, but not to the *gavetis*. Moreover, in the same *dastur* similar rates had been mentioned to be applied on the best (*awwal*) as well as second class (*dom*) land. The angry peasants justifiably questioned the application of such an anomalous *dastur*. In 1694, it was reported from many parganas that the peasants were too poor to carry on cultivation. There was no money-lender (*bohra)* ready to advance loans to them. In 1694, the *amil* of Toda Bhim sent the following report about his pargna:

> We are making arrangements for the cultivation of those lands which are close to the wells. The *patels* of *Sikrai* etc. came and told us that during the previous drought their condition was very miserable but because of the help given to them by the administration they came and settled in the pargana. Now conditions have become unbearable. They have been irrigating the land in the vicinity of wells. Many peasants are using the *laav-charas* (leather bucket and rope) which they made in the *rabi* season, for irrigating the *kharif* crops. In this way these peasants irrigated as much *kharif* crop area as was possible with the help of *laav-charas* made for use in the *rabi* season. But many peasants have been without *laav-charas* for long and at present they are not in a position to stay any longer because of the steep rise in the food-grain prices. There is no *bohra* in the pargana and the peasants cannot bear any more hardship. They have been hoping that the administration will give them *taqavi* (financial help) so that they can arrange for the *laav-charas*. In this way they will be in a position to produce *hasil* for the government and keep themselves alive. The peasantry of this pargana is very hardworking. So far I have been able to persuade them to irrigate the land around the wells. In order to ensure continuity of production it is necessary that a *bohra* of some other pargana may be asked to come here and distribute *taqavi* according to the need of each village. These loans may be recovered from the peasants at the time of harvest. In case *bohras* are reluctant to come here, then the administration should distribute *taqavi* among the peasants.[76]

It appears that the *amil* had collected the land revenue in 1693 strictly on the basis of the stipulations of the *dastur*, which according to the peasants amounted to 'overcharging'. Nothing was left with the peasants for a rainy day. This accounts for the peasants' inability to avert the crop-failure of the ensuing year. Irrigation was possible only with the help of the *laav-charas* which many were unable to afford. Production had become so uncertain that even the *bohras* refused to advance loans in parganas Kuthumbari, Hasanpur, and

Dausa.[77] Earlier in 1683 the *amils* of Bhairana and Chatsu had reported the misery of the *patels* and peasants of their respective parganas.[78] In 1665 poverty had caused a large-scale migration of the peasantry to Delhi and the trans-Jamuna areas.[79] In 1694, it was drought that forced the peasants of Bagar and Ajmer to migrate towards Mathura.[80]

The peasants were really reeling under the burden of various imposts. In 1646, the peasants of parganas Kotla and Bawal had complained against the burden of *seri* which was 4 *ser* per *man*.[81] The economic condition of the peasants of Niwai and Malpura was reported to be dismal in 1663-4.[82] For the peasants of Nainwai even the burden of *sehngi* appeared to have gone beyond endurance.[83] The entire peasantry of pargana Salawad was asked to pay two additional cesses, namely, *nyota* and *bhomi* at the rate of one per cent and two per cent of the *mal* respectively.[84] They refused on the plea that they were outside the *watan* (hereditary dominion) of the Amber Raja and could not be subjected to such levies. Even the *patwaris* and *patels* of the villages of Amber territories complained of an unbearable burden of levies such as the *peshkash* and *dihangi*.[85] In 1683, *jizya* was imposed on the cultivators (*haljotas*).[86] The peasants refused to pay this additional tax and told the *tahsildars* that *haljotas* had been exempted from *jizya* in the past. It was reported in 1685 that the entire pargana of Bahatri was ruined by the *dihangi* and *talbana*.[87] Again in 1686 the peasants of Malarna and Niwai were subjected to the payment of *jizya*.[88] In the year 1693, the condition of the peasants of Malpura was miserable.[89] The peasants of many other parganas strongly protested and those of Bayana rebelled against the arbitrary imposition of *virar*.[90] In the *jamabandi* of Toda Bhim *tahsildari*, *bhent*, *ghas* (a cess on grazing) and *lakri* (acess on wood taken from the forest) were entered as per the *dastur*. In the past the pargana was fully populated and the peasants could pay all these cesses. But during the concerned year there lived about 2 to 4 *asamis* (cultivators) in each of the villages. The officials chose to collect the entire amount of *tahsildari* from the latter who after having paid the land revenue were left with a small amount which was further taxed. Owing to this highhanded application of the *dastur* other peasants were not coming to repopulate the villages. The peasants mounted pressure on the *amil* of the pargana to remit the *tahsildari* cess. The *amil* agreed to do so, not out of altruistic concern but as a device to attract migrant peasants the village. 'Once all the villages are fully repopulated, the actual rates of the *dastur* will be reinforced', wrote the *amil*.[91] In the year 1704, the peasantry of Jhilai, Bhagotgarh, and Sarsomp was restive because of the imposition of *virar* for paying *peshkash* and sundry other expenses.[92] The same year the peasantry of many other parganas was so impoverished that they emigrated in different directions to eke out their living.[93] Those who stayed behind immediately and repeatedly demanded *pattas* of concession in revenue rates. The peasantry of Bahatri was being coerced to pay *virar* in 1709.[94] When the target could not be raised from the peasants, a sum of Rs 6,500 was collected from the *mahajans* of *qasba* Baswa (Bahatri). Similarly, *virar* of Rs 9,000 was collected from the peasants of Chatsu.[95] In 1712, *bhom* at the rate of 2 per cent of the *mal* was imposed and *virar* worth Rs 20,000 was realized from pargana Khohri.[96] In 1726, it was reported that *ghughari* was overcharged from the peasants of Toda Bhim and in many other parganas of Amber state the peasants felt the pinch of the *kharach* and *talbana* levies.[97] Everywhere peasants vigorously protested against the mounting fiscal pressure of the state.

The rapacity of the *bhomias* also made its own contribution to the misery of the peasantry. As early as 1649, it was reported that the Tanwar and Shekhawat *bhomias* of Behror plundered the peasants of the pargana.[98] In 1683, the peasants of Tonk fled because of this reason.[99] The peasants of pargana Saner were pauperized and could not carry on cultivation due to the intimidatory forays of the Chauhan *bhomias* into their villages.[100] Owing to the unending disturbances (*fisad*) of the Rajput *bhomias,* the *hasil* of Malarna declined and the annual *hasil* of another pargana, Mehmudabad, came down to 42 per cent of its *jama-i-kamil* in 1686.[101] In 1693, the *amils* of Toda Bhim reported that the peasants of their pargana had migrated due to the terror of the *bhomias*.[102] In 1694-95, three villages of pargana Boli and some of Chatsu were deserted due to the highhandedness of the Rajawat *bhomias*.[103] In 1695, migration of the peasants of Toda Bhim and Malarna was caused due to the terror of the *bhomias*.[104] Sardar Singh Rajawat, a *bhomia*, attacked the peasants of Shahjahanpur and arrested the *patels* of Vagri, a neighbouring village. He freed them only after extorting a sum of Rs 900 as ransom.[105] The terror of the *bhomias* was said to be the cause of the impoverishment of the peasants of Niwai. Kushal Singh Rajawat, a *bhomia* arrested many *patels* and demanded Rs 2,000 from them as ransom.[106] The peasants were so harassed that they left their villages to escape from *bhomia'* oppression. After a lapse of ten years these peasants were brought back from neighbouring parganas and resettled in their respective villages.[107] They returned only on the firm assurance given by the administration to protect them from any eventual harassment by the *bhomias* as well as of concessions in the revenue rates.[108] Two years later it was alleged that Sanwal Singh Rajawat was terrorizing the peasants of Chatsu and imposing arbitrary and unauthorized fines on them.[109] The cumulative impact of the plundering raids of the *bhomias* peaked when *hasil* in the *jagir* villages of the Amber territories started to decline.[110] In 1718, the villages of pargana Chatsu were abandoned due to harassment and uncertainty caused by the rivalry between various *bhomias* over the *bhom* cess.[111]

If this was not enough, the pargana officials also added to the misery of the peasantry through their acts of harassment. It was reported in 1666 that there were more *sehnas* (watchmen) than peasants in pargana Khohri. As such they were harassing the peasants.[112] The highhandedness of the *amils* and *chaudhuri* of pargana Malpura compelled the peasants to lodge a complaint against the officials with the *subadar*. The only action which Sadulla Khan took, however, was to transfer the overbearing *amils* and temporarily suspend the *chaudhuri*.[113] Similarly, the peasants of Nainwai were forced to abandon cultivation due to the oppressive acts of the *amils*.[114] The imperial *faujdars* of Mewat, Mathura, Hindaun, Bairath, Sambhar, and Ranthambore had made it a regular habit to send their armies to the villages without any provocation. The Amber Raja's agents had to bribe the *faujdars* to postpone or cancel of such 'punitive' expeditions. This money was ultimately collected from the peasants under the head of the well-worn *virar* cess.[115] In 1684, peasants and *mahajans* went to Amber and lodged complaints in the court of the *diwan* against the highhandedness of local officials.[116] The peasants of Bahatri and its adjacent parganas protested against oppressive acts of the officials in 1685.[117] In 1696, Prince Azam indulged in rioting in the parganas of Amber territory and the peasants had to pay for his adventure.[118] A large scale migration of the peasants led to the desertion of 62 villages in Bahatri. The severity of the famine was compounded by the oppression of the *amils* of Bahatri.[119] In the same year Nuruddin Ali Khan son of Nawab Abdullah Khan *subadar* of Ajmer, harassed the peasants and *mahajans* of Sanganer in a concerted bid to extort some unauthorized money from them.[120] Instead of protecting the peasants from the terror of the *bhomias*, the *amils* of Niwai chose to inflict their own oppression on them, and the pargana was completely ruined as per the report sent by the new *amil*.[121] The situation further worsened when the *subadar* of Ajmer sent his deputies (Hussain Ali Khan and Sarandaz Khan) to realize *peshkash*. The movement of their armies caused enormous dislocation and ruination in pargana Niwai.[122] Some efforts were made by the new *amils* of Niwai and Amber to resettle those peasants of their parganas who had emigrated due to the harassment of the earlier *amils*.[123] The peasants of pargana Ferozepur Jhirka revolted against the appointment of a new *amil* in 1710 and went to Shahjahanabad to fetch an *amil* of their choice.[124]

Though famine (*kahat*) in the region was quite frequent, on three occasions it became particularly severe, leaving a disastrous impact on the peasants of almost all the parganas. These occasions were the years 1660-3,[125] 1694-8[126] and 1717-18.[127] It resulted in considerable disruption of agricultural production. The cries of scarcity, misery, indigence and inability to live came written on documents emanating from almost all the parganas affected by famine. The peasants were totally at the mercy of moneylenders who invariably declined to advance loans to the impoverished.[128] Their misery did not end with the end of the drought. During years of good harvest the heavy hand of the revenue collector would revisit them. In 1685, there was good rain in 10 parganas but the state insisted on collecting the backlog of taxes.[129] Finding it impossible to stay, the peasants fled; their migration caused a decline in food grain prices.[130] In order to meet the drought situation in 1693, the state ordered that *taqavi* loans on the basis of Rs 2 per *bigha* may be advanced to the peasants.[131] In a similar situation the peasants of Malarna were granted *pattas* of concession in the land revenue in 1699.[132] The same year it was reported that drought and harassment by the *bhomias* combined to bring ruin to the peasantry of Chatsu, Malarna, Niwai, and Maujabad.[133] The total *jama* of pargana Fagi declined due to the unprecedented famine.[134] Whenever famine occurred in the Amber territories, the tendency was to leave for either the Ganga-Jamuna Doab or the *suba* of Malwa.[135]

The heavy demand of revenue in cash and the extreme uncertainty of production and movement of prices made the peasants increasingly dependent on moneylenders. The uncertainties of the period made the moneylenders reluctant to advance loans to the peasantry without proper surety. The peasants sought the intervention of the state for loans.[136] The moneylenders eagerly lent money to the Amber rulers so long as the latter were able to protect them from the plundering raids of the *bhomias*. The growing convergence of interest of the Amber rulers and the moneylenders inescapably increased the share of the moneylenders in the total surplus. Most of the moneylenders of the region had an agreement with the Amber Raja to lend him money at the flat rate of interest which was Rs 0.75 per cent per month.[137] The rulers spent this money largely on salaries but a portion of it was distributed among the peasants as *taqavi* loans at a relatively high rate of interest.[138] This alone can explain, even if other factors are ignored, why the rulers were so keen to protect the moneylenders from the aggressive *bhomias*[139] for moneylenders were the lynch-pin in the apparatus of revenue administration. Frequent mention of the dearth of *bohras* was due to the forced migration caused by the terror of the *bhomias*. On the other hand the *bohras* who stayed back in the *qasbas* and villages developed cold feet due to the non-availability of adequate surety and uncertainty of returns.[140] The *amils*, therefore, repeatedly sought permission to advance loans to the peasants from the treasury.[141]

Heavy and increasing fiscal burden on the peasantry formed the backdrop of the rural scenario. As the general tendency of the administration was to collect taxes in cash, the moneylender became a key player in the system. The peasantry opted for various forms of resistance whenever and wherever it was necessary, and resistance rendered cultivation and collection of revenues precarious. This was the intricate web of exploitation in which the peasantry was caught. The joint complaint of the peasants of eight parganas clearly betokened that they were at the end of their tether.[142] No wonder that peasant rebellions were soon to spread over the political landscape of Braj and Mewat regions.

NOTES

1. In pargana Khohri (1713: *kharif*) about 73.43 per cent revenue was realized according to the *batai* system, while in the same year and season in Hindaun the revenue collected under the *zabt* system constituted about 76.36 per cent of the

mal. Within pargana Khohri the amount of revenue realized under the *zabt* system changed from 5.24 per cent (1666: *kharif*) to 26.52 per cent in 1713: *kharif*. In our document *kharif* is mentioned as *syalu* and *rabi* as *unhalu*. Revenue collection operations normally began around Holi (in March) for *unhalu* and around Dussehra (in October) for *syalu*.

2. *Arzdasht*, dt. Vaisakh Sudi 3, VS 1741/1684.
3. Irfan Habib, *Agrarian System*, p. 274n.
4. *Arsatthas*, pargana Khohri, VS 1769-73/1712-16.
5. See *Arsattha*, pargana Khohri, Hindaun, Toda Bhim, Pahari, etc., for various years.
6. Ibid.
7. The market prices and the amount collected is mentioned in the *arsatthas*.
8. Irfan Habib, *Agrarian System*, p. 232.
9. In Khohri *mal* formed 97.24 per cent while *sair-jihat* accounted for the remaining 2.76 per cent of the total *jama* in 1666 (*kharif*). In Hindaun *mal* formed 95.59 per cent in *rabi* and 96.37 per cent in *kharif* of 1713 while *sair-jihat* accounted for the other 4.41 per cent and 3.63 per cent respectively. In Toda Bhim and Pahari the picture was almost same.
10. Their numbers ranged between 10 and 40 in our parganas. For variation in their magnitude see references 16, 19, 24 and 25 of this chapter.
11. *Dastur amal*, pargana Antela, VS 1784/1727; *Dastur amal*, pargana Niwai, VS 1800/1743; *Dastur amal*, pargana Gijgarh, VS 1794/1737; *Dastur amal*, pargana Sonkhar, VS 1773/1716; *Dastur amal*, pargana Khohri, AD 1049-50/1642; *Dastur amal*, pargana Chatsu, VS 1769/1712.
12. *Dastur amal*, pargana Khohri, AD 1049-50/1642. It must be the same in case of other parganas' *dasturs*.
13. *Arsattha*, pargana Malarna, VS 1771/1714.
14. *Arsattha*, pargana Kotla, VS 1722/1665; *Arsattha*, pargana Malarna, VS. 1722/1665; *Arsattha* pargana Chatsu, VS 1721/1664; *Arsattha*, pargana Niwai, VS 1721/1664.
15. *Arsatthas*, pargana Niwai, VS 1721/1664 and pargana Kotla, VS 1722/1665. According to Irfan Habib the rate of this levy was one *dam* per *bigha*. See his *Agrarian System*, p. 287.
16. *Arsattha*, pargana Kotla, VS 1722/1665; 2 per cent; *Arsattha* pargana *Udai*, VS 1769/1712; 3 per cent.
17. *Arsattha*, pargana Toda Raisinghpur, VS 1774/1717; *Arsattha*, pargana Malarna, VS. 1722/1665.
18. *Arsattha*, pargana Bahatri, VS. 1722/1665; *Arsattha*, pargana Pahari, VS. 1773/1716. The collection of various cesses in *dams* whose value had appreciated in relation to silver during the 17th century, was obviously to the disadvantage of the peasants, though not to the extent postulated by Moreland. Irfan Habib, *Agrarian System*, pp 280-1, provides a corrective to Moreland's position on this issue.
19. *Arsattha*, pargana Bahatri, VS. 1722/1665; 4 *sers*; *Arsattha*, pargana Niwai, VS 1721/1664; 5 *sers*; *Arsattha*, pargana Dausa, VS. 1722/1665; 3 *sers*; *Arsattha*, pargana Ponkhar, VS 1797/1740; 2 *sers*; *Arsattha*, pargana Fagi, VS. 1754/1697; 5 *sers*; *Arsattha*, pargana Chatsu, VS. 1721/1664; 2 *sers*; *Arsattha*, pargana Hindaun, VS. 1775/1718; 3 *sers*; *Arsattha*, pargana Jalalpur, VS. 1723/1666;

2 *sers*; *Arsattha*, pargana Pahari, VS 1723/1666; 2 *sers*; *Arsattha*, pargana Khohri, VS 1759/1712; 2 *sers*.

20. *Arsattha*, pargana Bayana, VS 1750/1693; *Arsattha*, pargana Maujpur, VS. 1771/1714; *Arsattha*, pargana Kotla, VS. 1722/1665; *Arsattha*, pargana Pahari, VS. 1773/1716.
21. Ibid.
22. *Arsattha*, pargana Banawar, VS 1748/1691; *Arsattha*, pargana Niwai, VS 1721/1664; *Arsattha*, pargana Kotla, VS 1722/1665; *Arsattha*, pargana Malarna, VS 1722/1665; *Arsattha*, pargana Tonk, VS 1765/1708; *Arsattha*, pargana Punkhar, VS 1797/1740; *Arsattha*, pargana Chatsu, VS 1721/1664; *Arsattha*, pargana Udai, VS 1769/1712; *Arsattha*, pargana Bhusawar, VS 1773/1716; *Arsattha*, pargana Jalalpur, VS 1723/1666; *Arsattha*, pargana Khohri, VS 1721/1664.
23. *Arsattha*, pargana Niwai, VS 1721/1664; *Arsattha*, pargana Khohri, VS 1721/1664.
24. *Arsattha*, pargana Bahatri, VS 1722/1665; *Arsattha*, pargana Maujpur, VS 1771/1714; *Arsattha*, pargana Dausa, VS 1722/1665; *Arsattha*, pargana Malarna, VS 1722/1665; *Arsattha*, pargana Tonk, VS 1765/1708.
25. *Arsattha*, pargana Antela, VS 1784/1727.
26. *Arsattha*, pargana Bahatri, VS 1722/1665; *Arsattha*, pargana Dausa, VS 1722/1665; *Arsattha*, pargana Fagi, VS 1754/1697; *Arsattha*, pargana Chatsu, VS 1721/1664.
27. *Arsattha*, pargana Bayana, VS 1750/1693; *Arsattha*, pargana Tonk, VS 1768/1708; *Arsattha*, pargana Fagi, VS 1754/1697; *Arsattha*, pargana Chatsu, VS 1721/1664.
28. Ibid.
29. *Arsattha*, pargana Hindaun, VS 1769/1712; *Arsattha*, pargana Udai, VS 1769/1712.
30. *Arsattha*, pargana Malpura, VS 1771/1714; *Arsattha*, pargana Udai, VS 1769/1712; *Arsattha*, pargana Hindaun, VS 1769/1712; *Arsattha*, pargana Jalalpur, VS 1723/1666; *Arsattha*, pargana Bayana, VS 1750/1693.
31. *Arsattha*, pargana Dausa, VS 1722/1665; *Arsattha*, pargana Udai, VS 1769/1712; *Arsattha*, pargana Malpura, VS 1771/1714; *Arsattha*, pargana Hindaun, VS 1769/1712; *Arsattha*, pargana Bhusawar, VS 1773/1716; *Arsattha*, pargana Toda Bhim, VS 1790/1733.
32. *Arsattha*, pargana Bahatri, VS 1765/1708; *Arsattha*, pargana Dausa, VS 1722/1665; *Arsattha*, pargana Ponkhar, VS 1797/1740 (4 per cent); *Arsattha*, pargana Jalalpur, VS 1723/1666 (4 per cent); *Arsattha*, pargana Khohri, VS 1721/1664; *Arsattha*, pargana Niwai, VS 1721/1664.
33. *Arsattha*, pargana Bahatri, VS 1722/1665.
34. *Arzdasht*, dt. Bhadwa Sudi 10, VS 1783/1726.
35. *Arsattha*, pargana Bahatri, VS 1763/1706 (Rs 4); *Arsattha*, pargana Bayana, VS 1750/1693 (Rs 4½); *Arsattha*, pargana Banawar, etc., VS 1748/1691 (Rs 8); *Arsattha*, pargana Malpura, VS 1771/1714 (Rs 5). These levies have been declared as 'forbidden extortions' by the imperial administration. See Irfan Habib, *Agrarian System*, p. 288. But our sources clearly show the unabated collected of these prohibited cesses.
36. Dilbagh Singh, 'Caste and Structure', p. 311.

37. *Arsattha*, pargana Malpura, VS 1771/1714; *Arsattha*, pargana Bayana, VS 1750/1693 (Rs 1½) on every Rs 1,000.
38. *Arsattha*, pargana Bahatri, VS 1722/1665.
39. *Arsattha*, pargana Toda Raisinghpur, VS 1774/1717.
40. *Arsattha*, pargana Bayana, VS 1750/1693; *Arsattha*, pargana Maujpur, VS. 1771/1714.
41. *Arsattha*, pargana Dausa, VS 1722/1665; *Arsattha*, pargana Udai, VS 1769/1712; *Arsattha*, pargana Hindaun, VS 1769/1712.
42. *Arsattha*, pargana Toda Bhim, VS 1790/1733.
43. *Arsattha*, pargana Hindaun, VS 1769/1712 (Re 1 *Chithawan* on each village); *Arsattha*, pargana Bayana, VS 1750/1693 (Rs 3.5 for *balkati* on each village), and *Arsattha*, pargana Bhusawar, etc., VS 1789 and 1732. *Hasil faslana* was collected at the rate of Re. 1 annually from each village of parganas Bhusawar, Kuthumbar, Sonkhar, etc.
44. *Arsattha*, pargana Hindaun, VS 1769/1712; *Arsattha*, pargana Jalalpur, VS 1723/1666.
45. *Arsattha*, pargana Bahatri, VS 1722/1665; *Arsattha*, pargana Bahatri, VS 1754/1697; *Arsattha*, pargana Pahari, VS 1773/1717 (1 per cent).
46. *Arsattha*, pargana Pahari, VS 1773/1717.
47. *Arsattha*, pargana Ponkhar, VS 1797/1740. The literal meaning of *ghiwai* is not clear.
48. S. Nurul Hasan and S.P. Gupta, 'Price of Foodgrains in the Territories of Amber (*c*. 1650-1750)', *PIHC*, 29th Session at Patiala, 1967, Patna, 1968, pp. 345-68.
49. S. Nurul Hasan, K.N. Hasan and S.P. Gupta, 'The Pattern of Agricultural Production in the Territories of Amber (*c*. 1650-1750)', *PIHC*, 28th Session at Mysore, 1966, Aligarh, pp. 244-64.
50. Irfan Habib, *Agrarian System*, p. 232 and 'Distribution of Landed Property in Pre-British India', *Enquiry* (Winter, 1965), p. 193n.
51. *Arsattha*, pargana Hindaun, VS 1770 to 1805 and AD 1713 to 1742.
52. *Arsattha*, pargana Khohri, VS 1769 to 1810 and AD 1712 to 1753.
53. *Arsattha*, pargana Dausa, VS 1722/1665.
54. *Dastur amal* pargana Khohri, AD 1049-50/1642.
55. These taxes have been written as *pachotra* (5 per cent), *Satotra* (7 per cent), *nirotra* (9 per cent), *barahotra* (12 per cent), etc. in the *Arsatthas*. See *Arsatthas* of the above mentioned 11 parganas for the year mentioned against them.
56. *Arsattha*, pargana Hindaun, VS 1774/1717. Everywhere this numerical tax seems to have been occasional due to the rise in prices of those crops only which were assessed under the *zabt* system.
57. *Arzdashts*, dt. Kati Sudi 14, VS 1760/1703; Falgun Badi 13, VS 1761/1704; Falgun Sudi 12, VS 1761/1704 and Mangsir Vadi 12, VS 1766/1709.
58. The literal meaning of this term is still unknown but it was frequently used in all kinds of revenue records. For example, *virar-waqai-naqis* in Hindaun, VS 1769/1712 and *virar kot naramati* in Udai, VS 1769/1712. It appears therefore to be an indigenous version of the term for special levy.
59. See *Arsatthas* of these five parganas for the years mentioned against them.
60. For similar rate in other Mughal territories see Irfan Habib, *Agrarian System*, pp. 233-6 and Shireen Moosvi, *The Economy of the Mughal Empire c. 1595: A*

Statistical Study, OUP, 1987, pp. 107-8, 118. S.P. Gupta, *Agrarian System*, pp. 59-60, shows lower revenue demand (32 per cent to 40 per cent). Actually Gupta has lumped together all the differential revenue rates and given their average. Indeed both the *dasturs* and *Arsattha,s* clearly mention the collection of revenues at the rate of 25 per cent of the gross produce from the rural gentry and 50 per cent from the mass of the peasantry.

61. *Dastur amal*, pargana Khohri, AH 1049-50/1642.
62. *Arsattha*, pargana Bhusawar, VS 1771/1714.
63. *Arsattha*, pargana Hindaun, VS 1791/1734. Though figures for all the villages are available, only representative villages have been mentioned here.
64. *Arzdasht*, dt. Vaisakh Sudi 12, VS 1702/1645.
65. *Arsattha*, pargana Chatsu, VS 1721/1664.
66. *Arzdasht*, dt. Vaisakh Vadi 13, VS 1722/1665.
67. *Arzdasht*, dt. Jeth Sudi 12, VS 1740/1683.
68. *Arsattha*, pargana Niwai, VS 1721/1664.
69. *Arzdasht*, dt. Jeth Sudi 12, VS 1740/1683. The imposition of *jizya* on the non-Muslims by Aurangzeb in 1679 was 'an important increase in the magnitude of rural taxation'. See Irfan Habib, *Agrarian System*, p. 285.
70. *Arzdasht*, dt. Sawan Vadi 2, VS 1721/1664.
71. *Arzdasht*, dt. Sawan Sudi 13, VS 1750/1693.
72. *Arzdasht*, dt. Vaisakh Sudi 3, VS 1741/1684,
73. *Arsattha*, pargana Salawad and Gudha, *sarkar* and *suba* Akbarabad, VS 1768/ 1691
74. *Arzdasht*, dt. Chet Sudi 4, VS 1750/1693.
75. *Arzdasht*, dt. Sawan Vadi 13, VS 1750/1693.
76. *Arzdasht*, dt. Asoj Vadi 12, VS 1751/1694.
77. *Arzdashts*, dt. Falgun Vadi 2, VS 1743/1686 and Bhadwa Vadi 5, VS 1762/1705.
78. *Arzdasht*, dt. Jeth Sudi 10, VS 1740/1683.
79. *Arzdasht*, dt. Vaisakh Sudi 14, VS. 1722/1665.
80. *Arzdasht*, dt. Kati Vadi 6, VS 1751/1694.
81. *Arzdasht*, dt. Jeth Vadi, VS 1701/1646.
82. *Arzdasht*, dt. Asadh Sudi 2, VS 1721/1664.
83. *Arzdasht*, dt. Sawan Vadi 2, VS 1721/1664.
84. *Arzdashts*, dt. Jeth Vadi 12, Asadh Sudi 13 and Falgun Sudi 3, VS 1740/1683.
85. *Arzdashts*, dt. Jeth Sudi 10 and 12, VS 1740/1683. *Dihangi* was charged at the rate of 6 *annas* to the rupee per head each day. Its imposition was quite arbitrarily exercised by the *amils*.
86. *Arzdasht*, dt. Jeth Sudi 12, VS 1740/1683. Interestingly the peasants were protesting as *haljotas* and not as a religious group.
87. *Arzdasht*, dt. Mah Sudi 12, VS 1742/1685.
88. *Arzdasht*, dt. Jeth Sudi 12, VS 1743/1686.
89. *Arzdasht*, dt. Kati Vadi 11, VS 1750/1693.
90. *Arzdasht*, dt. Chet Sudi 4, VS 1750/1693 of Sawan Sudi 2, VS 1750/1693, Kati Sudi 14, VS 1760/1703, Falgun Sudi 2, VS 1766/1709 and Vaisakh Vadi 1, VS 1767/1710.
91. *Arzdasht*, dt. Falgun Sudi 9, VS 1752/1695.
92. *Arzdasht*, dt. Falgun Sudi 9, VS 1752/1695.
93. *Arzdashts*, dt. Kati Vadi 14 and Posh Sudi 15, VS 1761/1704.

94. *Arzdasht*, dt. Mah Vadi 11, vs 1766/1709.
95. *Arzdasht*, dt. Vaisakh Vadi 1, vs 1767/1710.
96. *Arsattha*, pargana Khohri, vs 1769/1712.
97. Copy of *parwana*, dt. Bhadwa Vadi 14, vs 1783/1726.
98. *Arzdasht*, dt. Jeth Vadi 4, vs 1706/1649.
99. *Amber Records*, dt. Asadh Sudi 13, vs 1740/1683.
100. *Amber Records*, dt. Chet Vadi 13, vs 1741/1684.
101. *Arzdasht*, dt. Falgun Vadi 9, vs *1749/1692*.
102. *Arzdasht*, dt. Sawan Vadi 13, vs 1750/1693.
103. *Arzdashts*, dt. Asoj Vadi 7, vs 1751/1694 and Falgun Sudi 15, vs 1752/1695.
104. *Arzdasht*, dt. Sawan Vadi 13, vs 1750/1693.
105. *Arzdasht*, dt. Falgun Sudi 9, vs 1752/1695.
106. *Arzdashts*, dt. Asadh Sudi 14, vs 1760/1703 and Kati Sudi 14, vs 1760/1703.
107. *Arzdasht*, dt. Asadh Sudi 2, vs 1760/1703.
108. *Arzdasht*, dt. Kati Vadi 2, vs 1753/1696.
109. *Arzdasht*, dt. Asadh Vadi 4, vs 1755/1698.
110. *Arzdasht*, dt. Asadh Vadi 9, vs 1762/1705.
111. *Arzdasht*, dt. Jeth Vadi 11, vs 1775/1718.
112. *Amber Records*, dt. Chet Sudi 13, vs 1773/1666.
113. *Arzdasht*, dt. Bhadwa Vadi 11, vs 1721/1664.
114. *Arzdasht*, dt. Sawan Vadi 2, vs 1721/1664.
115. *Arzdashts*, dt. Falgun Vadi 11, vs 1739/1682, Bhadwa Sudi 5, vs 1754/1697, Sawan Vadi 14, vs 1754/1697 and Mangair Sudi 5 and 12, vs 1766/1709.
116. *Arzdasht*, dt. Sawan Sudi 3, vs 1741/1684.
117. *Arzdasht*, dt. Jeth Sudi 4, vs 1742/1685.
118. *Arzdasht*, dt. Falgun Sudi 8, vs 1753/1696.
119. *Arzdasht*, dt. Asadh Vadi 1, vs 1754/1697.
120. *Amber Records*, dt. Sawan Vadi 14, vs 1754/1697 and Posh Vadi 4, vs 1761/1704.
121. *Arzdasht*, dt. Asadh Sudi 2, vs 1761/1704.
122. *Arzdashts*, dt. Posh Sudi 15, vs 1761/1704 and Falgun Vadi 13, vs 1761/1704.
123. *Arzdasht*, dt. Asadh Sudi 2, vs 1762/1705.
124. *Arzdasht*, dt. Asadh Vadi 2, vs 1769/1712.
125. *Arzdashts*, dt. Vaisakh Sudi 14, vs 1722/1665 and Asoj Vadi 9, vs 1751/1694.
126. *Arzdashts*, dt. Kati Vadi 2, vs 1753/1696, Asadh Sudi 7, vs 1755/1698 and Asadh Vadi 4, vs 1755/1698.
127. *Arzdashts*, dt. Kati Sudi 15, vs 1774/1717 and Sawan Vadi 3, vs 1775/1718.
128. *Arzdasht*, dt. Asoj Vadi 9, vs 1751/1694.
129. *Arzdashts*, dt. Falgun Sudi 7, vs 1742/1685 and Sawan Sudi 3, vs 1742/1685.
130. *Arzdashts*, dt. Kati Vadi 6, vs 1751/1694, Asoj Sudi 13, vs 1751/1694 and Bhadwa Sudi 11, vs 1751/1694.
131. *Arzdasht*, dt. Kati Sudi 10, vs 1751/1694.
132. *Arzdasht*, dt. Asoj Sudi 12, vs 1756/1699.
133. *Arzdasht*, dt. Asadh Vadi 4, vs 1755/1698.
134. *Arzdashts*, dt. Falgun Sudi 8, vs 1753/1696 and Posh Sudi 15, vs 1761/1704.
135. *Arzdahst*, dt. Vaisakh Sudi 14, vs 1722/1665.
136. *Arzdashts*, dt. Kati Sudi 10 and Vadi 11, vs 1751/1694 and Asoj Sudi 13, vs 1751/1694.

137. *Arzdashts*, dt. Mangsir Vadi 3, vs 1730/1673, Bhadwa Sudi 13, Vadi 5 and 7, vs 1742/1685. In 1673 the Amber Raja borrowed Rs 60,755 from the *bohras* at the rate mentioned above.
138. See *Arsatthas* of Khohri for various years.
139. *Arzdashts*, dt. Asadh Sudi 13, vs 1740/1683 and Jeth Vadi 4, vs 1761/1704. *Amber Record*, dt. Chet Sudi 4, vs 1743/1686, Posh Sudi 1, vs 1753/1696 and Jeth Vadi 4, vs 1761/1704.
140. *Arzdashts*, dt. Sawan Sudi 3, vs 1741/1684, Asoj Sudi 2, vs 1751/1694 and Bhadwa Vadi 1, vs 1762/1705.
141. *Arzdashts*, dt. Asadh Sudi 2, vs 1721/1664, Kati Vadi 11, and Asoj Vadi 12, vs 1751/1694.
142. *Arzdasht*, dt. Vaisakh Vadi 13, vs 1722/1665.

4

The Domain of the Zamindars

'Zamindar' is a broad-spectrum category that encompassed an array of entities stretching from the ruler of a large kingdom to the holder of a tiny share in the village produce.[1] The blanket use of the term zamindar for the entire rural gentry can be traced to the fourteenth century in India.[2] By the time of the compilation of the *Ain-i-Akbari* the zamindars seem to have crystallized into a distinct class of rural potentates, having many features in common. They were claimants to a fiscal right which was basically an allowance outside the land revenue but a set percentage thereof.[3] The zamindars normally raised their militias from among their own caste members. The possession of a *garhi* or fortress was an important hallmark of the power of a zamindar.[4] The zamindari right contained all the ingredients of private property: it could be sold, purchased, and mortgaged.[5]

The zamindari right seems to have emanated from multiple channels. Many zamindars emerged out of the detritus of the Hindu kingdoms defeated by the Delhi Sultans. Other the leaders of victorious castes, especially the Rajput clans, colonized peasant-held villages and proceeded to subject them to their zamindari claims. Many enterprising village headmen too may have become zamindars.[6] However, historically the zamindari right emerged independent of any imperial design.

In the course of the enlargement of his empire in western India, Akbar encountered powerful Rajput chiefs and myriads of obscure zamindars occupying the political landscape of Rajasthan. With an adroit application of force and diplomacy, Akbar was able to obtain the partnership of these chiefs and zamindars at suitable levels in the structure of the empire. Consequently, many Rajput chiefs of Rajasthan who had been induced to join the imperial ruling class rose to the highest echelons of the Mughal bureaucracy. A multitude of ordinary zamindars were co-oped into the imperial land revenue machinery at subordinate levels.

The political exigency of the Rajput zamindars' integration with the Mughal empire has been differently explained. For one Iqtidar Alam Khan has suggested that the Rajputs began to align with the Mughal empire under mounting military pressures.[7] On the other hand Norman P. Ziegler has argued that the Rajput allegiance to the Mughal empire was largely determined by their own notions of ranking and political loyalties that were quite fluid.[8] Recently J.F. Richards has opined that the inclusive system developed by Emperor Akbar was a crucial facilitator in enlisting and cementing the loyalty of chiefs and the zamindars to the empire.[9] It may, however, be stressed that the process of integration of different layers of zamindars was seldom a smooth and complete affair. Mughal history is replete with events showing zamindars negotiating and re-negotiating their integration with the empire.[10]

The Kachhwahas, who had a fledgling state at Amber, were the first to align with the Mughal empire in this region.[11] Soon thereafter they emerged as key players in imperial politics. Their elevation in the Mughal court tremendously boosted their status in their *watan* (homeland). Also, enormous fiscal resources flowed to them in the form of *tankhwah-jagirs* or salary assignments. From Mirza Raja Jai Singh (1621-67) onwards successive Kachhwaha rulers were assigned *jagirs* adjacent to their *watan* of Amber.[12] Gradually this group began to play a pivotal role in the political management of the region. The Mughal emperors intended to control and stabilize the turbulent region through the agency of the Amber house and this gave an opportunity to the Kachhwaha clan to proliferate through the region. This amalgam of Mughal and Kachhwaha political objectives bode ill for the traditional zamindars of the region, as we shall see.

In our region the zamindars were known by the local term of *bhomia*.[13] *Bhomias* were entitled to a variety of superior rights in the land and its produce. They owned large land holdings which were assessed at lower rates of revenue as compared to the land cultivated by the peasants. According to some seventeenth century *dasturs* or revenue manuals the *bhomias* had to pay 25 per cent of their gross produce as land revenue.[14] Aside from this the *bhomias* were entitled to a set percentage of the land revenue collected from the peasantry under their jurisdiction. Unfortunately our documents do not enable us to determine the size of each *bhomia*'s share from the peasants' surplus. When the Kachhwaha rulers began to claim *bhom* rights on a large number of parganas outside their hereditary *watan*, they imposed a *bhom* tax ranging between 2 and 3 per cent of the land revenue.[15] But our sources are conspicuously silent about the total income of the ordinary *bhomias*. Irfan Habib has estimated the total remuneration of the ordinary zamindars of northern India somewhere between 15 and 20 per cent of the land revenue.[16] In view of the silence of our documents on this vital matter, we may accept Habib's calculation as an approximation. Apart from this fixed share, the *bhomias* were also entitled to sundry other customary levies, such as *vagdum, dhol,* etc., from the peasants.[17] The peasants were also under obligation to feed the *bhomia* and his retainers by extending invitations *(nyota)* to them.[18] Similarly traders passing through their territories had to pay *kori bhomi-ki* cess to the *bhomias*.[19] On sundry occasions the *bhomias* extorted unpaid work *(begar kotri-ki)* from the peasants, artisans, and menials living within their *bhoms*.[20] As the pitch of the revenue demand was already very high, these irregular levies added to the financial woes of the peasants. On many occasions, conflict (*khenchal*) broke out between the *bhomias* and peasants on the issue of *begar*.[21] Where the *bhomias* and peasants did not belong to the same caste, their volatile relations could degenerate into open clashes.[22] There is no reason, therefore, to assume that tension between the *bhomias* and the peasants remained latent everywhere.[23] However, the larger conflict between the higher echelons of the imperial administration, the *jagirdars*, on the one hand and the zamindars on the other, over the sharing of revenue greatly determined the latter's attitude towards the peasantry—the chief source of this revenue. As long as the *bhomias* were placed in an uneven contest with the *jagirdars* they preferred to let the increasing fiscal burden pass on to the peasants. Evidence of the *bhomia* intervening in defence of his *raiyat* against the caprice of the *jagirdars* is scarce. For instance in 1665—four years before the outbreak of the Jat revolt—when the peasants of eight parganas spread across Braj and Mewat were protesting against the excessive fiscal demands by the *jagirdars* of their respective villages, the *bhomias* of the region did not come out in support of the aggrieved peasants.[24] But when the peasants became increasingly restive, the *bhomias* did not have qualms about mobilizing them for their own interest.[25]

Occasionally, the *bhomias* extended much-needed support in the form of cash, seeds, and agricultural implements to the needy peasants.[26] Whenever the impoverished peasants contracted loans from the moneylenders, the *bhomias* stood surety for them.[27] Needless to say, by participating in these usurious transactions, the *bhomias* could keep the hapless peasants at their mercy.

If the *bhomias* had made substantial gains due to their multi-dimensional role in village society, the *bhom* right had also become vulnerable to the operation of various factors. For instance, the laws of inheritance leading to the division of *bhom* among various heirs had rendered many *bhoms* unviable. The increasing inroad of money into the expanding *bhom* market had in general deprived many traditional *bhomias* of their *bhoms*[28] although the transfer of the *bhom* rights through monetary transactions was limited in our region. The sovereign prerogative of the Mughal emperor to remove or appoint a zamindar was used as a weapon to tame refractory elements. Such punitive action became frequent during the second half of the seventeenth century. Putative loyal elements were appointed in place of the evicted zamindars. Through such actions, the Mughals sought to break the monopoly of entrenched castes in certain localities.[29] Obviously, the losing zamindars would not accept such a fate so easily. Ensuing struggles to regain their lost zamindaris brought them in a headlong confrontation with the loyalists. In this struggle of shifting equations, some zamindars were permanently banished; only a few managed to bounce back.[30]

In our region the parallel processes of the creation of new *bhoms* and the expansion of existing ones can be discerned from the documents. The creations and expansions of *bhoms* were usually achieved by the use of force. At no point of time was the entire countryside under the complete sway of the *bhomias*. In each *pargana* there were sizable numbers of peasant-held villages, the *raiyati gaon*[31] The existence of the *raiyati* villages is amply recorded in the *arsatthas* of the parganas of the region. As the *bhomias* did not have any jurisdiction over the *raiyati* villages, these villages were always coveted by neighbouring *bhomias*. Attempts to annex *raiyati* villages into *bhoms* become increasingly manifest during the late-seventeenth and early-eighteenth century. A few instances out of many about the occupation of the *raiyati* villages by bellicose *bhomias* are given here. One Roop Singh Kalyanot had his ancestral *bhom* in village Bhanpur of pargana Toda Bhim. Many *raiyati* villages of *tappa* Rini of pargana Bahatri were contiguous to his *bhom*. In 1693, Roop Singh forcibly annexed some of these *raiyati* villages, despite the opposition of the peasants.[32] Similarly, one Devi Singhmal occupied a *raiyati* village, Rohero Hindui of pargana Tonk and claimed his *bhom* rights there.[33] A similar attempt was made by the zamindars of Alwar to forcibly occupy some *raiyati* villages.[34] There are many more instances of the conversion of the *raiyati* villages into *bhoms*, especially in the Dhundhar region, a hotbed of competing Rajput lineages.

The pattern of distribution of zamindaris in the parganas under study clearly bears the imprint of the dispersal of entire castes in the region. Blocks of parganas which were contiguous (*mutsal*) to each other were occupied by the *bhomias* belonging to a single caste or clan. The detailed list of the *bhomias* appended to this chapter clearly indicates this kind of geographic distribution. Thus the Jats had the bulk of their zamindaris in *sarkar* Sahar in the centre of the Braj country.[35] The Meos were concentrated in the *sarkars* of Alwar and Tijara, both of which together constituted the Mewat region.[36] The Dhundhar region was occupied by the *bhomias* of miscellaneous Rajput clans.[37] The pattern of displacement of the *bhomias* of one caste by another also bears the imprint of group incursions. Clearly, the class of zamindars was 'largely made up of a number of castes which had for long been uprooting and subjugating each other'.[38] Even the paramount Mughal power could not permanently fix the boundaries of the zamindaris, despite its intention to do so.

Throughout the seventeenth century, considerable changes affected the position of all categories of *bhomias* of the region. The flux overwhelmed all levels, groups, and castes of zamindars. While those of some castes and clans were elbowed out, others forged ahead to fill the vacuum. The entire landscape of the zamindari right underwent a massive transformation. Before the contours and the inner mechanism of the changes in the *bhom* right are analysed, we may look at the traditional claims of different zamindari castes as recorded in the *Ain-i-Akbari*.

At the beginning of the seventeenth century the hereditary dominion *(watan)* of the Amber Raja was confined to three parganas of eastern Rajasthan. These were Amber, Dausa, and Baswa (also known as Bahatri).[39] The Amber Raja was a chieftain among zamindars and occupied a very prominent position in the Mughal nobility. The rest of the *bhomias* who were living in the neighbourhood of his *watan* were ordinary in status. They belonged to miscellaneous Rajput clans and other peasant castes. These *bhomias* were unevenly spread out in the parganas of the region.

The detailed inventory of the 'twelve provinces', in the *Ain-i-Akbari* shows that the Kachhwahas had zamindaris in *sarkar* Ajmer along with the Chauhan and Afghan zamindars,[40] while in all the 73 *mahals* of *sarkar* Ranthambore, Rajputs of the Hara clan held exclusive zamindari rights.[41] In *sarkar* Nagor the Kachhwahas had their zamindaris in 1 out of 31 *mahals*.[42] In *suba* Agra the Kachhwahas had 1 (out of 16 *mahals*) in *sarkar* Kalpi, 1 (out of 16 *mahals*) in *sarkar* Irij, 1 (out of 43 *mahals*) in *sarkar* Alwar, and one-third of the total zamindaris each in *sarkars* Narnaul (out of 16 *mahals)* and Sahar (out of 7 *mahals*).[43] In both of these *subas* the Haras, Chauhans, Bargujars, and Tanwars had far more extensive zamindaris than those of the Kachhwahas at the time of the compilation of *Ain*. There were other castes holding impressive zamindaris in the adjoining regions of Mewat and Braj. Six out of 32 parganas in *sarkar* Agra have Jats entered as zamindars, 1 out of 21 in Kol, 1 out of 41 in Alwar, 2 out of 16 in Narnaul and 5 out of 7 in Sahar.[44] In *sarkar* Alwar of *suba* Agra, the Khanzadas of Mewat and the Meos are entered as zamindars in 18 and 12 parganas respectively out of a total of 43 *mahals*.[45]

When we look at the pargana-level records covering the events of the late seventeenth and early eighteenth century, we find a startling change in the zamindari possessions of various castes. The change is remarkable, but does not find sufficient mention in the contemporary chronicles and travelogues. Perhaps these changes remained invisible to them as these were local affairs. As the balance of political power was shifting in favour of assertive zamindars, these changes have been widely reported by the local *faujdars* and *amils* posted in these parganas. A perusal of the *thikana* documents also corroborates the occurrence of such changes. Let us now see who replaced whom (Table 4.1).

A cursory glance at Table 4.1 suggests that various lineages of the Kachhwaha clan had successfully replaced the traditional zamindars in a number of parganas. The *bhomias* of Hara clan were the main losers in *sarkar,* Ranthambore. The Badgujars, Chauhans, Meos and the Khanzadas of Mewat were uprooted from their zamindaris in *sarkar* Alwar. The Meo zamindars of pargana Kama and Pahari of the *Pahat pal* were the worst affected by such changes. Similarly the Shaikhzadas of pargana Udai were displaced by the Kachhwahas. The principal gainers were the Rajawat, Naruka, Khangarot,

TABLE 4.1: THE CHANING IDENTITIES OF ZAMINDARS IN SOME PARGANAS

Pargana	*Sarkar*	*Caste of zamindars in the Ain: 1595*	*Caste of zamindars in the reign of Aurangzeb*
Ao	Agra	Rajput	Jat
Sonkhar-Sonkhari	Agra	Rajput	Jat
Bhusawar	Agra	Rajput	Jat
Kuthumbar	Agra	Rajput, Jat	Jat
Banawar	Agra	Bargujar	Naruka
Toda Bhim	Agra	Rajput, Thathar	Kalyanot
Udai	Agra	Shaikhzada	Panchanot
Wazirpur	Agra	Rajput	Naruka
Kama	Sahar	Meo, Jat, Ahir	Kachhwaha
Pahari	Sahar	Meo	Kachhwaha
Bairath	Alwar	Baqqal	Shaikhawat
Bharkol	Alwar	Khanzada of Mewat	Naruka
Baswa	Alwar	various	Naruka, Kalyanot
Devti-Sanchari	Alwar	Bargujar	Naruka
Khohri	Alwar	Khanzada of Mewat	Kachhwaha, Jat
Mandawar	Alwar	Chauhan	Naruka
Maujpur	Alwar	Abbasi	Naruka
Banhetta	Ranthambore	Hara	Rajawat
Malpura	Ranthambore	Hara	Kachhwaha
Tonk	Ranthambore	Hara	Kachhwaha, Solanki
Chatsu	Ranthambore	Hara	Rajawat
Jhilai	Ranthambore	Hara	Rajawat
Sarsomp	Ranthambore	Hara	Naruka
Malarna	Ranthambore	Hara	Chauhan, Jadam, Panchanot
Niwai	Ranthambore	Hara	Rajawat
Toda-Raisinghpur	Ranthambore	Hara	Khangarot, Naruka

Panchanot and Kalyanot lineages of the Kachhwaha clan in the Dhundhar and Mewat regions. The Jats had also made inroads into the zamindaris of some Rajputs in a few parganas of *sarkar* Agra.

Now instead of an entire *sarkar* being occupied by the zamindars of a particular caste or clan, we find their zamindaris here and there in small clusters. This fragmentation was the result of a simultaneous process of segmentation of various Kachhwaha lineages, a phenomenon quite conspicuous in the Dhundhar and Mewat regions. Evidently, this trend was in conflict with the Amber ruler's attempt to centralize political power in the region.

Of the factors which led to significant changes in the pattern of zamindari possessions, the role of money was nearly negligible in our region.[47] The merchants and moneylenders were reluctant to purchase *bhom* rights. Mercantile groups did not find it a sound business proposition to invest in such dubious ventures when better avenues of enhancing their income were still open to them.

Elsewhere in the empire 'numerous transfers, depositions and appointments' of zamindars were effected in the reign of Aurangzeb.[48] The zamindars' reluctance to pay revenue and their defiance of authority are stated to be the causes. Aurangzeb may have favoured a section of the Muslims elsewhere in the empire but in our region Muslims received no such affectionate regard from the orthodox emperor.[49] In fact the Meos and the Khanzadas of Mewat were unsuccessfully struggling to save their zamindaris from the combined Kachhwaha-Mughal onslaught and the beneficiaries, were various Rajput lineages of the Kachhwaha clan.

The process of change in the zamindari possessions needs to be discussed for an understanding of the political turbulence that had spread in our region from the mid-seventeenth century onwards. It appears that the ordinary zamindars in some of the parganas of the Braj-Mewat-Dhundhar territories had become restive long before Aurangzeb's ascendance to power.[50] The recalcitrance of the Chauhan *bhomias* of pargana Gijgarh and Salawad in 1640s and the rebellion of the Meo zamindars of *pargana* Kama and Pahari in 1649-50, became a turning point in the relations between the local zamindars, Amber state, and the Mughal empire. Shah Jahan ordered Mirza Raja Jai Singh to deal with the unruly Chauhans with a heavy hand and wipe out the Meo insurgents from Mewat. The Amber Raja was granted extensive powers to achieve quick results. From now on the Amber ruler was expected to ensure peace in his own *jagirs* as well as the *jagirs* of other imperial *mansabdars* and *khalisa* lands adjacent to his *watan*.[51] In his new administrative role, the Amber Raja was to act as a watchdog of imperial interests in the region. Such an important assignment was deftly utilized by successive Amber rulers to enlarge their influence and in the process imperial interests began to be compromised. The alienation of zamindars began, indicating a failure of zamindar management policy of the Mughals.

Mirza Raja Jai Singh adopted a two-pronged strategy for restoring peace in the region. To begin with, insubordinate zamindars were outrightly evicted from their zamindaris. The Chauhans were thrown out of pargana Gijgarh and Salawad.[52] Similarly the insurgent Meo zamindars of *pargana* Kama and Pahari were expelled from their zamindaris.[53] and these were handed over to members of the Kachhwaha clan. In doing so the Raja seems to have underestimated the power of the expelled zamindars to resist. Both the Chauhans and the Meos entered into a prolonged conflict with the Amber *watan* and the Mughal empire.

The ruler of Amber also assigned a large number of villages to his soldiers *(chakars)* in the parganas of his own *jagirs*. The *chakars* of the Raja were to deal with actual or potential turbulence from the *bhomias*. This arrangement was surreptitiously utilized by the Raja's *chakars* to carve out their own zamindaris in the sub-assigned villages.

An *arzdasht* written by Shyam Singh Rajawat, *faujdar* of Bahatri in 1689 gives a detailed account of the circumstances in which new zamindari claims were made over a vast area in Mewat. This *arzdasht* in fact clearly bares the subtle mechanism of new zamindari acquisitions. According to Shyam Singh, the Amber Raja was assigned 14 *mahals* of Mewat in 1650 by the Mughal emperor. In his capacity of being the main *jagirdar* the Raja further sub-assigned his *jagir* to his own soldiers by way to meeting their pay claims. When the main *jagir* of the Raja was transferred from these parganas, some of the sub-assignees also left their allotments along with him. But a large number of them, instead of relinquishing their charge, preferred to stay on as *ijaradars* of the new imperial *jagirdars*. When the disturbances of the Jats of Braj gathered momentum, these soldiers of the Amber Raja, taking advantage of the escalating political instablity, began to embezzle the entire *hasil* (collected revenue) of such villages. The testimony given by the *chaudhuris, qanungos, patels* and *raiyats* of these parganas corroborates the contention of Shyam Singh Rajawat that these erstwhile *chakars* (soldier servants) of the Raja were not the *bhomias* of the allotted or farmed-out villages even at the time of the uprising of the Jats.[54] But the contention of Shyam Singh was vehemently disputed by these *chakars*-turned-*bhomias*, mainly from the Naruka and Kalyanot lineages.[55] This became a bone of contention between the Narukas and the Amber rulers in the years to come.[56]

In Ajmer and Ranthambore also the zamindaris of Thakur *chakars* (soldiers) of the Raja increased manifold. They adopted a similar mechanism to convert villages of their *chakari* into their *bhom*. An *arzdasht* dated 1685 narrates the unfolding of this phenomenon. It says that those Thakurs who were the *chakars* of the Amber Raja had become *bhomias* of the sub-assigned villages and did not fulfil their obligations as servants of the Raja.[57] By adopting this strategy many lineages of the Kachhwaha clan—Mansinghavats, Valibhadravats, Khangarots, Sultanots, and Narukas—had successfully replaced the Hara *bhomias* of pargana Tonk by 1698.[58] A similar trend, replacement of the old *bhomias* by the new ones, is observable in pargana Malpura. At the time of the *Ain,* Malpura (known as Todri) was under the zamindari of the Haras.[59] In 1681 the zamindari of all Malpura was transferred to Hari Singh Khangarot apparently 'with the concurrence of the local *muqaddams*.[60] The total marginalization of the Hara zamindars in most of the parganas of *sarkar* Ranthambore by the end of the seventeenth century by the Kachhwahas looks like a political coup in the history of zamindari rights in medieval India.

If the imperial administration aimed at taming seditious zamindars through the agency of Amber state, it seems to have erred in its assessment. The Amber ruler could achieve only ephemeral peace in the region. Those hereditary zamindars who were displaced became permanent enemies of the empire. On the other hand many leaders of various Kachhwaha lineages who had participated in this process of displacement of the refractory zamindars had considerably increased their political clout and fiscal strength. The creation of a large number of *bhoms* and their subsequent expansion into *thikanas* by various Kachhwaha lineages can be traced to this forcible usurpation of others' zamindaris. As long as the *bhomias* of various Kachhwaha lineages were extending the area of their influence in the zamindaris of non-Kachhwahas, the Amber ruler gave his tacit approval to their drive. But this relentless pursuit by some aggressive Kachhwaha lineages to further expand their *bhoms*, tended to disturb the balance of power within the larger Kachhwaha clan. The rising power of the Narukas and the Kalyanots began to threaten the interests of the Rajawats and the Khangarots, closely aligned with the Amber house. Such a situation was hardly conducive for centralizing political power in the region. Therefore, Raja Bishan Singh decided to put curbs on the zamindari pretensions of his erstwhile *chakars*. He himself began to acquire zamindari rights in more and more parganas outside his *watan*. As Raja Bishan Singh was fighting against the Jat rebels of Braj, the Emperor was favourably inclined to grant more powers and resources to him. During the last two decades of the seventeenth century the zamindari of twelve parganas was accorded to the Amber Raja. All these parganas—Niwai, Chatsu, Jhak, Mauzabad, Bhairana, Bharkol, Umarni, Banawar, Jalalpur, Khilohra, Vadhera, and Toda Raisinghpur—were contiguous to the Amber *watan*.[61] At the same time 'negotiations' for getting the zamindari of seven more parganas were going on between the agents of the Raja and various officials of the imperial administration.[62] All of these 19 parganas had traditional *bhomias* entrenched in them. In other words the Raja's agents were not taking zamindari in the *raiyati* villages alone, but the ordinary *bhomias*' villages were also taken. Thus the Jadon and Panchanot *bhomias* of pargana Malarna were asked to vacate their ancestral *bhoms* as these had come under the zamindari of the Amber Raja.[63] In 1712 all the incumbent *bhomias* of pargana Khohri were dispossessed of the ancestral *bhoms* that had been granted to the Amber ruler.[64]

Similarly, when Mir Muhammed Hussain, the *amil* of pargana Alwar tried to collect the *bhom* cess on behalf of the Amber Raja in 1726, the incumbent zamindar and the peasants of those villages protested vehemently. They threatened to file a case against the Amber state in the imperial court (*ya gavan ki bhomi haal hi thhe, lyo chho ih baat ki nalsi zamindar waa raiyati jagirdar syo kare chhe*).[65] The agent (*gumashta*) of Nawab Khan-i-Jahan Bahadur, the then *jagirdar* of pargana Alwar, protested to the Amber *diwan* in this manner: *mhan ki jagir ka gavan syo ab tak bhomi ki khenchal hui nahi or ab mhan ka gavan syo bhomi ki khenchal kare chhe.*[66] (So far there had been no dispute about the *bhom* right in our *jagir*. But now a dispute has been started). The *amil* suspended the collection of the *bhom* cess but did not give up the Raja's *bhom* claim on those villages.

Obviously, such an indiscriminate drive on the part of the Amber Raja to sideline or uproot the hereditary *bhomias* spelled doom for them. In reaction they united against the imperial administration and the Amber Raja. Even the ordinary *bhomias* of various Kachhwaha lineages felt threatened and became enemies of the Amber ruler, notwithstanding his premier status among them. This internal tension within the Kachhwaha clan became so acute that it was open to deft exploitation by the Jat zamindars of the Braj region. The spill-over of this internal conflict and its linkages with the rebel zamindars of other regions will be discussed in detail in Chapter 6.

Our evidence shows a startling enlargement of the Amber zamindari by Raja Bishan Singh during the reign of Aurangzeb. Mughal Emperor, instead of directly controlling the recalcitrant or ambitious ordinary *bhomias*, found it more expedient to transfer their zamindaris to the Amber Raja, who was then expected to deal with them with a heavy hand. In whichever parganas the Amber ruler had acquired zamindari rights, the Kachhwaha chancery termed these as part of their *watan*. C.U. Wills, using evidence of a later period, wrongly assumed that the Amber *watan* was not enlarged before 1712.[67] In fact the expansion of the *watan* had already begun in the 1680s. Sawai Jai Singh merely pursued it to the logical end. A general revolt by those *bhomias* who were adversely affected by this trend became imminent. The Mughal *jagirdars* and *faujdars* who were partly instrumental in facilitating the redistribution of these *bhoms* also had to face the wrath of the affected *bhomias*. Five decades from 1680 to 1730 were to witness a fierce struggle over the zamindari right in the Agra, Alwar, Ajmer, Ranthambore and Sahar *sarkars* of Ajmer and Agra *subas* of the empire.

NOTES

1. Irfan Habib, *Agrarian System*, pp. 196-229; and S. Nurul Hasan, 'Zamindars Under the Mughals', in R.E. Frykenberg (eds.), *Land Control and Social Structure in Indian History*, Madison, University of Wisconsin Press, 1969, pp. 17-31.
2. Tapan Raychaudhuri and Irfan Habib (eds.), *The Cambridge Economic History of India*, vol. I, *1200-1750*, 1982, p. 58.
3. Irfan Habib, *Agrarian System*, p. 179.
4. The *bhomias* preferred to construct their *garhis* on hilltops. Thus according to an *arzdasht*, dt. Posh Sudi 15, vs 1761/1704, Kishna Naruka, a rebel *bhomia*, had his *garhi* on the *dungar* of village Kot of *pargana* Banawar. Similarly Hari Singh Rajawat had constructed his *garhi* in village Sumelya of pargana Niwai. See *arzdasht*, dt. Asadh Sudi 15, vs 1761/1704.

5. Irfan Habib, *Agrarian System*, p. 196.
6. Irfan Habib, *Essays in Indian History*, p. 236; and *Agrarian System*, p. 197.
7. Iqtidar Alam Khan, 'The Nobility under Akbar and the Development of His Religious Policy, 1560-1580', *Journal of the Royal Asiatic Society*, 1968, pp. 29-36.
8. Norman P. Ziegler, 'Some Notes on Rajput Loyalties During the Mughal Period', in J.F. Richards (ed.), *Kingship and Authority in South Asia*, Madison, 1978. Oxford University Press.
9. J.F. Richards, *The Mughal Empire*, p. 284.
10. '... usually there is some rebellion of the rajas and zamindars going on in the Moghul kingdom', observed Manncci, See his, *Storia do Mogor, 1656-1712*, translated W. Irvine, 4 vols, London, 1907-8, vol. II, p. 462.
11. Kanwar Refaqat Ali Khan, *The Kachhwahas Under Akbar and Jahangir*, New Delhi, Kitab Publishing House, 1971.
12. S.P. Gupta, *The Agrarian System of Eastern Rajasthan*, pp. 5-8.
13. James Tod, *Annals and Antiquities*, I, 133, 136. S.P. Gupta, *Agrarian System of Eastern Rajasthan*, 130-40. *Bhomia* is a *dhundhari* rendering of the Hindi term *bhumia*. The *bhomia* appellation was largely used for the Rajputs. Non-Rajputs were usually addressed as zamindars, though there are instances when both the terms were interchangeably used for all. See *arzdashts*, dt. Mah Vadi 7, vs 1732/1675; Kati Vadi 14, vs 1754/1696 and Mangsir Sudi 15, vs 1759/1702.
14. *Arzdasht*, dt. Sawan Vadi 9, vs 1783/1726.
15. *Arsatthas*, pargana Banawar vs 1748/1691; Maujpur vs 1771/1714; Dausa vs 1722/1665; Malarna, vs, 1722/1665; Tonk vs 1765/1708; Fagi vs 1754/1697; Chatsu vs 1721/1664; Hindaun, vs 1764/1712 and Jalalpur vs 1723/1666.
16. Irfan Habib, *Agrarian System*, p. 187.
17. *Arsattha*, pargana Lalsot, vs 1797/1740 and *arsattha*, pargana Pindayan, vs 1789/1732. On the occasion of the marriage of the daughter of a man of the *ponjati* (menial caste) (menial and artisan) a *vagdum* cess of 8 *annas* was to be paid to the *bhomia*. Whenever a marriage party belonging to any caste, left its village, a *dhol* tax was paid to the *bhomia*.
18. Dilbagh Singh, *The State, Landlord and Peasants*, p. 45.
19. Ibid., pp. 45-6.
20. Ibid., pp. 46-7.
21. Harbans Mukhia, 'Illegal Extortions ....', *IESHR*, April-June, 1977, pp. 234-5.
22. An open conflict between the *bhomias* and the peasants is a constant theme of a number of reports emanating from the *Dhundhar* region. See *arzdashts*, dt. Jeth Vadi 4, vs 1706/1649; Asoj Vadi 7, vs 1751/1694/Falgun Sudi 15, vs 1752/1695 and Amber records dt. Asadh Sudi 13, vs 1740/1683 and Chet Vadi 13, vs 1741/1684.
23. Irfan Habib, *Agrarian System*, p. 387, argues that the zamindars usually adopted a 'conciliatory attitude towards their peasants'. Perhaps this could be true when the zamindars and the peasants belonged to the same caste. If they belonged to different castes, their relationship tended to be hostile. Thus the upper caste Rajput *bhomias*' attitude towards the lower caste peasantry was far from conciliatory.
24. *Arzdasht*, dt. Vaisakh Vadi 13, vs. 1722/1665.
25. See Chapter 6.

26. Dilbagh Singh, *The State, Landlords and the Peasants*, p. 44.
27. Dilbagh Singh, 'Role of the Mahajans in the Rural Economy of Eastern Rajasthan', *Social Scientist*, May 1974, p. 22.
28. Irfan Habib, *Agrarian System*, pp. 195-6 and 107 where Habib has cited instances of zamindar*i* sales in pargana Sahar, the centre of Jat revolt.
29. Ibid, pp. 221-22.
30. For instance Dura Meo who was expelled from Mewat in 1650 launched a prolonged struggle to get back his zamindari. He was rehabilitated in his zamindari in 1709 by Churaman Jat. See *arzdasht* of Jait Singh to Sawai Jai Singh dt. Asadh Sudi 5, vs 1766/1709. Similarly the Chauhan *bhomias* of *pargana* Salawad once evicted, managed to recover their *bhoms* after a prolonged resistance against the Amber ruler. See *arzdashts*, dt. Mah Vadi 7, vs 1732/1675 and Sawan Sudi 9, vs 1743/1686.
31. *Arsatthas* parganas, Toda Bhim vs 1750/1693 to vs 1800/1743 and Udai vs 1743/1686 to vs 1800/1743.
32. *Arzdasht*, dt. Vaisakh Vadi 10, vs 1750/1693.
33. *Arzdasht*, dt. Sawan Sudi 3, vs 1742/1685.
34. *Chithi* to the *amil*, pargana Alwar, dt. Asadh Sudi 3, vs 1783/1726.
35. *Ain-i-Akbari*, tr. Colonel H.S. Jarrett, vols. II-III, Low Price Publications (LPP), Delhi, rpt. 1997, p. 206.
36. Ibid., pp. 202-4.
37. Ibid., p. 278.
38. Irfan Habib, *Agrarian System*, p. 207.
39. C.U. Wills, *A Report on the Land Tenures and Special Powers of Certain Thikanedars of the Jaipur State,* 1935, p. 10; and James Tod, *Annals and Antiquities of Rajasthan*, Delhi, Motilal Banarsidas, 1971, vol. II, p. 294.
40. *Ain-i-Akbari*, LPP, vols. II-III, p. 278.
41. Ibid., pp. 279-80.
42. Ibid., pp. 281-2.
43. Ibid., pp. 195, 199, 202-3 and 205-6.
44. Ibid., pp. 193-4, 197 and 205-6.
45. Ibid., pp. 202-3.
46. This table is based on the *Ain-i-Akbari*'s zamindar column and *arzdashts* mentioned in the Appendex to this chapter.
47. The purchase of zamindari right by some Vaishnavite establishments near Vrindavan seems to be an exception. See Irfan Habib, *Agrarian System*, p. 195.
48. Irfan Habib, *Agrarian System*, p. 220.
49. Ibid., 210, 222. The grant of zamindari of 25 villages to Sayyid Qasim near Mathura, is the sole instance of 'favour' done to the Muslims in our region.
50. S. Nurul Hasan, 'Further Light on the zamindars under the Mughals: A Case Study of (Mirza) Raja Jai Singh under Shah Jahan', *PIHC*, 39th Session, Hyderabad, 1978, pp. 497-502.
51. Ibid., p. 498 and S.P. Gupta, *Agrarian System of Eastern Rajasthan*, p. 6 Extensive *jagirs* worth about nine crore dams were granted to Mirza Raja and his son in the parganas Amber, Chatsu, Fagi, Mauzabad, Jhak, Bhairana, Khohri, Deoti-Sanchari, Bawal, Chal Kalyana and Pachwara which included Gijgarh, Saner, Salawad, Boli, Kuwawa, Lalsot, Toda Bhim, Liwali and Behror. In addition, the *faujdari* of Mewat was given to his son, Kirat Singh.

52. *Arzdashts*, dt. Mah vadi 7, vs 1732/1675 and Sawan Sudi 9, vs 1743/1686
53. *Arzdasht*, dt. Asadh Sudi 5, vs 1766/1709.
54. *Arzdashts*, dt. Mah Vadi 5 and 7, vs 1746/1689.
55. *Arzdasht*, dt. Bhadwa Vadi 5, vs 1749/1692.
56. *Arzdashts*, dt. Kati Vadi 6, vs 1759/1702; Vaisakh Vadi 3, vs 1760/1703; Mangsir Sudi 5 and 14, vs 1759/1702; Mangsir Sudi 3, vs 1760/1703 and Jeth Vadi 1, vs 1761/1704.
57. *Arzdasht*, dt. Jeth Sudi 10, vs 1742/1685.
58. *Amber Records*, dt. Jeth Vadi 5, vs 1755/1698.
59. *Ain-i-Akbari*, vols. II-III, p. 280.
60. Satish Chandra, 'Some Documents Pertaining to Zamindari and Thikana Records in the Former Jaipur State', *PIHC*, 29th Session, Patiala 1967, pp. 261-5.
61. *Arzdashts*, dt. Asoj Vadi Amavasya, vs 1742/1685; Bhadwa Sudi 13, vs 1749/1692; Asadh Sudi 2, vs 1759/1702 and Kati Vadi 6, vs 1759/1702.
62. *Arzdashts*, dt. Falgun Sudi 12, vs 1740/1683; Posh Vadi 7, vs 1746/1689; Sawan Vadi 7, vs 1746/1689; Asadh Vadi 1, vs 1754/1694; Kati Vadi 14, vs 1761/1704; Chet Sudi 12, vs 1762/1705 and Vaisakh Sudi 10, vs 1762/1705. These parganas were: Bairath, Mandawar, Jhilai, Boli, Bhagotgarh, Abhaneri and Rajore.
63. *Arzdasht*, dt. Chet Sudi 10, vs 1746/1689.
64. *Arzdasht*, dt. Chet Sudi 6, vs 1769/1712.
65. *Chithi*, dt. Asadh Sudi 8, vs 1783/1726.
66. *Chithis*, dt. Asadh Sudi 3 and 15, vs 1783/1726. The simultaneous existence of an *amil* of the Raja and the *gumashta* of the *jagirdar* in the same *pargana* was possible because Alwar then was under the *ijara* of the Amber Raja.
67. C.U. Wills, *A Report on the Land Tenures*, p. 9.

5

Resisting Dominance

In this chapter we shall challenge the existing historiographical notions associated with the work of Jadunath Sarkar and recently resurrected, that the Jat uprising was provoked by Aurangzeb's policy of religious discrimination against Hindus. It will be argued that the Jats did not belong to any particular religious tradition, and cannot be freely clubbed with high caste Hindus. In fact from the seventh to the seventeenth century they were at the receiving end of the Brahmanical order. As the Jats have been resisting identities ascribed to them by dominant discourses, it becomes important to expatiate upon their past social structure and religio-cultural practices.

The antiquity of the Jats is shrouded in mystery, but they appear to have invited the attention of rulers from the early medieval period. The first recorded description of the Jats is given, in considerable detail, in the *Chachnama*, an account of the Arab conquest of Sindh (AD 710-14). When the Arab conqueror asked about the Jats, he was told: 'Among them there is neither great nor small. They possess a savage temperament, are continuously rebelling and disobedient to the rulers and commit highway robberies.'[1] Arab historians refer to clusters of Jats inhabiting the swamps, mountains, and deserts of Sindh at the time of the Arab conquest. Besides tending cattle, they were also soldiers, sailors, and guides. The Brahman dynasty of Chach encumbered these Jats with the following social constraints.

> That they should never wear any swords but sham ones. That they should never wear undergarments of shawl, velvet, or silk, but they might wear their outer garments of silk, provided they were of a red or black colour. That they should put no saddles on their horses, and should keep their heads and feet uncovered. That when they went out they should take their dogs with them. That they should carry firewood for the kitchen of the chief of Brahmanabad. They were to furnish guides and spies.[2]

It is amply clear from these prescriptions that the Jats were living on the fringes of Brahmanical society. Rebellion and armed conflict with the Brahman ruler of Sindh were constant. It is equally clear that the Jats were an aggressive horse-riding people whom Chach tried to discipline and disarm. Subjection to various loathsome constraints was an operative part of this endeavour. It is not known to what extent these prescriptions actually worked on the ground, but these disabilities remained embedded in the memories of the Jats.

The Arab conquerors of Sindh continued to oppress the Jats.[3] It would be germane to mention here that there is no evidence of a direct assault from the Muslims on the inequity of the caste system.[4] On the contrary there is sufficient evidence to suggest that 'Muslim institutions served partially to legitimise and continue the caste system in Arab Sindh'.[5] In AD 836, an Arab governor not only intensified these disabilities but also asked the Jats to pay *jizya*.[6] In the early eleventh century the Jats are reported to have engaged the army of Mahmud of Ghazni on the banks of river Indus with their many thousand boats.[7] The *Tarikh-i-Baihaqi* refers to the Jats as 'seditious Hindus' fighting on horses.[8] Eventually they began to be profiled as an aggressive and predatory people.

In his Lahore-centred portrayal of India Alberuni (*c.* 1030) described the Jats as 'cattle owners and low Shudra people'.[9] Other evidence points to a northward migration and dispersal of the Jats.[10] The exact tempo of their migrations remains obscure, but the general social outcome of their dispersal in the succeeding centuries is clear. They seem to have occupied the sparsely populated plains of the Punjab. In 1260s, the Jats are mentioned as having occupied the Sutlej-Beas *barr* and the Beas-Ravi *barr*.[11] Babar too describes the presence of the Jats in the Sindh Sagar Doab and Sialkot region. According to Babar the Jats were prone to turbulent and predatory habits.[12] By the close of the sixteenth century the Jats had spread beyond the Punjab. The *Ain-i-Akbari*'s record of zamindar castes is eloquent testimony to Jat dispersal over vast territories of the Mughal *subas* of Multan, Lahore, Delhi, and Agra.[13] Such a wide dispersal also postulates a great increase in Jat population. Concurrently, a massive transformation of the Jats from nomadic pastoralists to settled agriculturalists was well on its way. It appears that the sedentrization of the Jats took place between the eleventh and sixteenth centuries and continued even after that. Their transformation from a pastoral to an agricultural economy, went in tandem with sedentrization. It may be noted that the Jats continued agriculture and animal husbandry as mutually supporting activities. The growing population of the Jats in the Punjab and other parts of north-western India in the medieval period has been generally explained in terms of migration and a diffusion from their original homeland in Sind. It may, however, be suggested that the demographic expansion of the Jats may have also been caused by a process of the social amalgamation of various tribes that were making the transition from mobile pastoralism to sedentary agriculture in these regions. 'Jat' became the identity of newly emerging peasant communities. For instance, Krishna's foster parents, the Yadavas, have been referred to by Alberuni as Jats.[14]

It seems that the Jats had to bear the main brunt of the tightening grip of the Arabs on Sindh—the turbid frontier of India. Not only were existing social disabilities intensified on them, they were also subjected to an enhanced fiscal burden.[15] Their response was to set out on a long itinerary from Sindh to the Punjab. Though the sources are silent about the trauma of this dislocation, the Jats might have come to the Punjab with harrowing memories of their past and still confined to the margins of the Brahmanical social order.[16]

Richard M. Eaton has concluded that before the beginning of their settlement in the Punjab (1000-1300) the Jats had not been integrated into 'Hindu society'.[17] He seems to suggest that this integration began to take shape when, during the pre-Mughal centuries, the Jats acquired a higher social status, that of a peasant caste, as a result of their gradual sedementarization among peasants.[18] Irfan Habib also emphasizes that it was the shift from pastoralism to peasant agriculture that led to an improvement in the status of the Jat communities. By the seventeenth century they had become peasants 'par excellence'.[19] However, a mid-seventeenth century work still describes the Jats as a low caste among the Vaisyas.[20]

Upward mobility in the Brahmanical social order through a process of occupational transformation and sanskritization was not an all-pervasive or universal phenomenon among the Jats of north-western India. Moreover, as we shall show, integration into the Brahmanical order of castes did not always imply an immediate acceptance by Jats of Brahmanical gods, rituals, and systems of worship. The formation and crystallization of the Jats as a caste of peasants did not extinguish their own religious beliefs or forms of worship, distinctly non-Brahmanical. Resistance to dominant

Brahmanical culture was an integral part of Jat religiosity and would have constituted an important element in the ideological dimensions of Jat rebellions in the late seventeenth and early eighteenth centuries. The intense hostility of the Jats to the Vaishnavite establishments in the Braj region are a clear manifestation of this. Obviously, the Jats considered the rulers and the religious elites as an integral part of the same order.

Two distinct alternatives to sanskritization and resultant integration into the Hindu caste system were historically available to the Jat peasants of the Punjab. First, many Jat clans came to be associated with the shrine of Baba Farid in Pak Pattan from the late fourteenth century onward. The simple religious *adab* of the shrine as elaborated by Eaton, not only integrated the Jats with the ritual and religious practices of the shrine, but also provided a 'universal cultural system'.[21] Though it was a gradual and slow moving process, it ultimately brought a large number of Jat clans within the orbit of Islam.

The other opening was provided by the Sikh Gurus, who not only rejected the social order based on Brahmanical dominance and caste hierarchy, but also raised the Jats to respectable positions within the Panth.[22] From the time of Guru Amar Das, Jats began to show allegiance to the Panth.[23] During the seventeenth century a massive incursion of Jats into the Panth seems to have taken place.[24] Irfan Habib gives a lucid explanation for this: 'In the guise of a Sikh or a Satnami, a Jat peasant could assert a dignity which was previously denied to him.'[25]

Muslim observers, both critics and sympathizers, characterized the religions of all non-Muslims in India collectively as 'Hindu'. In reality, what this involved, was a Brahmanical religion that Jats, in their given condition, would be loath to follow. In other words the Jats were not only escaping from the seamless web of a Brahmanical social order but also resisting integration into a Brahman-ordered society at a subaltern level. The favourable ambience created by the shrine of Baba Farid and the teachings of the Sikh Gurus greatly strengthened their power to resist.[26] A careful study of the religious beliefs and practices of those Jats who remained outside the ambit of both Islam and Sikhism is a basic desideratum. In the case of the Jats of the Braj-Mewat region, this lacuna becomes all the more irksome since all kinds of religious motives have been attributed to the Jat revolts that led to the formation of the Bharatpur state. In the considered opinion of Jadunath Sarkar, these Jats were 'Hindus' fighting Aurangzeb's religious bigotry.[27] Recently some scholars have suggested that the Jat uprising was against Aurangzeb's iconoclastic policies and in defence of the Vaishnava temple of Govinddeva.[28] Irfan Habib, on the other hand, finds having no connection of the Jat rebels with any religious movement.[29] Habib sees the Vaishnavite establishments of the Braj region as victims rather than as co-religionists of the Jat rebels. Kishan Charan Gosain, a Vaishnav leader of Vrindavan, was forced to flee from his establishment in the wake of the Jat rebellions and was only able to return after the rebels were suppressed by the Mughal officer, Bishan Singh.[30] It may now be worthwhile to expand upon the ascription of such a religiosity to the Jat uprising, even though it is difficult to reconstruct and recover all the elements that shaped the religious outlook of the Jat peasantry of the region. This task becomes all the more arduous as the unlettered peasants have not left any written record. However, some threads can be picked up from the tangled fabric of folk religion when some vernacular textual sources, including the Vallabhite hagiographies, are closely scrutinized.[31]

The recently published Vrindavan documents are of immense help for understanding the relationship between the Gaudia Vaishnavite sect, the Mughal state and the local populace.[32] Of paramount importance in this regard are, of course, the ethnographic investigations of Growse and Powlett.[33] We can also draw on the literary works of modern historians of Vaishnavism, well versed in the religious and cultural traditions of the Braj region.[34]

There is sufficient evidence to indicate a gradual Vaishnava takeover of the Braj region in the sixteenth and seventeenth centuries.[35] Two Vaishnavite sects, the Vallabhites and the Gaudias, had a widespread presence in the Braj region. Both were actively fostered by the Mughal emperors and their Kachhwaha allies, with extensive revenue-free land grants to them.[36] Thus Vaishnava occupation of the Braj region was at its peak when Aurangzeb ascended the throne. By making these endowments the Mughals perhaps aimed at stabilizing the region politically, as Braj was inhabited and bordered by turbulent elements.[37] It may be argued that the incorporation of the Brahmanical and other non-Islamic religious elites into the Mughal patronage system was an integral part of the political process of imperial integration. The entry of the Rajput chiefs into the Mughal nobility especially accelerated the process of extension of Mughal patronage to the Brahmanical institutions that in their turn became important centres of imperial legitimation. A systematic study of the hagiographic literature of these sects and the Vrindavan documents supports such inferences. Incidentally, these sects were dominated by Gujarati (Vallabhite) and Bengali (Gaudia) Brahmans. Much of their following also came from the upper castes: Brahmans, Thakurs, Banias, and Khatris.[38] On the other hand local people, known as Brajvasis largely belonged to the peasant castes such as Jats, Gujars, and Ahirs and were a nominal Vaishnav segment.[39] Indeed the Vaishnavite movement never questioned caste as the basic principle of ordering society.[40] Arguably the Vaishnavite movement in the Braj region was a renewed incarnation of Brahmanism and its rituals and practices could hardly enthuse the Brajvasis.

A perusal of the *varta* literature clearly shows one Dhagu Jat boycotting a Vaishnava feast on the plea that its organizer was a Samchora Brahman and 'an outsider'. Dhagu also disputed the superiority of the Brahmans by posing as a 'Pande' (a learned man) himself.[41] Such claims on the part of a rustic Jat seems to be symbolic of an inversion of the caste hierarchy. Conversely, he could have been negotiating for himself and his constituency for a secure and equal space in the Vaishnava sect. Similarly, one day a Brajvasi who was serving in the cattle-pen (*kharak*) of cows happened to cross the path of Gosainji early in the morning. Gosainji, the head priest of Srinathji temple, considered this to be inauspicious. In anger he asked the Brajvasi to stay away from the temple and its environs.[42]

In yet another *varta* it is said that one day Gosainji and a group of Vaishnavas lost their way between Gujarat and Braj. A *balahi* (member of a low caste) told them they were traversing a path infested by bandits, showed them a safer path. While travelling on, the Vaishnavas instead of giving him suitable food, gave the Balahi their leftovers (*jhuthan*) with much glee.[43] The relations of dominance and subordination are deeply embedded into the structures of these *vartas*. The piety of the pastoralists was in sharp contrast to the arrogance of the high-caste Vaishnavas. Charlotte Vaudeville, therefore, says, '. . . the pastoral people of Braj never had a share in official Vaishnava rituals. Today, as in the days of yore, they remain mountain and cattle worshippers'.[44] Actually the managers (*adhikaris*) and priests (*pujaris*) of the Vaishnava monasteries (*matha*) did everything to relegate the Brajvasis to an inferior position within the sect.[45] Such ritual marginalization was resented by the Jats who had a chequered history of resistance against constant lowering of their social status by the Brahmans. They were also indignant at the usurpation of their Devadham by the Vallabhites.[46]

The Vrindavan documents throw interesting light on the relationship between the Mughal state, the Gaudias, and the villagers of the Braj country. They reveal the attempt by the Gaudias to occupy the Brajbhumi with the active support of the Mughal emperors.[47] Incidentally, some of these documents also reveal persistent hostility between Jats and Gaudias. According to one document, Kishan Charan Gosain of the line of Rup Goswami had fled to the Rajput country (*mulk-i-Rajputan*) due to the disturbances by the Jats (*futur-i-Jatan*).[48] Similarly, a *sevak* (devotee) of the Madan Mohan temple had lost his *chaknama* (demarcation document) of about 89 *bighas* of land granted to him in village Rajpura during the 'disturbances of the accursed Jats' (*futur-i-Jat-i-mughuri*).[49] In another document we read a stream of coarse invectives against the Jats (*Jat-i-bad-zat*) and find that Gopal Das and Harkishan have asked for the restoration of their land near Vrindavan. They claim to have lost the *farman* of this land in the course of the 'tumult raised by the wretched Jats'.[50] All these documents seem to have been lost in the period when the Jats were in the midst of a life and death struggle with the Amber general (Hari Singh Khangarot) who was baying for their blood.[51] Apart from these instances of open hostility, there is ample evidence of latent tensions between the Gaudias and the local people of Braj. No wonder that Kishan Charan and the likes of him became the target of the fury of the Jat rebels. These Vaishnava revenue grantees had frequent land disputes with the local residents.[52] At times the zamindars refused to pay land revenue to the grant-holders.[53] Elsewhere, disputes over grazing rights between the Brajvasis and the Vaishnava revenue grantees also came to the fore.[54] Apparently, with such large scale endowments the Vaishnava institutions had emerged as formidable landowners, rivals to the interest of the Brajvasis.

The Brajvasis in general and the Jats in particular were not only outside the ambit of the Vaishnava creed but in conflict with the Gaudias and Vallabhites. The Jat rebels looked on the Vaishnavite sects with considerable suspicion as the latter were the protégés of the Mughals and Kachhwahas. The religious grants made in the parganas of Braj and its neighbourhood during the seventeenth century show striking similarity in the approach of the Mughals and Kachhwahas towards these sects. For example, when Aurangzeb ordered the cancellation of all grants to Hindus, he allowed two important Vrindavan grants, one of 135 *bighas* for the Govinddeva temple and another of 89 *bighas* for Madan Mohan temple to continue, 'with full official cognizance'.[55] Similarly, Mukhtar Khan, the *subadar* of Akbarabad, issued a *parwana* in 1705 to the revenue officials of pargana Islamabad (Mathura) ordering them to direct the zamindars to collect Re 1 from each village of eighteen parganas of Braj every year for the maintenance of Roop Dharam Das and his *bairagi* associates.[56] A similar levy of Rs 2 on each village within the *jagirs* of Raja Ram Singh was imposed for the maintenance of one Swami Mohan Rai.[57] These levies were an addition to the existing revenue demand. The Amber rulers also made large-scale *punya-udik* (charitable) grants to many Brahmans, Bhats, and Charans and various Vaishnava institutions in some key parganas of Braj. This policy was vigorously pursued in those parganas where the Jat rebellion was intensive and widespread. Needless to say, these *udik* holders willingly acted as apologists and propagandists of the Kachhwaha regime.

For example pargana Khohri had only one *udik* village in 1666.[58] The number of *udik* grants increased up to six villages in Khohri by 1716.[59] In the ensuing ten years the number of *udik* villages had gone up to thirteen in Khohri.[60] A similar trend can be seen in pargana Hindaun. Here the total number of *udik* grants was in fourteen villages in the year 1712.[61] The *arsattha* of 1718 shows 24 villages under *udik* grants in Hindaun.[62] Similarly in pargana Kama the number of *udik* grants had increased from two in 1650 to twenty in 1768.[63] All the three parganas were severely affected by the Jat revolts.

Though many parganas had villages granted to the *aimmadars*,[64] the number of such grants was on the wane due to a tilt in Sawai Jai Singh's policy in favour of Brahmans. In pargana Khohri the number of *milk* grants (two villages) remained constant whereas the area of *udik* grants increased manifold.[65] In the beginning of eighteenth century pargana Hindaun had a large number of *milk* grants scattered in 21 villages.[66] Their total area was 1,070 *bighas,* of which 859 were *farmani* and 211 *hukamiya*.[67] The cash value of these grants was Rs 2,553 *farmani* and Rs 610 *hukamiya*.[68] The total amount of *sayurghal* grants mentioned in the *Ain* was much more in Hindaun towards the end of sixteenth century than in the eighteenth century.[69] This was the result of resumptions made by the Kachhwahas during the intervening period. Surprisingly, the *milk* grants disappeared from Hindaun by the middle of the eighteenth century.[70] This could be the result of the erosion of Mughal power in the region and Sawai Jai Singh's inclination to make more grants to Brahmans and other Hindu orthodox elements.[71]

The increasing tension between the revenue officials of the Jaipur state and the *milk* grantees in the region must be viewed in the context of Jai Singh's penchant for orthodox Hinduism. Only a few cases of harassment of the *milk* grantees are given here to highlight the emerging trend. Hazi Saiyid Ahmad had his *milk* of 200 *bighas* in village Baroda of pargana Mathura. The *amil* appointed by the Jaipur Raja forced the said Saiyid to pay various cesses from which *milk* grantees were normally exempted.[72] The peasants who customarily cultivated the *milk* land in *qasba* Pahari were asked by the *amil* of Pahari not to do so.[73] Similarly, the *qazi* of *qasba* Pindayan complained that his *milk* land in village Rulpahari was not allowed to be cultivated.[74] Needless to say, such complaints were routinely glossed over by the Jaipur administration.

Interestingly, the attitude of smaller zamindars towards the *milk* and *udik* grantees was similar. As such these conflicts were motivated more by mundane considerations than any religious rancour. Some cases of hostility between the zamindars and the grantees would make it more clear. For instance the villages endowed for the maintenance of Akbar's tomb at Sikandra refused to pay revenue for many years at the behest of Jat zamindars of the area.[75] Similarly the Jats attacked ten of the thirty villages endowed for the maintenance of the Taj Mahal.[76] It is a well known fact that rebels usually attack anything having a conneetion with their adversary. Jats' attacks on the sources of the maintenance of these monuments should be viewed as such. In another case Prem Singh Naruka, a *bhomia,* forcibly took the *hasil* of village Bhogor in pargana Alwar. The looted *hasil* was from the *milk* (70 *bighas*) of Shaikh Alahyar.[77] A village called Vadhalwara near Ajmer had been granted in *milk* by Emperor Akbar to the ancestors of Mir Ahmad Pirzada. Amar Singh Gaur, a neighbouring *bhomia,* not only looted this village in 1742 but also carried and all its cultivators as captives. Mir Ahmad also complained that another village called Kahanpura granted to him in *milk* was forcibly annexed by Amar Singh into his zamindari.[78]

A similar kind of tension existed between the zamindars and the *udik* grantees in the region. The nature of hostility between the Jat zamindars and the Vaishnavite grantees of Vrindavan has already been discussed at length. The smaller Rajput *bhomias* also exhibited a similar hostility towards the *udik* grantees of their area. For example, it was reported by Vijay Ram Bhatt that his *udik* village Chhaparwara in pargana Mauzabad was customarily exempted from the *bhom* cess. In the same report is a complaint that the local *bhomia* forced Vijay Ram Bhatt to pay the *bhom* cess.[79] One Mahadev Bhatt had his *udik* grant in village Khedri-khurd of pargana Chatsu. According to a complaint, the Mansinghvat *bhomias* took away all the cattle and the entire *hasil* of the said village in 1718.[80] In another instance it was reported that five carts full of grain meant for *bhog* (offerings) were being brought by Radha Kishan Vyas from village Chhani of pargana Udai when Amar Singh Panchanot, a local *bhomia* looted all the carts with the active support of the *patels* of village Sewa of Hindaun.[81]

Indeed the Kachhwahas had been nurturing territorial ambitions in the Braj country. Various forms of largesse extended by the Kachhwahas to the religio-cultural activities of the Vaishnavites were a part of this strategy. On the other hand the Jat zamindars who were well entrenched in *sarkar* Sahar,[82] the heartland of Braj, could not afford to ignore the Amber Raja's increasing political hold on the area. Such a situation was bound to create conflict between the Jats and the land revenue grantees (the legitimation machinery) of the Amber state. This spat between the land revenue grantees and the zamindars developed into open hostility in the course of the Jat rebellion. In the neighbouring *suba* of Awadh, the Mughal state had specially bolstered up the grant holders 'with a view to arrest the growth and expansion of the rural disturbances'.[83] It becomes meaningful, in this context, to discover that in a number of cases the zamindars' hostility began to be directed against the *milk* as well as *udik* grantees. For their part the land grantees did nothing to buy peace with the recalcitrant zamindars. The grantees were probably acting as conduits of information for their respective patrons regarding the day-to-day movements of the refractory zamindars.

It has already been argued that Vaishnavism in the Braj country was primarily the religious universe of high-caste Hindus. It could even be termed an official religion, for it was closely aligned to the Mughal empire and the Amber state during the seventeenth century.

Its patrons and practioners lived off the surplus product of the peasants, who largely belonged to the lower castes. These peasants and the peers of their caste had their own views on religion.

The existence of an elite-folk binary opposition within the conduct of religious life has been questioned,[84] yet such a dichotomy cannot be totally denied. At the interface of elite and popular cultural traditions, there always existed a vast terrain where contestations, negotiations, and re-articulations could take place. In this interactive space, mutual appropriations, inversion, and marginalization of some of the elements of the contending cultures was a constant feature. During the sixteenth and seventeenth centuries, the Braj-bhum had become a battle-ground of two rival cultures. The fabled discovery of Braj by the founders of the Vaishnavite sects grew into such a powerful legend that it tended to obscure the already existing religious traditions in the region.[85] These Vaishnavites tried to belittle the culture of the Brajvasi by belittling all forms of popular worship. As their behaviour and actions were to some extent influenced by their view of the Puranic past, this was resented and resisted by the local people. In fact a resistance against cultural domination was one of the hidden dimensions of the Jat revolts, for the elements and forms of protest were against the culture of the powerful.[86]

The most notable feature of popular religion in Braj-bhum was the ubiquitous presence of *lok-devis* (folk goddesses) at various annual fairs. The most widely venerated among the *lok-devis* is Nari-Semri, known as the protectoress of Braj. An equally important *devi* is Sayal-Mata, worshipped by women at the Ahoi festival. Mansa-devi is also held in reverence and ardently worshipped by all the Brajvasis.[87] Between 1600 and 1800 the worship of these *devis* was popular among the Jats and other peasant communities. In an important contemporary document it is mentioned that Churaman Jat, with a large entourage undertook a *yatra* (pilgrimage) to a popular *devi* in village Vaharkhoh, *tappa* Rini, pargana Bahatri. On the way Churaman was given a tumultous welcome by the villagers. Hearing this uproar the *faujdar* of Bahatri was enraged and had the *devi* uprooted from its place before the arrival of Churaman.[88] The importance of this event lies in the fact that the said *devi* was becoming a rallying point for the rebels and a matter of grave concern for the administration. In fact the Narukas, an important rebellious clan allied with the Jats, would embark on a rebellion only after worshipping their *kul-devi* at *qasba* Sanchari.[89] Indeed the *yatra* of such *devis* was a common feature in the months of Chet and Bhadwa.[90] For the Amber state these *yatras* were merely a source of income, but for the participants these occasions could be a way of forming community bonds and fostering ideological religious unity. These *devis* and the *yatras* around them were an object of contempt for high-caste Vaishnavas who were closely allied with the Mughals and the Kachhwahas. One important dimension of the official Vaishnavite propaganda against non-Vaishnavite forms of worship among local groups is that rather than eliminating these forms, they are sought to be subordinated to the Krishna worship. The *devis* are made to acknowledge the superior position of the Vaishnavite pantheon. Thus Vaishnavite forms were superimposed on pre-existing forms of worship. Charlotte Vaudville brings out this conflict clearly when she writes, 'In spite of Vaishnava abhorrence of the bloody rites associated with the devi-worship, the pastoral castes, especially the Jats and the Gujars who formed the bulk of the autochthonous population of Braj-bhum, did remain attached to the cult of their local goddesses.'[91] The extent to which the prevalence of this *devi* or *shakti* worship imparted an aggressive edge to the Jat rebellion is only a matter of conjecture.[92]

Another striking feature of popular religion in Braj is the abiding importance and precedence of *prakriti-puja* (nature worship) over *murti-puja* (idol worship). In the realm of the common man's devotion, woods, cows, pasture and mountains are the main objects of adoration; images and shrines are secondary.[93] All kinds of sources are unanimous about the presence of an impeneterable *jungle* (forest) that provided the safest cover to the Jat rebels. The existence of this thick forest wall frustrated the Mughal generals engaged in counter-insurgency campaigns.[94] It was perhaps in recognition of this in their struggle that the Bharatpur rulers later fixed a severe penalty on anyone who was found cutting the trees.[95] Regarding the forest-friendliness of the Jats there is a popular saying in Rajasthan: *Jungle Jat na chhediye, hattan beech kirad,*[96] never pick up a fight with a Jat in the forest, or with a trader in the market place. The purport of the saying is that for the Jats forest was an abode of unrestrained freedom. Similarly the Govardhan mountain occupies a central place in the mythical landscape of Braj. In fact *govardhan-puja*, the cult of mountain and cattle, is widespread and popular among the Brajvasis. The worship of Govardhan without assistance from the Brahman is a common feature.[97]

Cults of various folk-deities emerged among the pastoral and peasant communities of medieval north India. Some of these cults cut across Hindu-Muslim religious boundaries and freely drew upon the elements of both religions.[98] Guga Pir, whose primary prowess lay in curing his worshippers of snake bite, was one of the reigning folk-dieties in our region. In the contemporary sources annual fairs around the cult of Guga Pir have been reported. For instance, a *Guga-ka-mela* was held every year in village Vadhari, pargana Khohri, on the sixth day (*chhath*) in the bright part of the month of Bhadwa.[99] On the same day, a similar fair, known as *Guga-Pir-ka-mela,* was also held at village Hathangaon of pargana Pahari.[100] People belonging to all castes, especially those of the lower order, thronged to these fairs. The location of both villages is significant because they lay at the interface of Braj and Mewat. Annual meetings of the Brajvasis and Mewatis at these fairs created unstructured solidarities among them. Some aspects of this solidarity came to the fore in the course of the Jat uprising.[101] Reciting the name of Gugaji/ Guga Pir became an important ceremony among the peasants at the time of the beginning of the agricultural season and ploughing.[102] The idea perhaps was to save the peasant and his bullocks from snake-bite. Guga Pir was seen as the protector of both the ploughman and his bullocks. Most of the folk-deities of medieval north India were historical personages,[103] associated with certain concerns which were essential for the welfare and survival of peasant communities. Many great deeds of valour are attributed to these deities.[104] Their followers among the subaltern groups believed that these deities possessed powers to preserve and enhance pastoral and agricultural resources.

In much of northern India a vibrant *sant*-inspired anti-Brahmanical culture was pervasive during the seventeenth century.[105] Lal Das (1540-1648), born in a Meo family, was a leading *sant* who had a considerable following in Mewat and its neighbourhood. His teachings were similar to those of Kabir.[106] In a legendary account of his life, he is alleged to have been imprisoned by the local *faujdar* for not making distinctions between Hindus and Muslims. In various hostile encounters with local Mughal administrators, Lal Das emerges unscathed due to his *karamat* (miraculous powers).[107] For these deeds he became very popular among the peasants especially the Meos and the Jats.[108] When caught in difficult circumstances the peasants used to invoke the name of Lal Das for succour. For instance, two peasants (Dasodhi and Nayamat) of village Maharajpur in pargana Khohri had concealed some cultivated land from the prying eyes of revenue officials. When caught, they said that the crops neither belonged to them or the state, but to Lal Das. The officials imposed a fine of Rs 40 on the 'culprits'.[109] This episode shows that the name of Lal Das had a place of pride in the life of the peasants, if not the officialdom.

It is clear from our discussion so far that the Jats did not adhere to any particular sacred tradition, and they cannot be freely clubbed with the high caste Hindus. In fact from Sindh to Braj the Jats were at the receiving end of the Brahmanical order. On the other hand the Brahmans and the Vaishnavas were patronized by the Mughals and their Kachhwaha allies in the Braj region. It seems that Aurangzeb's temporary religious rage was the result of chinks that had developed in Mughal-Kachhwaha relations. The Jats and other peasant pastoral communities of the Braj region practised forms of worship ranging from the deification of natural phenomena to the glorification of living or dead *sants*. While these forms of worship may have been mutually contradictory, they remained integral to the religious and cultural universe of the common people and linked to their everyday lives. They were mobilized during religious and cultural resistance to external forces. As these modes of faith and practice were not approved by the Brahmanical and Vaishnavite establishment, the rebellions of the Jats and Satnamis cannot be treated as constituting any 'Hindu' reaction. While rebelling against the Mughal/Kachhwaha authority, the Jat peasantry drew upon its own religious/cultural resources, neither Brahmanical nor Vaishnavite.

NOTES

1. *The Chachnama: An Ancient History of Sindh*, by Mirza Kalichbeg Fredenbegi, Delhi, Idarah-i Adabiyat-i Delhi, 1900 (rep. 1979), p. 37.
2. *Chachnama*, p. 37.
3. *Chachnama*, tr., p. 170.
4. Irfan Habib, 'Economic History of the Delhi Sultanate – An Essay in Reinterpretation', *IHR*, 4(1977), p. 297.
5. Derryl N. MacLean, *Religion and Society in Arab Sindh*, Leiden, E.J. Brill, 1989, pp. 48-9.

6. *Futuh al-Buldan*, tr. Elliot and Dowson, *History of India as Told by Its Own Historians*, Kitab Mahal Edition, vol. I, p. 128. According to Derryl MacLean these restrictions were part of a general policy of the Abbasids towards the rebellious Jats. See his *Religion and Society*, p. 47.
7. Elliot and Dowson, *History of India*, vol. II, p. 478.
8. *Tarikh-i-Baihaqi*, quoted by Irfan Habib, 'Jatts of Punjab and Sindh', in H. Singh and N.G. Barrier (eds.), *Punjab Past and Present: Essays in Honour of Ganda Singh*, Patiala, 1976, p. 95.
9. Edward C. Sachau, *Alberuni's India*, S. Chand of Company, 1910 (rpt. Delhi, 1993), p. 401.
10. Irfan Habib, 'Jatts of Punjab and Sindh', in H. Singh and N.G. Barrier (eds.), *Punjab Past and Present: Essays in Honour of Ganda Singh*, Patiala, 1976, pp. 95-6.
11. Richard M. Eaton, 'The Political and Religious Authority of the Shrine of Baba Farid', in Barbara Daly Metcalf (ed.), *Moral Conduct and Authority: The Place of Adab in South Asian Islam*, University of California Press, 1984, p. 342.
12. *Babarnama* (Memoirs of Babur), tr. or Turki Text by A.S. Beveridge, vols. I and II, 1922, rpt. 1979, New Delhi, p. 454.
13. Irfan Habib, 'Jatts of Punjab and Sindh', pp. 100-1. Habib has prepared a table of *sarkars* where Jats are recorded as zamindars in the *Ain-i-Akbari*.
14. Edward C. Sachau, *Alberuni's India*, p. 401.
15. Derryl MacLean, *Religion and Society*, p. 45.
16. Richard M. Eaton, 'The Political and Religious Authority of Baba Farid', p. 343.
17. Ibid.
18. Ibid., p. 345.
19. Irfan Habib, 'The Jatts of Punjab and Sindh', p. 99 and 'Caste in Indian History', p. 175.
20. *Dabistan-i-Mazahib*, tr. by Anthony Troyer and David Shea, *Schools of Religion*, 3 vols., London, 1843. The section dealing with the 'religious systems of the Hindus' have been reproduced as *Hinduism* during the Mughal India of the 17th Century, Patna, Khudabaksh Library, rpt., pp. 252, 270.
21. Richard M. Eaton, 'The Political and Religious Authority of the Shrine of Baba Farid', p. 355.
22. Irfan Habib, 'Jatts of Punjab and Sindh', p. 98.
23. W.H. McLeod, *The Evolution of the Sikh Community*, Oxford University Press, Delhi, 1996, pp. 8-9.
24. J.S. Grewal and Irfan Habib (eds.), *Sikh History from Persian Sources*, Tulika, 2001, see the Introduction by Grewal.
25. Irfan Habib, 'Historical Background of the Popular-Monotheistic Movement of the 15th and 17th Centuries', in Bisheshwar Prasad (ed.), *Ideas in History*, Bombay, 1969, p. 3.
26. Romila Thapar in her Presidential Address, 'The Scope and Significance of Regional History', to the Punjab History Conference, Patiala, 1976, said, 'Brahmanism never seems to have had deep social root in the plains' of Punjab. She based this observation on an 'absence of evidence' which at best shows only an institutional weakness of Brahmanism in the plains. Yet the Sikh Gurus' constant harping on caste equality and the lower-caste ardour for Sikhism, shows

the strong ideological presence of Brahmanism even in the plains of Punjab.

27. Jadunath Sarkar, *History of Aurangzeb*, vol. III, 3rd edn., Calcutta, 1926, Chapter XXXV.
28. R. Nath, 'Sri Govinddeva's Itinerary from Vrindavana to Jayapura, *c.* 1534-1727', in Margaret K.H. Case (ed.) *Govinddeva—a Dialogue in Stone*, New Delhi, 1996, p. 164; Monica Hortsmann, *In Favour of Govinddevji: Historical Documents Relating to a Deity of Vrindaban and Eastern Rajasthan*, New Delhi, 1999. In a well researched recent paper on the causes of desecration and destruction of Hindu temples in medieval India, Richard M. Eaton, somewhat erroneously, connects two distinct events of the Jat rebellion near Mathura in 1669-70 and the demolition of the famous Keshava Deva temple in that city in the same year. *Essays on Islam and Indian History*, Oxford University Press, 2000, p. 120. However, Saqi Mustad Khan, the author of *Maasir-i-'Alamgiri*—the source cited by Eaton in support of the imagined links—treats the two events separately and does not see any connection between them. After giving an account of the suppression of Gokula Jat's rebellion, he narrates an other episode before turning to the destruction of the temple by Aurangzeb in the month of Ramzan 'abounding in miracles'. See Saqi Mustad Khan, *Massir-i-Alamgiri*, tr. J. Sarkar, Calcutta, Royal Asiatic Society of Bengal, 1947, p. 60.
29. Irfan Habib, *Agrarian System*, p. 393.
30. Ibid., P. 393 n. 26.
31. *Chaurasi Vaishnavan Ki Varta*, Bombay, Khemraj Shrikrishnadas, 1988; *Do Sau Bavan Vaishnavan Ki Varta*, Bombay, Khemraj Shrikrishnadas, 1986. All the eighty-four Vaishnavas were the followers of Vallabhacharya (1478-1530) who had founded the *Pushti-Marg*. The two hundred and fifty-two devotees were the disciples of Vithalnath (1515-64). The *Vartas* (tales) were transmitted through oral tradition and compiled in late seventeenth century. Another *Varta*, the *Sri Nath Ji Prakatya Ki Varta*, was composed in the middle of the seventeenth century by Sri Hariray.
32. Tarapada Mukherji and Irfan Habib, 'Akbar and the Temples of Mathura and its Environs', *PIHC*, 48 (1987), pp. 234-50; 'The Mughal Administration and the Temples of Vrindavan during the Reigns of Jahangir and Shahjahan', *PIHC*, 49 (1988), pp. 234-300 and 'Land Rights in the Reign of Akbar (The Evidence of the Sale-Deeds of Vrindavan and Aritha)', *PIHC*, 50 (1989-90), pp. 236-55 and R.A. Alvi, 'Persian Documents of the Reign of Aurangzeb', *PIHC*, 49 (1988). Most of these documents have been reproduced by Irfan Habib, 'A Documentary History of the Gosains (Goswamis) of the Caitanya Sect at Vrindavan', in Margaret H. Case (ed.), *Govinddeva: A Dialogue in Stone*, New Delhi, 1996, pp. 131-59.
33. F.S. Growse, *Mathura: A District Memoir*, Ahmedabad, 1978, reprint of the 3rd edn., 1883 and P.W. Powlett, *Gazetteer of Ulwur*, London, Trubner and Co., 1878.
34. Seth Govinddas, *Braj Aur Braj-Yatra*, Delhi, 1959, and P.D. Mittal, *Braj Ka Samskritik Itihas*, Delhi, 1966 and *Braj Sampardayon Ka Itihas*, Mathura, 1968.
35. Charlotte Vaudeville, 'The Goverdhan Myth in Northern India', in C. Vaudeville (ed.), *Myths, Saints and Legends in Medieval India*, Delhi, Oxford University Press, 1999, pp. 72-139.
36. Tasrapada Mukherji and Irfan Habib, 'Akbar and the Temples of Mathura and

its Environs', and 'The Mughal Administration and the Temples of Vrindavan during the Reign of Jahangir and Shahjahan'.

37. Irfan Habib, *The Agrarian System*, pp. 390, 398. Habib cites various authorities showing the presence of rebellious and predatory elements on both sides of the Yamuna and in Mewat.
38. The *Vartas* contain the names of innumerable Vaishnavas together with their caste, indicating a clear preponderance of high castes, and only a sprinkling of lower caste persons in the sects.
39. Charlotte Vaudeville, 'The Goverdhan Myth in Northern India', p. 99.
40. R.P. Bahuguna, 'Some Aspects of Popular Movements, Beliefs and Sects in Northern India during the Seventeenth and Eighteenth Centuries', unpublished Ph.D. thesis submitted to University of Delhi, 1999, p. 210.
41. *Do Sau Bavan Vaishnavan Ki Varta, Varta* no. 243, p. 312.
42. Ibid., *Varta* no. 87, p. 236.
43. Ibid., *Varta* no. 168, p. 349.
44. Charlotte Vaudeville, 'The Goverdhan Myth in Northern India', p. 91.
45. Ibid., p. 113.
46. Ibid., p. 117.
47. Tarapada Mukherji and Irfan Habib, 'Akbar and the Temples of Mathura' and 'Mughal Administration and the Temples of Vrindavan'.
48. Irfan Habib, 'A Documentary History of the Gosains (Goswamis)', in Margaret H. Case (ed.), *Govinddeva: A Dialogue in Stone*, p. 145.
49. Ibid., p. 142.
50. Ibid., p. 140.
51. K.R. Qanungo, *History of the House of Diggi*, ed. Shyam Singh Ratnawat, Jaipur, 1997, pp. 62-86.
52. Irfan Habib, 'A Documentary History of the Gosains (Goswamis)', in Margaret H. Case (ed.), *Govinddeva*, p. 137.
53. R.A. Alvi, 'Persian Documents of the Reign of Aurangzeb', Document no. 8, *PIHC*, 1988.
54. Tarapad Mukherji and Irfan Habib, 'The Mughal Administration and the Temples of Vrindavan', Document nos. 33 and 34.
55. Irfan Habib, *Agrarian System*, p. 357n.
56. R.A. Alvi, 'The Temples of Vrindavan', *PIHC*, 1988. These parganas were: Mathura, Sahar, Udai, Mangotta, Ao, Pahari, Khoh, Kama, Khoh Muzahid, Noh, Khohri, Hodal, Baluchi (?), Faridabad, Mahaban, Sadabad, Jalesar, Kol, and Anup Nagar.
57. *Arzdasht* from Kesore Das to Maharaja Ram Singh, dt. Kati Vadi 7, vs 1741/1684.
58. *Arsattha*, pargana Khohri, vs 1723/1666.
59. *Arsattha*, pargana Khohri, vs 1773/1716.
60. *Arsattha*, pargana Khohri, vs 1783/1726.
61. *Arsattha*, pargana Hindaun, vs 1769/1712.
62. *Arsattha*, pargana Hindaun, vs 1775/1718. The names of these grantees are: Bhattacharjee, Srikishan Bhatt, Ram Nath Kanauji, Churamani Bhatt, Nandan Bhatt, Swami Santosh Rai, Rai Singh Bhatt, Nand Lal Brahman, Jai Ram Bhatt, Fateh Singh *Charan*, Bhav Singh Bhat, Hari Singh, Daulat Ram Gujrati, Rakhesur Gujrati, Swami Ram, Ram Kishan Pathak and the widow of Ratan

Ram. Temples endowed with grants are: Srinathji, Thakur Gopinathji, Thakur Sri Shyam Sunderji, Thakur Sri Radha Madhoji, Thakur Madan Mohanji, Thakur Ram Gopalji and Thakur Govinddevji (two).

63. *Arsattha*, pargana Kama, vs 1825/1768. In this pargana six grants were for temples. Others were for Brahmans, Charans and Bhats.

64. Irfan Habib, *Agrarian System*, p. 342n. Grants made by the Mughals were known by many appellations: *milk, sayurghal aimma* and *madad-i-maash* ('aid for subsistence'). In our documents the terms *milk* and *aimma* have been used.

65. Village Lawan-bujurg was assigned to Qazi Abdul Rashid as *milki-aimma* grant. Village Nangal-Alif Khan has been termed as the *inam* land for Shaikh Alif. See *arsattha* pargana Khohri, vs 1723/1666.

66. These grants are as follows:

Name of Village	*Name of grantee*	*Amount in Rs*
Hindaun	Qazi Rashid	941
Patoda	-do-	941
Jatwara	Mir Saiyid Hussain	193
Surauth	-do-	65
Somal-Ratla	Jaimal	22
Samalpur	Khuda Beg	82
Alipur	Hayat Khan, etc.	135
Jharora	-do-	
Raipur	-do-	
Arhera	-do-	
Salahpur	*Pir-ki-dargah*	17
Saidanpur	Maqbara Waris	2
Neesura	Bhure Waris	37
Nangla Mina	-do-	30
Harauli	*Dargah* Shaikh Abdul	24
Mandawra	Mir Muhammad	19
Aranya	Pir Muhammad Mufti	12
Kazanipur	Feroze Khan	8
Fulwara-Papat	Shah Murad and *Faqiran dargah*	18
Khedip	*Faqiran dargah*	20
Sherpur-Kagroli	-do-	4

Source: *Arsattha*, pargana Hindaun, vs 1769/1712.

67. *Arsattha* pargana Hindaun, vs 1770/1713. *Farmani* grants were sanctioned by the emperor. *Hukamiya* grants were made by the *amils* of the *jagirdar*.

68. Ibid.

69. *Ain-i-Akbari*, vols. II-III, p. 194.

70. The *arsatthas* of pargana Hindaun do not mention any *milk* grants after vs 1775/1718.

71. Gopal Narayan Bahura and Chandramani Singh, *Catalogue of Historical Documents in Kapad Dwara*, vol. I, Amber-Jaipur, 1988, p. 163. Some of these documents clearly prove that various Vaishnavite groups were acquiring more and more orthodox Brahmanical overtones.

72. *Chithi* for the *mutasaddian* of Mathura and Vrindavan, dt. Kati Vadi 13, vs 1801/1744.

73. *Chithi* for *amil*, pargana Pahari, dt. Asadh Sudi 12, vs 1797/1740.
74. *Chithi* for *amilan*, pargana Pindayan, dt. Bhadwa Sudi 3, vs 1802/1745.
75. K.R. Qanungo, *History of the House of Diggi*, p. 100.
76. *Vakil* Report, Kesho Rai to Raja Ram Singh, dt. 5th Jamadal award 1099 AH/ 168. *A Descriptive List of the Vakil Reports Addressed to the Rulers of Jaipur* (Persian), Rajasthan State Archives, Bikaner, 1974. All subsequent references of Vakil Reports are from this Description List. The total number of villages assigned in the *waqf* of the Taj Mahal was thirty with an estimated annual income of Rs 3 lakh. The Mughal Emperor himself was to be the *mutaawalli* (administrator of the *waqf*). See Irfan Habib, *Agrarian System*, p. 359n.
77. *Chithi* to the *faujdar* and *amil* of pargana Alwar, dt. Vaisakh Vadi I, vs 1800/ 1743.
78. *Auzdasht* of Mir Ahmad Pirzada, dt. Sawan Sudi 10, vs 1799/1742. Akbar had made a grant of 18 villages to the shrine of Muinuddin Chisti at Ajmer. See Irfan Habib, *Agrarian System*, p. 359n.
79. *Arzdasht*, dt Sawan Vadi 13, vs 1750/1693.
80. *Arzdasht*, dt. Jeth Vadi 11, vs 1775/1718.
81. *Arsattha*, pargana Udai, vs 1806/1749.
82. Irfan Habib, *An Atlas of the Mughal Empire*, Oxford University Press, 1982, p. 19. This *sarkar* was subsequently enlarged by the addition of Mathura, to form the *sarkar* of Islamabad (Mathura). For the concentration of Jat zamindars in this *sarkar* see the *Ain-i-Akbari*, p. 206.
83. Muzaffar Alam, *The Crisis of the Empire in Mughal North India*, p. 117.
84. Peter Brown, *The Cult of Saints*, Chicago, 1981, p. 13.
85. Charlotte Vaudeville, 'Braj, Lost and Found', in *Myth, Saints and Legends in Medieval India*, pp. 45-71.
86. James C. Scott, *Weapons of the Weak, Everyday Forms of Peasant Resistance*, Oxford University Press, 1990, pp. 284-89. Scott makes insightful observations about the hidden or 'unedited transcripts' permeating peasant resistance, especially in power-laden situations.
87. See F.S. Growse, *Mathura, a District Memoir*, 1874, for a detailed description.
88. *Arzdasht* from Shyam Singh Rajawat to Maharaja Jai Singh, dt. Mangsir Sudi 3, vs 1760/1703.
89. *Arzdasht*, dt. Vaisakh Vadi 3, vs 1760/1703.
90. *Arzdasht*, dt. Chet Sudi 10, vs 1743/1686.
91. Charlotte Vaudeville, 'Braj, Lost and Found', p. 65.
92. W.H. McLeod attributes an energizing role to the devi cults of the Sivalik Hills on the culture of the embattled Sikhs. See, *The Evolution of the Sikh Community*, Oxford University Press, 1996, p. 13.
93. Seth Govinddas, *Braj and Braj-Yatra*, Delhi, 1959; and Prabhu Dayal Mittal, *Braj ka Samskritik Itihas*, Delhi, 1966, p. 86.
94. K.R. Qanungo, *History of the House of Diggi*, p. 96; where he cites a document describing the existence of a thick *forest*, 'One *kos* in depth and eleven *kos* in length'. There were about twelve *vans* in Braj.
95. Jean Deloche (ed.), *Wendel's Memoirs on the Origin, Growth and Present State of Jat Power in Hindustan* (1768), Pondichery, p. 106.
96. Devi Prashad Munshi, *Mardum Sumari Raj Marwar*, 1891, Jodhpur, Shri Jagdish Singh Gahlot Shodh Sansthan, 1997, p. 55.

97. Charlotte Vaudeville, '*The Govardhan Myth in Northern India*', in her, *Myths, Saints and Legends in Medieval India*, pp. 113-17.
98. Dominique-Sila Khan, *Conversions and Shifting Identities: Ramdev Pir and Ismailis in Rajasthan*, Delhi, Manohar, 2003, pp. 60-95.
99. *Arsattha*, pargana Khohri, *Kharif*, vs 1781/1725.
100. *Arsattha*, pargana Pahari, *Kharif*, vs 1781/1724 and vs 1793/1736.
101. See Chapter 6.
102. Munshi Devi Prasad, *Mardum Shumari*, p. 14.
103. Most of these folk-heroes—Tejaji, Gugaji, Pabuji, Ramdevji, etc.—existed between 1100 and 1500 centuries. See John D. Smith, *The Epic of Pabuji: A Study of Transcription and Translation*, Cambridge University Press, 1991, pp. 6-7; and Dominique-Sila Khan, *Conversions and Shifting Identity*, pp. 68, 69.
104. According to Dominique-Sila Khan, the beginning of 'Rajputisation' of these folk-deities can be traced back to the work of Munhata Nainsi, though the process acquired momentum only in the eighteenth century. Non-Rajput and popular elements can still be deciphered. Rajput values that were later brought to bear on the narrative can similarly be identified. *Conversions and Shifting Identities*, p. 65.
105. R.P. Bahuguna, 'Some Aspects of Popular Movements, Beliefs and Sects in Northern India During the Seventeenth and Eighteenth Centuries'. unpublished Ph.D. thesis, University of Delhi, Delhi, 1999.
106. P.W. Powlett, *Gazetteer of Ulwur*, London, 1878, pp. 52-9.
107. Ibid., pp. 53-5.
108. According to Shail Mayaram 'Lal Das is said to have enabled the Jat clan to find a treasure and thereafter establish an army and kingdom'. Suraj Mal later built a temple in his honour. See her *Resisting Regimes: Myth, Memory and Shaping of Muslim Identity*, Oxford University Press, Delhi, 1997, pp. 39-40.
109. *Arsattha*, pargana Khohri, *Kharif*, vs 1773/1716.

6
Agrarian Revolts

In the late seventeenth century large parts of northern India experienced spectacular rural uprisings.[1] A spate of agrarian revolts were triggered off and spread like a hurricane across many *subas* of the Mughal empire. More than a hundred parganas, spread across three Mughal *subas*, Agra, Delhi, and Ajmer, were affected.[2] In fact the entire countryside between Agra and Delhi at one end and Ajmer and Ranthambore at the other was disturbed by large-scale rebellions. Those who participated in these revolts belonged to miscellaneous peasant castes and Rajput clans. The intensity of these revolts also varied from pargana to pargana and year to year. The widespread rural disturbances in these regions were set in the background of increasing fiscal pressure of the state on the peasantry and resurgence of zamindari power. Caste affinity and territorial solidarity often formed a bridge between these two restive sectors of rural society. Most of the revolts took place, by and large, between 1665 and 1735. While some revolts persisted for decades, others were short-lived. The degree of success of these revolts varied, as indeed did their objectives. While the Jats ultimately succeeded in establishing a state at Bharatpur, the Naruka revolts laid the foundation for the subsequent emergence of the state of Alwar. Revolts by some of the other Rajput *bhumias* resulted in the creation of numerous *thikanas* in eastern Rajasthan.[3] Many other rebels considerably expanded their zamindaris. A large number of village headmen and other rural rich joined the ranks of zamindars. On the other hand, traditionally dominant groups such as the Meos, Khanzadas of Mewat, and Chauhans were further pushed into the political wilderness.[4] The revolts led to a complete erosion of imperial authority in a large number of parganas in the Braj, Mewat, and Dundhar territories.

This chapter deals with the Jat revolts and the circumstances leading to the formation of Bharatpur state, and if other revolts have also been discussed it is because they formed part of a larger scenario. It is true that without encouragement and timely support from the Jats, the revolts of other zamindars would have either not taken place or could have been suppressed easily. It is equally true that in the absence of solidarity expressed by the rebel zamindars of other castes in the rebellious (*zortalab*) areas, it would have been difficult for the Jats to sustain their insurgency for such a long period. It was clearly a two way process that had brought the Jats and other zamindars together in a common struggle against the Mughal empire.

The peasants of *suba* Agra were known for their 'rebelliousness and courage' even in the days of Emperor Akbar.[5] From the time of Akbar down to that of Aurangzeb, many military operations were organized against the rebellious peasants living on both sides of the river Jamuna.[6] Such is the pre-history of peasant rebellions against the empire in the region which later became the cradle of the Jat revolt. The earlier rebels were either Jats or Rajputs as parganas on both sides of the Jamuna have been entered as the zamindari of both these castes.[7] However, the actual history of the Jat rebellion dates from 1669 when Gokula Jat, a zamindar of Talpat near Mathura, took up arms against the Mughal *faujdar*. This was a daring uprising in which a small number of poorly-armed peasants took on the might of the empire. After a bloody encounter Gokula was captured and executed.[8] Although the revolt was crushed, it served as leaven for generations to come. Braj, Mewat and Dundhar were seething with peasant unrest when Gokula Jat revolted. As the severity and unequal incidence of revenue demand became increasingly unbearable, group after group of peasants from various parganas went to the imperial court for the redressal of their grievances. A large number of peasant 'deputations' to the Mughal court during the 1660s have been recorded.[9] The arrival of aggrieved peasants in the imperial capital was seldom liked by the rulers. Given this attitude, normalcy could hardly be expected in the villages.

Writing on peasant insurgency in colonial India, Ranjit Guha has observed that peasant uprisings are preceded by increase in rural crime.[10] A spate of rural violence directed against local revenue officials looms large in the reports emanating from the pargana headquarters during the years before Gokula Jat revolted. From 1664 onwards we come across a large number of reports sent by the *amils* and *faujdars* indicating a rise in the incidence of theft and violence in the villages. For instance the *amils* of pargana Bhusawar and Sonkhar reported a steep rise in the occurrence of theft in both the parganas.[11] Similarly, the *amils* of Kotla, Khohri, Kama, and Rewari complained that poaching of cattle by the peasants with the active connivance of the *patels* had become a common happening in the villages.[12] It was also pointed out that the Ahir and Gujar peasants of pargana Kotla particularly were bent on creating disturbances (*fisad per utaru chhe*).[13] Deterioration in the law and order situation in pargana Mandawar was also reported.[14] A common refrain in most of these reports is that the peasants in the parganas of Braj and Mewat had abandoned the path of obedience. Suddenly, officials began to give epithets such as 'bastard' (*haramzada*), thief (*chor*) and rioter (*fisadi*) to the peasants[15] indicating rising tempers in the countryside. However, the officials failed to recognize the participants as potential rebels. This situation was keenly watched by the local zamindars. Not all the zamindars of the region revolted but those who did so assumed very aggressive postures against the Mughal empire and its supporters. A regionwise account of the zamindars who revolted and the level at which they forged alliances among themselves and with the peasantry is given below. The narrative is broken in places with analysis of the unfolding situation.

A. REVOLTS IN BRAJ

After the suppression of the Jat revolt led by Gokula, the Jats were relatively quiet between 1670 and 1680. In 1681 they again revolted under the leadership of Raja Ram Jat who was a zamindar of village Sinsini of pargana Ao in *sarkar* Sahar.[16] The first shot fired by Gokula Jat at Talpat in 1669, proved to be premature. On the other hand the rebellion started by Raja Ram Jat in 1681 turned out to be a portentous event heralding an era of widespread insurgency. With the entire countryside seething with unrest it was not difficult for zamindars like Raja Ram Jat and others to defy the Mughal authority in their respective areas. The zamindars' open defiance, their refusal to pay revenue which they had collected from the peasants, invited immediately military action. The intensity of revolt alarmed those Mughals who held *jagirs* in this region and military action became inevitable. Though the zamindars of different castes/ clans were rebellious in a much wider area, there was no unity of action, purpose or direction among them in the initial stages. The repeated failure of the Mughal campaigns under the leadership of Muhammad Safi Khan (*subadar* of Agra) created conditions out of which a distinct leadership was thrown up from amongst the ranks of zamindars. Many who were so far lying low, were now emboldened to revolt. A zamindar-front was born out of the confrontation between the Mughal armies and the rebels.

Nawab Khan-i-Jahan Bahadur Kokaltash Jafar Jang organized two campaigns against the Jats. The Amber ruler and Mehrab Khan, *faujdar* of Mathura, were also asked to extend help to the Nawab. This campaign however ended in failure. The Jats not only repulsed the three armies, but extended their control over parganas Bhura, Kuthumbar, Hodal, and Palwal.[17] This victory of Raja Ram Jat over Nawab Khan Bahadur was due to the active support extended to him by all the Jats of the region. A general uprising of all Jats around Delhi and Agra seems to have taken place according to an *arzdasht* report.[18] Imperial revenue officials (*karoris*) and the agents of the *jagirdars* were driven out of the parganas lying between Delhi and Agra. The entire area went out of the control of the Mughals for a long period as Nawab Khan Bahadur was stranded at Kama.[19] The Nawab had to beat a retreat to Mathura after a month long unsuccessful campaign.

Nawab Khan-i-Jahan Bahadur marched against the Jats of Sinsini again. This time he besieged the fortress (*garhi*) of Soghar where Ram Chahar Jat lived. The *garhi* fell to the Nawab and Ram Chahar along with many other Jats, was killed. His death was a big loss for the Jats. With this victory the Nawab marched against Sinsini and dreamt of vanquishing Raja Ram Jat for good.[20] Near Sinsini an encounter took place between Raja Ram Jat and Nawab Khan Bahadur. The Nawab lost the battle. Many prominent Rajput leaders (*sardars*) who had been sent by the Amber ruler to help the Nawab were killed in the battle.[21] The Nawab again retreated to Mathura, and the Jats became more belligerent and removed his police posts (*thanas*) from Khohri, Bhusawar, Ao, Sonkhar and Sahar and established their own *thanas* there.[22] Nawab Khan Bahadur blamed his failure on the non-cooperation and pussilanimity of the *amins* and *amils* of the region.[23]

The Jats established an outpost at Harsana from where Bahatri, considered to be a buffer pargana between the Jats and Kachhwahas, was only a few miles away. Raja Ram Jat then sent letters to all the *bhomias* of the neighbouring parganas—especially the Narukas and the Kalyanots—asking them to join him immediately.[24] The Naruka and Kalyanot *bhomias* quickly responded to his call. The economic and political conditions in *sarkars* Ajmer, Ranthambore, and Alwar were similar to those prevailing in *sarkars* Agra, Kol, and Mathura. The only difference was that it is the Rajput *bhomias* of various clans who revolted in the first three *sarkars,* while the Jat and other middle caste zamindars were more active in the other three. Nonetheless all were pitted against the imperial *jagirdars*. Hence it was not difficult for some of them to coordinate their activities. Some *bhomias* openly took an anti-Mughal stance after Raja Ram Jat's victories over Nawab Khan Bahadur. The Narukas and Kalyanots who had been acting as a buffer between the Jats and the Amber Raja, joined the Jats after the failure of the campaigns of Nawab Khan Bahadur.[25] Earlier the Narukas had been vacillating between the rebels and the loyalists, but their increasing rivalry with Hari Singh Khangarot over the zaminderi of malpura had brought them close to the latter. Therefore the Jats and Narukas became allies in their struggle against the Mughals and Kachhwaha ruler.

The Narukas and other Rajput *bhomias* had a conflict with the Amber Raja over the zamindari right. In the *mahals* of Mewat the Narukas, Kalyanots and Panchanots wanted to expand their zamindaris and the Amber ruler aimed at incorporating the *sarkar* of Alwar into his expanding hereditary dominion (*watan*).[26] In order to contain his expansionist designs, the Jats supported the Narukas and others. The Narukas were strengthening their zamindari claims over the parganas of Mewat. The Amber Raja considered this as an effront and this was the objective basis for the formation of a united front consisting of the Jats Narukas, Kalyanots, Meos, Gujars, and Ahirs.

The Jat insurgency was at its peak in 1688 when they attacked the tomb of Akbar at Sikandra and raided all those villages that had been assigned for the maintenance of the Taj Mahal.[27] These attacks do not appear to have been to avenge an earlier injustice, as has been suggested by Manucci.[28] Perhaps the Jats were simply attacking Mughal symbols of power and splendour. The Jats were moving from Mathura to Ranthambore without fear or impediment. Disturbances were increasing day by day. The imperial *mansabdars, subadars* and *faujdars* posted in this region did not have sufficient force to curb the revolts.[29] This ascending scale of disturbances caused by the Jats forced Emperor Aurangzeb to pay more attention to the problem. He was particularly infuriated by the Jat attack on the tomb of Akbar. So far the main command of the forces sent to suppress the Jats was in the hands of prince Bedar Bakht, but in May 1688 Maharaja Bishan Singh of Amber was asked to march against the Jats and destroy them.[30]

The leadership of the Jat revolt was in the hands of ordinary zamindars. They were aiming at the expansion of their zamindaris in the neighbouring parganas. They went into tactical alliances with *bhomias* of various castes. In eastern Rajasthan their ambition clashed with the interest of the Amber rulers, themselves eager to take advantage of the disturbed conditions to expand their *watan* in *sarkars* Alwar and Ranthambore, and if possible up to Agra.[31] Therefore, a direct confrontation between the Jats and the Raja of Amber was inevitable. Gradually, as a result of repeated set-backs at the hands of the Jats the Emperor was veering around to the idea of transferring this command against the Jats to Amber.

Maharaja Bishan Singh gave an undertaking he would 'suppress the Jats and raze Sinsini to the ground within six months'.[32] In return he demanded extensive powers, adequate finances, and the *jagirdari* and zamindari rights of various parganas.[33] He knew how to get things done for he waited for the Emperor to send repeated directives through his *vakil* Kesho Rai before he slowly moved from Amber to Sinsini.[34] The prevarication was meant to be a message for the imperial court and soon he got most of what he had demanded. A *jagir* worth 20,00,000 *dams* was granted to him in Kama.[35] He was also asked to look after the *faujdari* of Kama.[36] Though he failed to secure the *faujdari* of Khohri and Sonkhar,[37] he was accorded the zamindari of the Jat villages in parganas Ao and Sonkh.[38] With such lavish assistance from the Emperor, Bishan Singh marched against the Jats of Sinsini cautiously, even lackadaisically. The fort of Sinsini was surrounded by a thick forest and a ring of other forts in various Jat villages: Ranghar, Kasot, Soghar, Rarh, Pingora, Sonkh, Sakora, Raisis, Bhattawali, Chakora, Gaddo, and Sonkhar-Sonkhari. These *garhis* and *naglas* (fortified block-houses) existed within a radius of 25 to 30 miles.[39]

On 30 July 1688 it was reported that Raja Ram Jat had been killed in an encounter with an advance party of the imperialists.[40] His son Zorawar Singh assumed leadership of the Jats for a short period. Soon he gave way to Churaman Jat. Yet, even after a concerted campaign of 14 months (December 1688 to January 1690) the imperial forces, having broken the ring of forts mentioned above were able to conquer Sinsini.[41] The Jats were evicted from their zamindaris and driven out of the parganas surrounding Sinsini. The expelled Jats not only waged guerrilla warfare in order to regain their lost places but also impeded revenue collection from these parganas.[42] The peasant population was hostile to the imperialists and extended its support to the rebel zamindars. Hence the temporary occupation of Sinsini, instead of containing the rebellion, forced the rebels to spread out in other directions.

One section of the Jats now turned its attention towards Mewat. The *watan* of Amber bordered on the parganas of *sarkar* Alwar. Here the Naruka and other zamindars (mostly members of the zamindar-front) were already rebellious against the Amber ruler. The Jat zamindars received unflinching support from the rebel zamindars of many other castes. Their help proved crucial to the Jats in their guerrilla war for the re-capture of Sinsini. The Jats divided themselves into four guerrilla bands. Three of these attacked Bhura, Mandawar and Rehlari, respectively, the fourth preyed on parganas Maujpur, Raipur and Antre. Thus the Jats became irresistible in these parganas.[43] After a month the combined forces of the Jats, Narukas and Meos conquered *tappa* Rini of pargana Bahatri.[44] Thus they had made inroads into the hereditary dominion of the conqueror of Sinsini. Bahatri was one of three parganas that comprised the original Amber *watan*.[45] The conquest of Rini not only contained the further expansion of the Amber Raja's *watan* in Mewat but also blocked various trade routes passing through the Amber territories. Moreover, the links that the Jat zamindars had forged with the other rebellious zamindars were further strengthened. It is evident from the fact that four Kalyanot zamindars—Ran Singh, Raj Singh, Chhattar Singh and Santokh Singh—were having correspondence with the Gaurva, Gujar and Jat zamindars. It was suggested to all the zamindars to coordinate their activities and pool their resources to face the imperial forces.[46] This swelled the ranks of the rebellious zamindars. They unanimously decided to revolt under the leadership of Churaman Jat. The tacit understanding among the rebels was that whenever any one of them was attacked others should extend their support to him, and this enhanced their confidence.

Kamaluddin Khan who was looking after the *faujdari* of Toda Bhim, Bayana, and Hindaun had been pursuing a policy of ruthlessness with the rebels. He had expelled the Kalyanots from Toda

Bhim,[47] and was determined to weed out all turbulent (*fisadi*) elements from Bayana and Hindaun. But with the solid backing of Churaman, the Kalyarots were able to re-conquer their lost *bhoms* in Toda Bhim.[48] Thus Kamaluddin Khan's victory in Toda Bhim, Hindaun, and Bayana proved to be as ephemeral as that of Bishan Singh in Sinsini.

The Jat zamindars of the trans-Jamuna region had also been rebellious since the days of Raja Ram Jat. They had occupied pargana Tapal and extorted an amount of Rs 9,000 from local officials.[49] When Sinsini was attacked by Maharaja Bishan Singh, the Jat zamindars of the trans-Jamuna parganas where the Raja had his *jagirs*, revolted against him. In pargana Kol (Aligarh) Amar Singh Chauhan who was a zamindar of 250 villages in *tappa* Khair revolted against the Mughal *jagirdars*.[50] In *tappa* Lagasma of Kol another zamindar, one Nanda Jat, had also revolted. Besides Amar Singh and Nanda Jat, eleven other zamindars of Kol revolted. The Jats had already brought pargana Antrauli under their control. One day the rebels came out of their *garhis* to join an important gathering of all the Jat zamindars on both sides of river Jamuna. In this gathering the rebel zamindars took the decision to attack the camp of Nawab Shaista Khan who was campaigning against them. After attacking the Nawab they removed the *thanas* of the Amber Raja from pargana Baliram.[51] When the *jagir* of the Amber Raja was transferred from Kol, the zamindars and peasants made it impossible for his *naib-faujdar* Gaj Singh Khangarot to collect revenue arrears from there.[52] The Jats beat up the revenue collectors of the Raja and themselves collected 5,000 *mans* of grain. After the death of Hari Singh Khangarot, the Jats reconquered the *garhis* of Varon, Hirpura, and Sukhpura in Kol.[53] In the neighbourhood of Mathura, the Jat zamindars and peasantry of villages Aruki, Tartu Rao, and Sarai Tavarkhan, became increasingly aggressive.[54] While Prince Bedar Bakht was carrying Jorawar Jat, who had been arrested at Sinsini, to the Deccan, a strong force of 500 Jats attacked *qasba* Maujpur in retaliation.[55] The Jats attacked *qasba* Pilgawa, plundered the bazaar, and imprisoned 700 *mahajans* from there. They also arrested Mir Fazil, the imperial *karori* from his office. Subsequently, the Jats made raids on the townships of Nogaon, Ferozepur, Kama and Pahari.[56] Such activities do not indicate that the Mughal authority was restored after the fall of Sinsini in 1690, as has been noted by Irfan Habib.[57] The fall of Sinsini forced the Jats to shift and spread out the area of their insurgency in Mewat and the Doab. In fact, in the Mewat and trans-Jamuna regions the Jats became more aggressive and volatile after the temporary loss of Sinsini.

The aggressive posture of the Jats in the two regions—one on the border of the Amber state and the other far away from his territories—compelled Bishan Singh to adopt a conciliatory attitude towards a section of the rebels. He began to placate the Jats of the trans-Jamuna region. In August 1692, Megh Raj, a *vakil* of the Raja in the imperial court, wrote to his master suggesting that prior permission of the Emperor should have been taken for rehabilitating the Jats at Pinghor.[58] Nawab Saadat Khan had alleged that the Raja was settling the Jats in the trans-Jamuna area and got one-third of the booty in return.[59] Kamaluddin Khan, who was pursuing a strict policy towards the rebels in Mewat, had also lodged similar complaints against the Raja regarding the settling of the Jats.[60] The fact that this policy earned him imperial displeasure shows that the step had been taken at Bishan Singh's personal initiative at a local level to win over a section of the Jats to his side. Clearly, he had not reckoned with other nobles with their own interests in the region, who would not let him displace the existing cultivators with whom they possibly had established links.

B. REVOLTS IN MEWAT

Mewat became a battle-ground for rebels and imperialists for many years. In Mewat, zamindars belonging to various castes had already formed a united front against the Mughal *jagirdars*. The region was a hub of Naruka *bhomia* revolts. Here Rao Hathi Singh, Kishan Singh and Udai Singh were the leaders of the Naruka insurgency. By 1686 they had established their military control over a vast area which included many parganas of *sarkar* Alwar.[61] The peasants of Jalalpur, Bharkol, and Umarni are reported to have extended their support to the Narukas.[62] All trade routes via Bahatri were closed due to the disturbances caused by the Narukas.[63] In 1702 the Narukas simultaneously revolted in the eight *mahals* of Mewat.[64] The *jagirdar* of Bharkol and Jalalpur, Sayyid Qasim, had to ask the Amber Raja either to expel Rao Udai Singh Naruka, a servant (*chakar*) of the Raja, from his *jagirs* or face a suit in the imperial court.[65] Bahatri was surrounded by the *bhoms* of Narukas and Kalyanots and it became practically impossible for the *jagirdars* to collect revenue from any of the pargana contiguous to Bahatri.[66] In 1703 the Narukas held a secret conference in a fair (*Devi ka mela*) at *qasba* Sanchari. In that conference they gave concrete shape to their aspirations. Their main demand was that they should be formally recognized as the *bhomias* of those parganas which were under their effective control.[67] Following this decision, Rao Udai Singh unilaterally declared himself a zamindar and staked his claim to the *bhom*, *faslana*, and *kharach* cesses.[68] Karan Singh and Amar Singh Narukas had already become the *de facto* zamindars of Jalalpur and Bharkol respectively.[69] Around Kuthumbar many parganas were under the effective control of Kishan Singh Naruka since 1692.[70] When Nawab Mukhtar Khan tried to farm out five *mahals* of his *jagir* to the Amber Raja, Kishan Singh Naruka openly revolted against the Nawab and the Raja. He had firm backing from the Jats in the form of men and material. Thus the move to give *ijara* of these *mahals* to the Raja was thwarted.[71]

As already stated, the Kalyanot *bhomias* fought most of the time as the allies of the Jat and Naruka zamindars. They held extensive zamindaris in parganas Toda Bhim, Machilpur, and Gudhala. They aimed at the further expansion of their zamindaris. In 1687, the Naruka and Kalyanot *bhomias* together attempted to annex some villages of Bahatri.[72] The watchmen (*sehnas*) sent by the Raja's *amil* to the villages of Toda Bhim to look after the crops were beaten up by the peasants at the instigation of the Kalyanots. The imperial *faujdar* was directed to expel the Kalyanots from their zamindaris of Toda Bhim. When evicted, some of the Kalyanot *bhomias* trekked to Bahatri, where they occupied various villages of *tappa* Rini without obtaining prior permission of the officials. From Rini they continued their efforts to regain their lost zamindaris in Toda Bhom.[73] Other dispossessed Kalyanot *bhomias* entrenched themselves in pargana Machilpur, from where they wrote letters to the Jats and Narukas for help.[74] This step of the Kalyanots had brought them into the vortex of a larger zamindar rebellion in Mewat. As members of the zamindar-front, they could rely on the help of other. For example, when the Mughal *faujdar* of Hindaun mounted his military pressure on the Kalyanots, Churaman Jat helped them by sending a contingent of 1500 soldiers.[75]

Thus between 1680 and 1700 the authority of the central government had weakened considerably over a large part of the three *subas*. The revolts of the zamindars, directly feeding on the rampant misery of the peasants, became uncontrollable in many parganas. The zamindars openly disobeyed the authority of the Mughals and refused to give revenue to the *jagirdars*. Some of the zamindars, evicted from their zamindaris, did not allow cultivation in the villages of their zamindari. The growing unity within the ranks of the rebel zamindars and corresponding weakening of the central authority made the situation worse for the *jagirdars*.

With the entire Amber territories seething with *bhomia* revolts and peasant unrest, the Amber ruler could hardly find time and resources to keep the Jats of Sinsini under check for long. He would rather put his own house in order. As soon as he turned his attention to the revolts within his territories, the Jats again became active in the Sinsini region. It should be noted here that during the last decade of the seventeenth century the Jats of Sinsini, when driven into wilderness, had succeeded in integrating the rebel *bhomias* of various castes into a common struggle against the Mughals. If the Jats of the Doab provided timely succour to the Jats of the Sinsini region, the Rajput *bhomias* of *sarkar* Ranthambore gave help to the rebel *bhomias* of Mewat. Thus the centre of the zamindar-front with its base in Mewat, was flanked on both sides by various groups of zamindars from Agra to Ajmer. No wonder that the rebellion could not be quelled despite the increasing attention paid by Emperor Aurangzeb to the problem.

At the turn of the eighteenth century the zamindars intensified their activities. A growing weakness and helplessness of the administration and an increasing arrogance on the part of the zamindars characterized the last seven years of the reign of Aurangzeb. In the parganas of Kama, Ao, and Pahari, the Jats had retrieved lost ground to a great extent. When Nawab Mukhtar Khan came to campaign against them in 1702, they were rebellious all around Agra.[76] The Nawab was beleaguered by the Jats at *qasba* Nagar. He was utterly ineffective against the rebels who had occupied all the parganas of his *jagir*. Under these circumstances, the Nawab thought it wiser to give five parganas of his *jagir* on *ijara* to the Amber Raja for Rs 1,80,000.[77] As signs of Mukhtar Khan's weakness grew, the rebel *bhomias* were emboldened to become more aggressive in Mewat.

In the parganas surrounding Bahatri, *bhomia* revolts had assumed serious proportions. In 1704 the revolts of the *bhomias* and peasants had spread from Agra to Ajmer.[78] Shyam Singh Rajawat, *faujdar* of Bahatri, wrote in two *arzdashts* that 'neither the *bhomias* nor the peasants are afraid of us. The *bhomias* are becoming increasingly arrogant and we do not have adequate force to deal with them firmly'.[79]

In Mewat the rebels got considerable strength when Dura Meo, a zamindar of the *Pahat pal* of the Meos, joined hands with them.[80] The Amber Raja considered Dura Meo a hereditary enemy of his *watan*. It was persistent hostility between Dura Meo and the Amber house that had forced Mirza Raja Jai Singh to expel the former from his zamindari of Kama, only to be rehabilitated by Churaman Jat.[81] Churaman would have known that this was unlikely to please the Amber Raja, but he preferred a new ally in Dura Meo. The zamindars created more disturbances in Kama and completely occupied the pargana after some time.[82] The loss of Kama was a serious setback to the Raja of Amber. He directed his *faujdar*, Shyam Singh Rajawat, to attack the Jat *garhi* at Vinani village of Kama. The Raja's army of 30,000 soldiers was routed by the combined strength of the rebel zamindars of the area.[83] After that the Jats, Meos, and Narukas began massive preparations for a bigger offensive against the Amber Raja. They recruited more soldiers, collected arms, and accumulated large quantity of foodgrain in the strategic fort of Maujpur.[84]

After coming to the throne Bahadur Shah followed a policy of curbing the powers of the rulers of Amber and Jodhpur for some years.[85] In order to mobilize the support of the rebel zamindars against the Rajput Rajas, Bahadur Shah conferred the title of *naib faujdar* of Mathura on Churaman Jat.[86] Thereafter, the imperial *faujdars* of Mathura and Hindaun from one direction and Churaman and his allies from the other launched a pincer movement against the Amber Raja.[87] The frontiers of Amber had become vulnerable. Churaman, encouraged by the developing cracks in the defences, occupied *qasba* Bhusawar and made an unsuccessful attempt to reconquer the fort of Soghar.[88] Mir Khan, the *faujdar* of Mathura and Churaman, overran the parganas of Kot, Kama, Khohri, Piragpura, Ghazi-ka-Thana, Bhangarh, Mungona, and Alwar.[89]

It may be noted here that acceptance of a title from the Mughal court by Churaman also caused some divisions in the ranks of the rebel zamindars. Though prominent Jat zamindars like Daya Ram, Girdhara and Kamaliha sided with Churaman, there were other Jats who dissociated themselves from him.[90] Other partners of the zamindar-front like Dura Meo, Ballu Sokya, and the Narukas stayed with Churaman.[91] Evidently Bahadur Shah had succeeded in winning over a significant section of the rebels, and pitched them against the Rajput Rajas. Earlier Aurangzeb had pitted the Rajputs against the Jats, now Bahadur Shah was mobilizing the Jats against the Rajputs. Taking advantage of this change in imperial outlook, Churaman began to occupy the villages of pargana Khohri. By the end of 1715 he had occupied 336 villages of Khohri.[92] When the zamindari of the entire pargana was transferred to the Amber Raja, it sparked off a massive uprising of all the traditional zamindars of Khohri against the imperial *faujdar* and the Raja.[93] They looked up to Churaman to provide leadership. From Khohri the rebels collected Rs 1,55,380 out of which Churaman got the lion's share of Rs 90,000.[94] Churaman also established his *thana* in the zamindari village (Alawara) of the Raja in pargana Ferozepur.[95] This provoked the Amber Raja to impose a special tax on the Jat peasants of 21 villages as a punishment. While many Jat peasants abandoned their villages and went to Thoon to join the army of Churaman, others remained in the fields to cultivate for him.[96]

Elsewhere Churaman had opened many fronts to harass his adversaries. He kept on supplying arms and grain to the Narukas who had placed themselves in full command of the fort of Maujpur.[97] As the peasantry of Bayana was perpetually rebellious, the Jats stepped up their activities there too.[98] Near Hodal they swooped on a traders' caravan of 13 carts carrying mechandise. When they were chased by the guards, the villagers of the nearby villages attacked the guards.[99] According to Shiv Das, property of the value of Rs 20 lakhs was plundered.[100]

The Jats again became very aggressive during the second decade of the eighteenth century under the leadership of Churaman, but the nature of the Jat rebellion had undergone a change. In the beginning (the 1680s) the Jat zamindars, like others, had expressed their hostility by refusing to pay revenue to the *jagirdars*. The empire saw the sign clearly and expeditions were sent against the rebels to force them to pay revenue. But after the death of Aurangzeb the rebellion was becoming more of a political battle between the zamindars and the Mughal empire. Agra and Alwar *sarkars* were the main arena of this contest.[101] Churaman's nephews, Bhika and Jait Singh, occupied many villages of pargana Sahar and Hodal respectively and claimed the zamindari right there.[102] A climax was reached when the Jats and Narukas again occupied *qasba* Rini of Bahatri and plundered it.[103] The Meos in general and the Brahmans of Jatmai in particular helped the Jats to occupy these areas.[104]

After the death of Aurangzeb, the growing political instability reached a high pitch. The contribution of the uprisings led by the zamindars in various parts of the country in weakening the central authority cannot be gainsaid. In hastening this process the role of the rebel Jat zamindars of the region under study was substantial. Aurangzeb treated the Jats as rebels whom he would not allow to be clothed with the briefest scrap of legitimacy. He called them 'wolves', and *badzat* (of lowly origin).[105] To crush the Jat revolt was his obsession for some time, as is evident from the *vakil* reports written from the imperial court. 'The Jat is moving like a lion' (Jat *sher dagre chhe*) was written in many reports sent by the *amils* and *faujdars* from the parganas.[106] Such reports underlined the most obvious change in the politics of the region by referring to the Jats as virtual masters. These are clear indications of the emergence of Jat power. The Jat rebellion under the leadership of Churaman acquired legitimacy when Aurangzeb's successors, in their quest to 'use' him against their rivals offered berth to him in the imperial bureaucracy.[107] Churaman reciprocated the imperial mood by participating in campaigns against the Rajput states of Amber and Jodhpur.[108]

Churaman also participated in various battles fought among the contestants for the imperial throne after the death of Aurangzeb.[109] His role in these wars was seldom of a decisive nature, but these occasions enabled him to acquire a lot of political clout in the eyes of those nobles who were now emerging as king-makers. Through his token presence and penchant for looting the loser, Churaman had also earned the enmity of many Mughal nobles. If Khan-i-Dauran and Sayyid brothers became his patrons in the imperial court, Chhabila Ram Nagar and Sawai Jai Singh became his sworn enemies.[110]

The circumstances in which the last campaign against Churaman was ordered throws some light on his ambitions and the limitations imposed on him by the mercurial nature of the politics of eighteenth-century northern India. Like most of his contemporaries Churaman was an ambitious zamindar. He had a clear idea of his social base and the territorial extent of that base. His zamindari was limited, but the area of his military operations was very vast. Therefore, he had to find fiscal resources from outside his little zamindari. For this he had brought many parganas under his *de facto* control without legal claims over them. The actual area under his permanent control was scattered and dispersed in many *sarkars*.[111] Because of the uncertain and undefined nature of his claim and hold over so many parganas, he could hardly have desisted from interfering with the *jagirs* of other nobles.[112] These affected nobles always mounted pressure on the Emperor to chastise Churaman.

Though Churaman had been made an official custodian of the road between Agra and Delhi in 1709, and a principal watchdog of the highway from Delhi to the banks of river Chambal, normalcy could not be restored there. Churaman could not have been unaware that these reconciliatory gestures on the part of the Mughal Emperor were born of necessity rather than of change of attitude; as such these would endure merely so long as he had the strength to stand on his own feet. Accordingly, he occupied many more parganas, and constantly interfered with others *jagirs*.[113] He constructed a fort at Thoon which he made into the headquarters of his operations.[114] His *modus operandi* was first to construct a *garhi* at a strategic place. From there his armies would make forays into the neighbouring parganas. The arrival of his army would cause a general fear (*vahda*) among the local officials, who would flee. Thereafter it became easy for his men to collect revenues from that pargana. For instance in 1713 Churaman constructed five *garhis* in different villages of pargana Kotla. Soon peasants of about 15 villages refused to give revenue to the *jagirdar* and joined hands with Churaman. In 1714, he constructed a *garhi* at village Bawali in pargana Alwar. Thereafter, the Jats established their control on the villages of Maujpur, Punkhar and Bharkol parganas.[115] These moves of Churaman naturally annoyed the Emperor when complaints reached him. In September 1715, Farukh Siyar directed Jai Singh to march against the Jats.[116] This was the time when Farukh Siyar and Jai Singh were moving towards unity against the Sayyids, a situation bound to help the Jats, who were ever watchful of dissensions at the Mughal court.

In November 1716, Jai Singh invested the fort of Thoon with a large army. The Jats put up a fierce resistance. The geographical location of Thoon also helped the Jats. There existed an impenetrable forest belt on the outskirts of Thoon, and the area usually became a cauldron of heat and dust in summer and swamp in monsoon. Jai Singh had to pass through the swampy forests in order to lay his hands on Churaman. Despite his best efforts, he could not force the Jats to surrender so long as Churaman was alive. Meanwhile Sayyid

Abdulla Khan mounted his pressure on the Emperor to withdraw the campaign against the Jats and enter into an agreement with them.[117] The Sayyids would thereby not only earn the Jats' gratitude, but also highlight Jai Singh's failure to handle a situation. Thus Churaman was bailed out of his predicament by factionalism in the imperial court.

If the issue of the Jats accentuated dissent at the court, within the camp of the Jats also two factions emerged. The surrender of Thoon to the imperialists was the cause. Those siding with Churaman and his sons Mohkam Singh and Zul Karan were Sardar Khem Karan Sogharia, Vijay Raj Gadasia, Faujdar Fateh Singh of Chhattarpur, Tula Ram, and Kesa Jat, one of the commanders of the fort. Badan Singh, the leader of the rival group, was supported by Faujdar Anup Singh, Raja Ram's son Fateh Singh, the Jat zamindars of Gairoo and Halena and some chiefs from other communities.[118] Most of the adherents of the former faction belonged to the generation of Jat rebels. The latter group was nurturing aristocratic aspirations. The Jats met in at village Mundhela where a decision against the total surrender of the fort was taken.[119] A small force sent by the Sayyids was allowed entry inside the fort, more as a token gesture on the part of the Jats to assuage the ruffled feelings of the Emperor.

The abrupt termination of this campaign lowered the prestige of Jai Singh and enhanced that of the Jats, if we go by the contents of an *arzdasht*.[120] Jai Singh's helplessness and Churaman's ability to pull strings at court became evident. Once relieved of immediate military pressure, Churaman was back to his old game of occupying others' territories and making unauthorized revenue collections. After that, most of the moves of the Jats were of a nature that was bound to incur the wrath of the Mughals.[121] In April 1722 Jai Singh was again asked to lead an army against the Jats.[122] Meanwhile, with the elimination of the Sayyids, Churaman had lost an important source of support against his adversaries in the court.

Jai Singh marched against them with enormous preparation and freedom from interference. Churaman's death and the ensuing conflict between Mohkam Singh and his cousin Badan Singh enabled Jai Singh to enter and occupy the fort of Thoon. Although Badan Singh succeeded to the leadership of the Jats and inherited the zamindari of Churaman, he always played second fiddle to the Amber Raja. Two factors seem to have played a significant role in determining the a policy of Badan Singh. First, Jai Singh had restored peace in the Amber territories by suppressing his unruly clansmen. Hence the Jats could not expect any help from the Rajput *bhomias* of eastern Rajasthan. Second, during the last few years of Churaman, the Jat rebellion had begun to subside due to divisions among their leaders. That is why Churaman had begun to look for support within the Mughal court. Badan Singh, instead chose to be an ally of Jai Singh and to consolidate his gains with his support. Jai Singh recognized the necessity of a settlement with the Jats for the up-keep of peace in this region. As a direct annexation of the Jat territory would have created a long drawn struggle with the Jats, a policy of conciliation towards them was preferred. Thus Jai Singh and the Jat zamindars under the leadership of Badan Singh reached a landmark agreement. 'But apparently, he was a good administrator, and under his watchful stewardship the Jat house of Bharatpur gained in power silently and steadily for the next two decades. Thus the setback to the growth of Jat power was more apparent than real', writes Satish Chandra.[123] The rise of Badan Singh marked a new phase in the history of the Jats, who were now transforming themselves from rebels to rulers.

Complete normalcy at the village level could never be achieved, notwithstanding Badan Singh's acceptance of the status of an ally of Jai Singh. The latter began to pay more attention to the hitherto unruly Jat zamindars. As a successor of Churaman, he inherited his zamindaris and other claims over a large tract lying between Agra and Alwar. Though Churaman had conquered many parganas, his hold over them was seldom legalised. On the other hand Badan Singh was recognized as a legitimate owner of his inheritance. In this task, he was encouraged by Jai Singh who had realized the importance of Badan Singh. Incidentally, Sawai Jai Singh and Badan Singh had some things in common. Both were fond of large harems and had utter disdain for their unruly kinsmen.[124] They trusted each other and flourished in tandem. Badan Singh ultimately founded the independent state of Bharatpur whereas Jai Singh restored peace in his dominion.

Having ensconced himself in the zamindari of Churaman, Badan Singh began to enlarge his resources and the area of his influence through the institutions of *taalluqdari, jagirdari* and *ijaradari*. In Akbarabad (Agra) Badan Singh started as a *taalluqdar* of 25 villages with an assessed revenue of Rs 26,358 in 1731.[125] In 1735, the number of villages under his *taalluqa* went up to 61 with an income of Rs 80,193.[126] In pargana Jafarnagar, his agent got an *ijara* of Rs 30,000.[127] In pargana Bhusawar he had 85 villages under his *taalluqa*.[128] Similarly in pargana Sonkhar his *taalluqa* comprised 21 villages.[129] Badan Singh also contracted the *ijara* of many villages in Bhusawar through his agent Bhupati Mahajan.[130] In pargana Khohri, Pratap Singh s/o Badan Singh was assigned a *jagir* worth Rs 18,000 in 17 villages.[131] Badan Singh himself got 3 villages in perpetuaty (*istimarari ijara*) for Rs 291.[132] In pargana Hindaun many Jat zamindars *chaudhuris,* and *patels* had been given the *ijaras* of many villages.[133] As the pargana was still disturbed, the Jats were able to inveigle more and more villages on *ijara*. In a significant move the zamindari of 5 villages of Pahari was conceded to Badan Singh by Sawai Jai Singh.[134] Many more villages were given to him on *ijara*.[135] Through these deft moves, the Amber ruler was successful in enlisting Badan Singh's support against the Meos who were still refractory in Mewat.

Evidently, Badan Singh had spread his wings from Akbarabad – Jafarnagar to Khohri and Pahari, though none of these parganas were entirely his zamindari. The nature of his claims over these villages was varied. If he was a *taalluqdar* in some villages, elsewhere he claimed *ijara* and the *jagir* rights. He had already firmly based himself on the zamindari of Churaman. In *modus operandi* Churaman, and Badan Singh seem to have differed in some ways. Churaman, a rebel and military adventurer, always believed in conquering the surrounding parganas in order to protect the core area of his zamindari. He had an army of 9000 cavalry (*sawars*) and 600 musteteers (*topchis*) for which raising of fiscal resources from outside his little zamindari became crucial.[136] Even though the area of his operations was very extensive, he always had an infirm and instable control over the conquered territories. However, Churaman succeeded in shaking and disrupting the existing Mughal administrative apparatus at the pargana level. Though he had the wherewithal, he lacked the vision to provide an alternative administration. However, the creation of a new focus of power at the intermediate level was a distinctive contribution of Churaman. Both in his success and fall Churaman had provided the Jats with a goal. He had pushed them in the military labour market, i.e. in politics.

Unlike Churaman, Badan Singh avoided confrontation with the Mughals and Kachhwahas. As we have seen, he made use of available avenues of growth, to the hilt. Therefore, he could provide some kind of administration in a region that had always been tumultous. Thus the emergence of a state with its capital at Bharatpur took place under conditions largely created by Churaman but astutely exploited by Badan Singh and his son Surajmal.

Gradually, Jats had established their control over extensive territories and agrarian resources in the Braj region. Their claims were not just over space, but also over manpower. They had captured all the local instruments of Mughal administration (*jagirdari*, *jaradari*, *thanadari* and *faujdari*) and turned them into their own ruling institutions. In the process the Jats had carved out a domain over which Mughal sovereign claims were firmly constrained. This was a clear manifestation of the seizure of political power by the Jats. A rudimentary Jat state with its capital at Bharatpur was established by Badan Singh in 1735. Subsequently, Bharatpur grew into a full-fledged state under Surajmal whose period is outside the scope of this study.

C. REVOLTS IN DUNDHAR

A study of the revolts of the Rajput and other zamindars is essential for understanding the larger milieu in which the Bharatpur state was born. In the absence of these revolts the Jat uprising could have perhaps been crushed with less effort and cost: the Amber ruler had to spend a considerable part of his strength for keeping his own clan under discipline. It is also true that without the timely help of the Jats, some of these zamindars would not have revolted and others could not sustain their rebellion for long. In other words their revolts fed on each other. The appointment of various rulers of Amber to lead campaigns against the Jats becomes intelligible in the context of the nature of this emerging tension within the Kachhwaha clan and the Jats meddling with that process.

The linkages between the Jats of Braj and Narukas of Mewat have already been noted above. Relations between the Jats and the rebel *bhomias* of Dundhar were mediated through the Narukas of Mewat.[137] Zamindari right was the principal bone of contention between the rebels and the rulers in Dundhar too.[138] As the Kachhwaha clan had branched into various lineages, each lineage either sought to carve out new *bhoms* or expand the existing ones.[139] The Amber Raja, the chieftain of the clan, was disturbed by this drive. As he tried to curb the ambition of these lineage members, a large number of them revolted. Though many of these *bhomias* were in revolt at the same juncture, absolute unity among them could not be forged in this region. They rebelled independently and under their own lineage leaders. In fact some of the lineages were fighting against each other.[140]

In terms of intensity, spread and duration, the revolts of the Naruka *bhomias* were next only to those of the Jats. The peak period of their uprising also coincided with that of the Jat revolt. While Rao Hathi Singh led the Naruka *bhomias* in the Mewat revolts, in Malpura they were led by Fateh Singh and Partap Singh.[141] Their common enemies were the Amber Raja and the *bhomias* allied to him. The dispute over the zamindari of Malpura was said to be at the root of Naruka hostility towards the Raja. The Naruka revolt created disorder in 15 parganas of Mewat and severely dislocated normal life in fourteen parganas around Malpura.[142] In Malpura Pratap Singh was opposed by the Khangarot and the Rajawat *bhomias* (allied to the Raja) and supported by the Hara and the Panwar *bhomias*.[143] In 1684, the Narukas gained a major victory over their enemies by physically liquidating Gaj Singh Rajawat—a prominent noble of the Raja and hardliner against Pratap Singh Naruka.[144] This victory resulted in the meteoric rise of Pratap Singh who attacked the Solankis of Tonk and the Nathavats of Hasanpur, and threatened other zamindars.[145] The parganas of Sherpur and Bhagotgarh became depopulated and the inhabitants of another ten parganas dispersed.[146] The plundering activities of the Naruka and Hara *bhomias* created fear for a long time. Pratap Singh coerced the *chaudhuris* of pargana Tonk to transfer the zamindari of the pargana from the Solankis.[147] He occupied all the *bhom* villages of the Khangarots in Malpura. Pratap Singh and Fateh Singh became the unchallenged masters of Toda Raisinghpur, Tonk, and Malpura. The Narukas opened three fronts to elude the imperial forces. When chased in Tonk and Malpura, they moved to Bahatri. From Bahatri, they moved towards Fagi, Niwai, Mauzabad, and Chatsu.[148] When Pratap Singh was at the peak of his power some differences developed between him and Durjan Singh Hara over the sharing of spoils. Taking advantage of this rift the Amber Raja sent an army to punish Pratap Singh. But the Naruka leader shrewdly won over the support of Sayyid Qutab, *faujdar* of Malpura, and succeeded in buying his neutrality in the ensuing conflict.[149] Meanwhile Fateh Singh and Durjan Singh Hara had joined hands and attacked Nawab

Mukhtar Khan who was campaigning against them in Tonk. It seems that in the Malpura region a durable zamindar-front could not be forged. That is why Pratap Singh and his allies took divergent courses when faced with the Mughal armies. Out of this struggle Pratap Singh emerged as a prominent *bhomia* in the region. The Amber Raja was hardly expected to view this development with approval. Therefore, military operations were intensified against him.[150]

The Chauhan *bhomias* also revolted in many parganas. Their rebellion was spread over five parganas of Pachewar: Salawad, Gijgarh, Kuwawa, Saner, and Lalsot.[151] They successfully disrupted the normal functioning of these parganas for many years. The issue on which the traditional relations between the Mughal *jagirdars* and the Chauhan *bhomias* broke down was again the zamindari right. In 1675, some Chauhan *bhomias* were expelled from pargana Salawad and their zamindari was transferred to the Raja of Amber.[152] The Chauhan *bhomias* of Gijgarh, Kuwawa, Saner and Lalsot, expressing solidarity with their kinsmen in Salawad, violently reacted to the transfer of their zamindari.[153] Even the Chauhan *bhomias* of Liwali and Malarna rebelled in support of the expelled Chauhans of Salawad.[154] In order to regain their lost zamindaris the evicted Chauhans organized a protracted fight (1676-86) from Hindaun where they had meanwhile settled. Under the pressure of the Chauhan *bhomias* the peasants began to abandon their villages.[155] The transfer of zamindari to the Raja added to the burden of the peasants as they had to pay certain additional taxes.[156] Soon it was realized by the revenue officials of Salawad that without the co-operation of the Chauhan *bhomias* it was impossible to repopulate the parganas of Salawad and Saner.[157] The Chauhans adopted a two-pronged strategy to regain their *bhoms*: outright appropriation of the land revenue from the villages of the Raja's zamindari and disruption of cultivation in their erstwhile *bhoms*. This strategy ultimately paved the way for their rehabilitation. When the Chauhans of Salawad expressed their desire in 1686, through Rawat Karan of Behror and Khetsi Nandwan (*bohra*), to resettle, they were immediately allowed to do so.[158] It may be mentioned here that the Raja was unable to punish the rebels because their cause had been taken up by other Chauhan *bhomias*. Second, no military action could be undertaken against the expelled *bhomias* because they had found asylum in Hindaun. The *subadar* of Agra and the *faujdar* of Hindaun would not brook interference within their jurisdictions.[159]

Hence the Amber Raja was unable to annihilate the Chauhans even after uprooting them from their *bhoms*.

The other centre of Chauhan *bhomia* revolt was Kol, where Amar Singh Chauhan of *tappa* Khair was the leading light of this clan.[160] The seriousness of his rebellion is evident from the fact that Nawab Shaista Khan personally had to lead an army against him in 1693.[161] While the Chauhans of the Salawad region revolted in defence of their ancestral zamindari now threatened by the Raja, the Chauhans of Kol became refractory in league with the Jats. The Amber Raja was keen to take over these parganas, whatever the pretext, in order to expand his *watan*. The imperial *jagirdars* being unable to collect revenue themselves from these parganas were also inclined to 'oblige' the Raja. But the Chauhan *bhomias*, like many other *bhomias* of the region, protested. It seems that by then most of the smaller *bhomias* had come to believe, and justly, that the farming out of territories to the Amber Raja was a prelude to the suppression of their zamindari rights.[162]

The revolts of the Rajawat *bhomias* were relatively limited in scale and scope. The main target of their attacks was non-Rajawat zamindars of the neighbouring villages. Sometimes the Rajawats attacked and occupied others' zamindari villages. In order to create panic they would harass the *patels* and the peasants of the targeted zamindaris.[163] Between 1694 and 1697 all the Rajawat *bhomias* of Chatsu were in revolt.[164] Sangram Singh Rajawat, a *taalluqdar* of 32 villages drove away the old inhabitants of some villages and put his own men there.[165] Many villages of Chatsu remained depopulated for a long time due to the terror of the Rajawat *bhomias*.[166] Kushal Singh, a *bhomia* of pargana Boli, was the most refractory among the Rajawats. He constantly meddled with the normal functioning of Malarna, Jhilai (*jagir* of the Raja), Niwai and Chatsu[167] After having embezzled the entire *hasil* of these four parganas he audaciously sent a share of a fourth to Abdullah Khan, then *subadar* of Ajmer.[168] The Amber authorities looked at this collaboration between the *subadar* and a refractory *zamindar*, in dismay. A similar policy was being pursued by the Khangarot, Panchanot, Solanki and Jadon *bhomias*.[169] Frightening away the neighbouring zamindars in order to annex their *bhoms* was a common feature. As a result the peasants of the rival zamindaris had to suffer considerably.[170] To collect land revenue from these *bhomias* was practically impossible.[171] Their plundering activities frightened the peasants and the traders alike.[172] If any *jagirdar* wished to farm-out his *jagir* to the Amber Raja these *bhomias* thwarted the move by raising the banner of revolt.[173] They even started occupying the *raiyati* villages and converted them into their zamindari.[174]

The Rajput *bhomias* of Chatsu were notorious for making various kinds of extortions from the *patels* and the peasants. In order to deal with the rebel *bhomias,* the Amber Raja adopted the policy of the carrot and stick. He tried to appease them by increasing the size of their respective *taalluqas.*[175] The *amil* of Salawad vainly intervened with the Raja against the increase in the *taalluqa* villages. The *amil* felt that appeasement would not lessen the inflated ambition of the *bhomias*; on the contrary it was fanning disorder in the parganas of the zamindari, *jagir* and the *ijara* of the Raja.[176] The Rajput *bhomias* to whom villages had been sub-assigned by the Raja kept collecting revenue from such villages but remained in their *bhom* villages.[177] They refused to fulfil the obligations attached to their assignments. About fifteen parganas around Sonkhar and the entire neighbourhood of Bahatri were in the grip of *bhomia* revolts in the last two decades of the seventeenth century.[178] The Naruka, Kalyanot, and Panchanot *bhomias* were busy constructing *garhis* in ten parganas in defiance of the order of the Amber Raja.[179] Also, *bhomias* from Abhaneri to Bhangarh raised the banner of revolt.[180] The Sanganer-Bundi route was rendered unsafe due to the plundering activities of the *bhomias.*[181] At the same time *bhomias* were turbulent all around Niwai.[182] The ranks of the rebel *bhomias* were swelling day by day. The villages of Niwai, Dausa, Chatsu, and Mauzabad were honeycombed with rioters (*fisadis*).[183] In 1698, the pargana officials expressed the view that without deploying a substantial force, the Kachhwaha *bhomias*—Mansinghawats, Valibhadrawats, Khangarots, Sultanots, and Narukas—of pargana Tonk could not be subjugated.[184] Obviously, *bhomias* belonging to various lineages of the Kachhwaha clan had been alienated from their chieftain.

Thefts with the active connivances or at the behest of the *bhomias*, forcible occupation of villages, looting of traders and harassment of peasants had become the order of the day in Dundhar.[185] This was a period of generalized disobedience by *bhomias* and peasants. All the trade routes became insecure. The imperial *faujdars* of the region were utterly helpless in overpowering the rebels. Sensing the imminent failure of their military operations against the rebels, they thought it prudent to farm out the parganas of their *jagir* to the Raja.[186] Officials posted in the parganas felt that the escalation of revolts was a direct spin-off of the victory of the Jats over the imperialist armies.[187]

In many parganas the rebel zamindars had amassed considerable wealth at the cost of the Mughal *jagirdars*. It has been argued in some recent writings that the zamindars thrived on the structures of the Mughal empire during the seventeenth century. Having benefited from their association with the imperial administration the wealthy zamindars certainly turned against the empire and brought about its downfall in the early eighteenth century.[188] But in our sources there is no evidence of the putative prosperity of the zamindars before they had revolted against the empire. In other words the zamindars acquired wealth only after they challenged the empire. Some evidence is discussed here in support of this contention.

The zamindars in twenty five parganas refused to pay the land revenue to their respective *jagirdars*.[189] It seems that they succeeded in collecting only a part of the revenue from the peasants. The collection of land revenue by the imperial *jagirdars* was at its nadir in about eleven parganas from 1683 to 1723.[190] And such revenue as was collected remained in the hands of the *bhomias* themselves, for refusal to pay land revenue had become by and large the norm. No wonder that under such conditions the tax claims of various *jagirdars* were overdue at different places. Part of these arrears (*baqaya*) were pending with the zamindars of the respective villages. Sometimes the amount running in arrears was startling. In pargana Udai a sum of Rs 40,514 was pending as arrears in 1683.[191] In 1694, the total assessed amount of revenue in pargana Kol was Rs 4,09,916-15, of which Rs 2,41,609-9 were shown as the arrears of various zamindars in the subsequent year.[192] The imperial *mansabdars* who had their *jagirs* in Dausa, Mauzabad and Chatsu refused to renew the *ijara* of their *jagirs* in 1697 because their past dues had not been paid.[193] Possibly, the *ijaradar*, the Amber Raja himself was in no position to collect the money from these parganas. When Saif Khan's *jagir* of pargana Punkhar was brought under *khalisa*, his arrears of 20,000 *mans* of grain was appropriated by the *bhomias*.[194] The *bhomias* refused to hand over land revenue to their *jagirdars* in sixteen parganas.[195]

Two Naruka *bhomias* had collected Rs 4 lakhs each from the *jagir* parganas of Mewat.[196] The *bhomias*, who were in the service of the Amber Raja, paid more attention to their *bhoms* than to their service obligations. They contrived to get their allotments in the proximity of their *bhom* village, so that in course of time they could claim a zamindari right over such villages.[197] Even the *amils* of the Amber Raja advised him not to take *ijara* in the sixteen disturbed parganas.[198] In 1689, the *jagirdars* were unable to collect revenues from six parganas.[199] The Amber Raja had taken pargana Dausa on *ijara* for Rs 1,39,322. When his *amils* went to collect revenue from the villages, the *patels* and peasants refused to pay up.[200] The Amber Raja could get nothing from pargana Nagar as it was under the control of the Jats.[201]

The Amber Raja had taken the zamindari of pargana Malarna against the wishes of the traditional Jadon zamindars of the area. The Jadon *bhomias*' retaliation ruined agriculture in these villages.[202] The *bhomia* disturbances remained unabated for many years in this pargana.[203] In pargana Bayana, the Panwars, Gujars, and Jadons made it impossible for the *jagirdars* to collect land revenue.[204] While the zamindars of Bayana were up in arms, the peasants refused to pay revenue.[205] Zamindars and peasants in Hindaun were rebellious during 1696.[206] More disturbances created by the *bhomias* of Dausa, Chatsu, Mauzabad, Tonk, and Niwai were reported.[207] The *bhomias* of these parganas declined to pay revenue to the *jagirdars*.[208] In 1703 revenue arears of Rs 1,80,000 could not be collected by Nawab Mukhtar Khan from five parganas of his *jagir*. These were under the occupation of the Jat and Naruka rebels.[209] Similarly, revenue arears of 58 villages in Tonk have been shown pending with miscellaneous *bhomias*.[210] Churaman and his allies (*humrah*) are said to have collected Rs 90,600 from Khohri in 1713.[211] The Amber Raja became reluctant to take the *ijara* from the imperial *jagirdars* due to the prolonged and widespread unrest.[212] Earlier, he had taken the *ijara* of many parganas assuming that he would be able to collect revenue at gun point, but the collective strength of smaller *bhomias* showed the limitations of his arms. The policy of eviction of rebellious *bhomias* fanned uprisings and enlarged the area of rebellion. Clearly, the prosperity of the zamindars is a post-rebellion phenomenon and not a result of their association with the empire.

D. THE SOCIAL BASE OF THE REVOLTS

As merchants had become an important element in operating the revenue system, their role in the situation is germane to our discussion. There were three types of merchants. Those who acted as revenue farmers (*ijaradar*) were generally known as *mahajans*. Those who gave loans to the state and credit (*tagai*) to the peasants were called *bohras*; grain-traders were *vyaparis*; sometimes the nomenclature *mahajan* was applied to all of them.[213] They were ubiquitous in the *qasbas* and big villages irrespective of their business status. The upswing in the political activities of the zamindars against the Mughal empire had caught the *mahajans* in the centre of a conflict from which to escape unhurt was difficult. The heavy drain of agricultural produce to the towns, necessitated as much by the urban character of the Mughal ruling class as by the concentric spread-out of its members throughout the empire, stimulated banking and commercial activities in medieval India.[214] Although this view attributes far too much of social and economic dynamism to the initiative of the Mughal ruling class, it is generally accepted by economic historians of medieval India.[215] The permanent dependence of the traders and creditors on the smooth functioning of this system, therefore, cannot be gainsaid. Inversely, the whole system depended on the small and big moneylender and money-changer. Though the revolts created tensions in the traditional relations between the trading and moneylending community and the Mughal ruling class, the world of business never posed a challenge to its beneficiaries. Instead, the traders initially financed all the activities of the *jagirdars* to curb the power of the rebel zamindars. This infuriated the zamindars, who began to blockade the crucial trade-routes and resorted to various means to fleece the traders. The rebel zamindars frequently attacked the *qasbas* and made prisoners of the *mahajans* and *bohras*, as noted earlier. On the other hand, successive victories of some of the zamindars forced a section of traders to shift their allegiance from *jagirdar* to zamindar. A chronological description of the nature of relations between the *jagirdars* and the traders on the one hand and zamindars and traders on the other would help to understand the process.

The *bohras* and *sarrafs* had entered into an agreement with the Amber rulers for mutual benefit. The terms of the agreement were that the *bohras* would lend money to the Raja at a flat rate of interest, 12 annas per month. The market rate ranged between 1.50 and 2.50 per cent. In return the *bohras* were assured of safety and the freedom to carry on their business in these parganas. As per this agreement the *bohras* regularly issued *hundis* to the Amber rulers for their expenses. These *hundis* could be encashed in most cities of

India. This facility was also available to other imperial *jagirdars* in the region. The *bohras* were assigned villages wherefrom they could realize the money thus advanced. They had only to pay the customary cess on their trade transactions. This business was disrupted when rebel zamindars began to extort excessive *rahdari* from the traders. Therefore, when Pratap Singh Naruka revolted, the *sarrafs* of Malpura promptly offered to finance the campaigns organized against him.[216] These campaigns failed rather miserably. The moneylenders of the region then realized that it was not possible to carry on their business in the Malpura region. Therefore, they refused to issue *hundis* to the agents of the Raja, unless and until Pratap Singh was pacified.[217] The subsequent escalation of the zamindar revolts resulted in the closure of all important trade routes.[218] The *sarrafs* of Manoharpur gave up their shops and sought asylum with the Chundawat *bhomias* of Rampura.[219] The traders of *qasba* Sanganer went on a 22 days strike against the local officials' failure to provide protection to them.[220] The *amils* reported from various parganas that there was dearth of *bohras* in the villages.[221] They felt that the flight of the *bohras* was due to the terror of the zamindars. The flight had caused a virtual money-famine in the parganas.[222] The *amils* recommended the exemption of *rahdari* to bring back the traders. The *bhomias* continued to extort un-authorized *rahdari* from them.[223] Under such circumstances grain-merchants stopped visiting these parganas.[224] The frequent imposition of an extra levy (*virar*) on the merchants forced many *mahajans* and *bohras* to migrate from the Amber territories.[225] An important trader of Bahatri had entered into a clandestine deal with the Jats in order to continue his trade at Hodal, a *qasba* under Jat occupation.[226] Meanwhile some traders had come to terms with Churaman Jat and his allies and diverted their trade towards Agra, Delhi and Thoon.[227] Churaman made fortunes out of temporary shifts in the traders' attitudes. Whenever he was besieged in the *garhis*, traders continued the grain supply to him. But this state of affairs was short-lived. The diversion of trade to the Jat country alarmed the Amber Raja, who issued quick instructions to his officials to assure safety and exemption of *rahdari* to the traders.

Thus even though the trading community was unwilling to help the rebel zamindars, the success of revolts did force some of them to come to terms with the rebels. This indirectly helped the rebels and weakened the position of the imperialists. Timely sales of grain collected by the rebels from the *jagirs* of others was of crucial importance. This could be ensured only by the merchants. Traders, besides, played a crucial role in converting the in-kind revenues into cash.[228] The medieval Indian trader was interested in profit and could not care less about where it originated. Hence his loyalties were always shifting, especially when the power of state and zamindar was evenly matched. Yet the rebel zamindars and merchants remained suspicious of each other.

To analyse the social base of such impressive zamindar revolts, it is essential to examine the extent of peasant participation. The extent of cleavages that had formed in the relationships between the *jagirdars* and zamindars and between zamindars and peasants varied from region to region. Our evidence shows that the social base of the rebel zamindars among the peasantry had regional variations, though in general the revolts were intensive and massive in scale almost everywhere. In the rebellious (*zortalab*) parganas of three *sarkars*, Agra, Mathura, and Kol (Aligarh), the zamindars enjoyed the explicit support of the *patels* and the *gaveti-palti* peasants. The frequent imprisonment of 'defaulting' *patels* and other well-to-do peasants by *faujdars* abundantly illustrates this point. The *chaudhuris* and the *qanungos* who had extensive holdings in *qasbas* and big villages largely remained loyal to the state. A few instances are mentioned here to highlight the degree of peasant participation in the revolts.

In 1693, Budh Singh *faujdar* appointed by the Amber ruler, arrested about twenty-seven persons from village Shergarh of Bayana. One of them was a *patel* and others were peasants. They were alleged to be supporters of Panwar zamindars.[229] In pargana Kuthumbar peasants of twenty-two villages were actively supporting the Jat zamindars.[230] An alliance between the Jat zamindars and peasants is borne out by a document containing the names of peasants imprisoned in the course of campaigns against the rebels.[231] Of the total number of imprisoned peasants, the size of land holdings of 9 ranged between 5 and 10 *bighas* each; 4 owned land up to 15 *bighas* each, and only one person was the owner of 47 *bighas*. Significantly, the arrested peasants belonged to various castes: Jats (5), Gujars (4), Balahis (2), Chamar (1) and Khati (1). Clearly the rebel Jat zamindars enjoyed support from a wide ranging section of peasants caste. Pargana Kuthumbar was the cradle of the uprising of the Jat zamindars and the peasants of many lower castes.[232]

Moreover, it may be emphasized that the Jat zamindars derived their strength mainly from the peasants of their caste. But peasants belonging to many other castes were in league with them. Largely, peasants followed zamindars of their respective castes.[233] In pargana Ao also the Jat zamindars were supported by peasants of their caste, and some Meos. When Thakur Hari Singh attacked Sinsini (Ao), he had to face the hostility of about fourteen villages surrounding Sinsini.[234] Similarly, six out of eight persons arrested in the villages of pargana Bhusawar were Jat peasants while the remaining two were *patels* of the same caste.[235] In Bhusawar many Jat *patels* had got *ijara* in about 12 villages. At the time of revenue collection they became rebellious and cast their lot with the Jat zamindars.[236]

Patels of many villages of Kama were imprisoned because of their alleged collaboration with the Jat zamindars.[237] In 1993, it was felt by the revenue officials that the revolts of the Jats of *tappa* Lagasma (Kol) could not be suppressed because the villagers were collaborating with the turbulent zamindars.[238] The peasants of seven our of twenty-seven villages of pargana Khohri fled to Thoon/Nagar and joined hands with the Jat zamindars in 1716.[239]

The next year, when about 23 carts carrying valuables were attacked by the Jats near Palwal, the guards could not chase the Jats because the latter enjoyed the active support of the peasants of nearby villages.[240] It was perhaps this persisting solidarity between Jat zamindars and Jat peasant that provoked the Amber Raja to take the unprecedented step of imposing a special tax exclusively on Jat peasants in twenty-one villages in pargana Khohri.[241] The general impression gathered from the documents relating to Kol is that the peasants were hostile to the revenue officials and co-operating with the rebels.[242] Similarly, the turbulent zamindars of Bayana and Secundra could not be weeded out of the villages because of peasants' support to them.[243]

The second region where massive revolts occurred was the *chakla* of Mewat in Alwar *sarkar*. Here the Khanzadahs of Mewat, the Meos, the Chauhans and Bargujars had more zamindaris around 1600 than did the zamindars of the intermediate castes.[244] In this region the uprisings were led by the Naruka, Jat, Kalyanot, and some Meo zamindars. The most remarkable feature of the Mewat revolts was the formation of a united zamindar-front which seems to have enjoyed at best uncertain support of the peasantry.[245] The zamindar-front was formed in a complex political situation. Kalyanots, who had negligible zamindaris, suddenly began to expand them by bringing new villages under their control. At the same time, the Amber Raja wished to expand his *watan* by bringing the parganas of Mewat under his control. The Jats also moved into Mewat with their own ambition. Thus the Narukas and the Kalyanots were sandwiched between the expanding Amber *watan* and the equally ambitious Jat zamindars. The peasantry of this region was composed of heterogeneous castes, Jat, Ahir, Gujar, Mina and Meo.[246] Together they constituted the majority. The peasantry had economic grievances against the Raja who was acting as the watchdog of the Mughal *jagirdar's* interests in Mewat. Most of the peasants had a caste affinity with some zamindars of the Braj or Mewat region. This combination should have ensured durable peasant support to zamindars. The peasants, instead of coming out openly in support of the Narukas, adopted a particularly pragmatic attitude. Whenever the Narukas established their *thanas* in the region, the peasants came and paid land revenue to them, but when the Raja re-established his *thanas* the peasants accepted his claims, though usually with reluctance.[247] Occasionally the Narukas succeeded in persuading the peasants not to pay cesses like *bhent, bhom,* etc., to the Raja's agents.[248] It was perhaps this ambivalence on the part of the peasants that persuaded the rebel *bhomias* to refrain from harassing the peasantry of the Mewat region, lest it be pushed into enemy ranks. Instead, many zamindars were busy coaxing peasants to join them.

In the third region of zamindar revolts, Ajmer and Ranthambore *sarkars*, there existed open hostility between the zamindars and the peasants.[249] Peasants were the special targets of *bhomia*' plunder. The activities of Pratap Singh Naruka and others in the Malpura and Chatsu regions were a constant source of terror for peasants. Refusal to pass on the collected revenue, burning down (*jalawatan karna*) the villages of rival zamindars, and waylaying traders, were some of the features of *bhomia* revolts in this region. The picture of a terror-stricken peasantry on the run inevitably emerges from the documents pertaining to the parganas of these two *sarkars*. It is possible that the lack of caste affinity was responsible for this hiatus between rebel zamindars and peasants. Almost all the zamindars of this region were Rajput by caste, while the peasantry belonged to miscellaneous intermediate castes (Jats, Gujars, Ahirs, and Minas),[250] and the social linkages remained tenuous. On the other hand, the peasantry compensated itself by wresting some concessions from the Amber Raja.[251]

In this region the zamindars of a particular lineage, however, acted in concert whenever any of them were attacked. When the Chauhan *bhomias* were expelled from their villages in pargana Salawad, the Chauhan' of neighbouring parganas revolted to express their solidarity with them. Indeed, the Chauhans were subsequently rehabilitated only because their seven *bhom* villages remained deserted due to the activities of other Chauhan *bhomias*. It was the solidarity expressed by the neighbouring Chauhans that paved the way for the expelled Chauhan *bhomias* of Salawad to return home. Solidarity among zamindars on lineage lines is a noticeable feature of political life in Dundhar.

Besides the zamindars' uprisings, peasant rebellions took place in all these regions with varying intensity. Our evidence suggests that large-scale peasant rebellions took place in Bayana, Nagar, Sahar, Khohri, and Kol. In 1693, and 1704 it was reported that zamindars and peasants were rebellious everywhere (*raiyat aur bhomia berah chale chhe*).[252] However, the more the Jat zamindars moved away from the Agra-Kol-Khohri complex, the further their mass support tended to shrink. Although the ferocity of the zamindar revolts was more or less equal in all regions, the degree of peasant participation was regionally variant, though none of these regions had a docile peasantry. Whenever the zamindars and the peasants acted together the revolts could be sustained for long and they had far-reaching political and social consequences. In areas where such unity could not be forged, zamindar revolts were shortlived. Clearly, unity was achieved through the interaction of a complex of economic, caste and political factors and wherever it was achieved, it worked to the advantage of the zamindars, who were particularly adroit in appealing to the sentiment of caste. This is clearly borne out by the fact that Churaman and his handiwork—the united zamindar front—had a definite social base among peasants of their own caste compared to the others.

Yet, the role of caste in this scenario need not be overrated. The widespread disturbances in our region were set in the background of a resurgence of zamindari power on the one hand, and a rapid impoverishment of the peasantry on the other. Although caste affinity often formed a bridge between these two restive sectors of rural society, their uprisings did not always coincide with each other;

nor did they adopt similar forms of protest. Indeed, there are three distinct patterns of relationship between zamindars and peasants in three sub-regions of the area under study, quite apart from the distinctive forms of struggle of each group. While zamindars lost no time in taking to arms, peasant protest would pass through certain stages, all the while directed primarily against the rising level of exploitation by almost every one in a position to lay his hands upon their produce. The first step the peasants took against any intrusion into their subsistence was to lodge a complaint with the imperial authorities; the second was the threat to migrate; the third was a refusal to pay revenue; the fourth was actual desertion of villages; and finally, resort to arms. It is only after passing through all these stages that peasant rebellion merged with zamindar revolt in the Agra-Kol-Khohri region. On the other hand, in the Mewat region peasant unrest did not merge with zamindar revolts completely. If the peasantry of the Mewat region did not become cannon-fodder for the zamindars, it did not co-operate with the administration's efforts to curb turbulent zamindars either. Face-to-face with a situation where the zamindars and the imperial authorities were equally balanced, the peasants preferred to organize resistance under the leadership of the village headmen (*patel*) who were also emerging as an alternative power bloc.

In the Ajmer-Ranthambore region, peasant unrest proceeded simultaneously with the zamindar revolts; however, the action of the two did not converge at any stage. The zamindars of this region relied mainly on their personal armed power rather than on any kind of support from the peasantry. Indeed, it is the plundering activities of the zamindars in this region that became the chief cause of the peasant misery and consequent restiveness.

It seems therefore that even though the apparent simultaneity of the peasant and the zamindar disturbances is seductive, the interconnections between the two are quite intricate in each region of rural disturbances. Clearly, the reality is far too complex to fit into a neat pattern. However, even as the Mughal power was waning, it is the zamindars who were exerting themselves at every level to inherit the empire they had done so much to destroy. The helpless peasantry had little reason to be grateful to the zamindars, who in turn did not take long to forget the caste bond between them and their lower class brethren once their zamindaris had been consolidated on a new footing.

NOTES

1. W.C. Smith, 'Lower Class Uprisings in the Mughal Empire', *Islamic Culture*, 1945, pp. 202-28; Irfan Habib, *Agrarian System*, pp. 390-405; Muzaffar Alam, 'Aspects of Agrarian Uprisings in Mughal India', in S. Bhattacharya and R. Thapar (eds.), *Situating Indian History*, Delhi, 1986; Chetan Singh, 'Conformity and Conflict: Tribes and the "Agrarian System" of Mughal India', *IESHR*, no. 3, 1988; and Gautam Bhadra, 'Two Frontier Uprisings in Mughal India', in Ranajit Guha (ed.), *Subaltern Studies*, II, 43-59 Delhi, 1984.
2. R.P. Rana, 'Agrarian Revolts in Northern India during the late 17th and early 18th Centuries', *IESHR*, 3 and 4, 1981, pp. 287-326.
3. A *thikara* was an autonomous zamindari. Some of these *thikanas* were at Diggi, Uniara, Khetri and Singhana. For details C.U. Wills, *A Report on the Land Tenures and Special Powers of Certain Thikanadars of the Jaipur State*, 1935, p. 10.
4. R.P. Rana, 'A Dominant Class in Upheaval: The Zamindars of a North Indian Region', *IESHR*, vol. 4, 1987, pp. 395-410.
5. Abul Fazl, *Akbarnama*, III, tr., p. 231.
6. Ibid., p. 391.
7. Abul Fazl, *Ain-i-Akbari*, II, tr., pp. 190-206.
8. Irfan Habib, *Agrarian System*, p. 392.
9. R.P. Rana, 'Everyday Forms of Peasant Resistance in Eastern Rajasthan (*c.* 1660-1750)', *Social Science Probings*, vol. 15, nos. 3-4, 2003, pp. 41-62.
10. Ranajit Guha, *Elementary Aspects of Peasant Insurgency in Colonial India*, Oxford University Press, Delhi, 1983, pp. 77-108.
11. *Amber Records*, dt. Posh Sudi 7, VS 1722/1665 and Sawan Sudi 2, VS 1722/1665.
12. *Amber Record*, dt. Chet Sudi 13, VS 1723/1666.
13. *Amber Record*, dt. Asadh Sudi 4, VS 1722/1665.
14. *Amber Record*, dt. Mah Sudi 13, VS 1721/1664.
15. *Amber Records*, dt. Mah Sudi 14, VS 1721/1664; Mangsir Sudi 13, VS 1723/1666 and Asadh Vadi 8, VS 1723/1666.
16. Sahar ceased to be a *sarkar* at some stage and was merged into a new *sarkar* called Islamabad (Mathura). See Irfan Habib, *An Atlas of the Mughal Empire*, p. 19.
17. *Arzdashts*, dt. Kati Vadi 9, VS 1748/1686 and Jeth Sudi 8, VS 1744/1687.
18. *Arzdasht*, dt. Posh Vadi 7, VS 1743/1686.
19. *Arzdasht*, dt. Vaisakh Vadi 14, VS 1744/1687.
20. *Arzdasht*, dt. Bhadwa Vadi 7, VS 1744/1687 and *Amber Records*, dt. Bhadwa Vadi 3, VS 1744/1687.
21. *Arzdasht*, dt. Kati Sudi 4, VS 1744/1687.
22. *Arzdasht*, dt. Mangsir Vadi 2, VS 1744/1687.
23. *Arzdasht*, dt. Asoj Vadi 13, VS 1744/1687.
24. *Arzdasht*, dt. Mangsir Vadi 2, VS 1744/1687.
25. *Arzdasht*, dt. Mangsir Vadi 2, VS 1744/1687.
26. Chapter 4.
27. Vakil Report, Kesho Rai to Raja Ram Singh, dt. 5th Jammadal Awwal, 1099/AH 1688.

28. N. Manucci, *Storia Do Mogor* or Mogul India: 1653-1708 (tr. William Irvine), vol. II, Indian Edition, Calcutta, 1966, p. 301.
29. *Arzdasht*, dt. Jeth Sudi 8, VS 1744/1687.
30. Vakil Report, Kesho Rai to Bishan Singh, dt. 28 Jammadal Akhir, 1099/AH 1688.
31. R.P. Rana, 'Agrarian Revolts in Northern India', pp. 318-22.
32. *Akhbarat*, dt. Vaisakh Sudi 10, VS 1745/1688.
33. Vakil Reports, Kesho Rai to Bishan Singh, dt. 13 Rajab 1099 AH/May 4, 1688; 4 Sabban 1099 AH/25 May 1688 and 24 Ramajan, 1099 AH/July 18, 1688.
34. Kesho Rai wrote about 40 letters (between May 1688 to September 1689) to Bishan Singh exhorting the latter to march against the Jats.
35. Vakil Report, Kesho Rai to Bishan Singh, dt. 24 Ramjan, 1099 AH/July 13, 1688.
36. Vakil Report, Kesho Rai to Bishan Singh, dt. 13 Zilkada, 1099 AH/August 21, 1688.
37. Vakil Report, Bhawani Das to Bishan Singh, dt. 15 Zilhijja, 1099 AD/October 1, 1688.
38. Vakil Reports, Kesho Rai to Bishan Singh, dt. 11 Zilkada, 1100 AH/August 17, 1689 and 20 Safar, 1101 AH/November 23, 1689.
39. K.R. Qanungo, *History of the House of Diggi*, p. 63.
40. Vakil Report, Kesho Rai to Bishan Singh, dt. 11 Shawwal, 1099 AH/July 30, 1688,
41. Vakil Report, Kesho Rai to Bishan Singh, dt. 8 Jamadal akhir, 1101 AH/March 9, 1690.
42. *Arzadasht*, dt. Mangsir Sudhi 2, VS 1746/1689.
43. *Amber Records*, dt. Kati Vadi 4, VS 1747/1690.
44. Ibid., dt. Mangsir Sudi 3, VS 1747/1690.
45. C.U. Wills, *A Report on the Land Tenures*, p. 10.
46. *Arzdasht*, dt. Jeth Vadi 13, VS 1752/1695.
47. *Arzdasht*, dt. Vaisakh Vadi 10, VS 1750/1693.
48. *Arzdasht*, dt. Vaisakh Vadi 14, VS 1750/1693.
49. *Arzdasht*, dt. Kati Vadi 13, VS 1740/1683.
50. U.N. Sharma, *A New History of the Jats*, Jaipur, 1977, p. 176. Sharma tells us that Amar Singh was a Jat zamindar. But in the records of the 1857 Rebellion, the Chauhans of Khair are mentioned as Rajputs. See Eric Stokes, *Peasant and the Raj: Studies in Agrarian Society and Peasant Rebellion in Colonial India*, Cambridge University Press, 1978, pp. 192-3. In fact Stokes is surprised at the alliance of the Jats of Lagasma and the Chauhan Rajputs of Khair—supposedly 'hereditary enemies'. Little did Stokes know that the Jats and the Rajputs of this area had earlier fought together against the Mughals.
51. *Arzdasht*, dt. Vaisakh Vadi 11, VS 1749/1692.
52. *Arzdasht*, dt. Mangsir Vadi 5, VS 1750/1693.
53. *Amber Record*, dt. Vaisakh Sudi 5, VS 1752/1695.
54. *Arzdasht*, dt. Jeth Sudi 8, VS 1753/1696.
55. *Arzdasht*, dt. Sawan Vadi 14, VS 1754/1697.
56. *Arzdasht*, dt. Mah Vadi 4, VS 1747/1690.
57. Irfan Habib, *Agrarian System*, p. 393n.
58. Vakil Report, Megh Raj to Bishan Singh, dt. 10 Zilhijja, 1103 AH/Aug. 13, 1693.

59. Vakil Report, Megh Raj to Bishan Singh, dt. 1 Jamadal akhir, 1104 AH/January 28, 1693.
60. Vakil Report, Megh Raj to Bishan Singh, dt. 11 Jamadal akhir, 1104 AH/ February 7, 1693.
61. *Arzdasht*, dt. Mah Vadi 11, VS 1743/1686.
62. *Arzdasht*, dt. Bhadwa Sudi 13, VS 1749/1693.
63. *Arzdashts*, dt. Sawan Sudi 4, VS 1749/1692; and Mangsir Vadi 10, VS 1761/ 1704.
64. *Arzdasht*, dt. Bhadwa Vadi 5, VS 1759/1702.
65. *Arzdasht*, dt. Kati Vadi 6, VS 1759/1702.
66. *Arzdasht*, dt. Mangsir Sudi 3, VS 1760/1703.
67. *Arzdasht*, dt. Vaisakh Vadi 3, VS 1760/1703.
68. *Arzdashts*, dt. Vaisakh Vadi 3, and Kati Vadi 6, VS 1760/1703.
69. *Arzdasht*, dt. Mangsir Vadi 5, VS 1749/1692.
70. *Arzdasht*, dt. Bhadwa Vadi 5, VS 1749/1692.
71. *Arzdasht*, dt. Asadh Sudi 14, VS 1760/1703.
72. *Arzdasht*, dt. Kati Vadi 14, VS 1744/1683.
73. *Arzdasht*, dt. Vaisakh Vadi 10, VS 1750/1693.
74. *Arzdasht*, dt. Jeth Vadi 13, VS 1752/1695.
75. *Arzdasht*, dt. Mangsir Vadi 10, VS 1761/1704.
76. *Arzdasht*, dt. Falgun Vadi 4, VS 1759/1702.
77. *Arzdasht*, dt. Asadh Sudi 14, VS 1760/1703. The parganas were Sonkhar (under Jats, Narukas, Kalyanots and Chauhans), Kuthumbar (under Jats), Banawar, Mandawar and Toda Thek (under Narukas).
78. *Arzdashts*, dt. Mangsir Sudi 3, VS 1760/1703; Asadh Sudi 15, Asadh Vadi 6 and Bhadwa Sudi 5, VS 1761/1704.
79. *Arzdashts*, dt. Asoj Vadi 14, Asadh Sudi 15, VS 1761/1704 and Jeth Vadi 2, VS 1762/1705.
80. *Arzdasht*, dt. Asadh Sudi 5, VS 1766/1709.
81. *Arzdasht*, dt. Asadh Vadi 14, VS 1766/1709.
82. *Arzdasht*, dt. Asadh Sudi 8, VS 1766/1709.
83. *Arzdashts*, dt. Asadh Sudi 8 and Asadh Vadi 14, VS 1766/1709.
84. *Arzdasht*, dt. Sawan Vadi 6, VS 1766/1709.
85. Satish Chandra, *Parties and Politics*, pp. 122-5.
86. *Arzdasht*, dt. Kati Sudi 11, VS 1766/1709.
87. *Arzdashts*, dt. Kati Vadi 6 and 12, VS 1766/1709.
88. *Arzdasht*, dt. Kati Vadi 11, VS 1766/1709.
89. *Arzdashts*, dt. Kati Vadi 14, Mangsir Sudi 6 and Mah Sudi 6, VS 1766/1709.
90. *Arzdasht*, dt. Posh Vadi 10, VS 1766/1709.
91. *Arzdashts*, dt. Posh Sudi 2 and 13, VS 1766/1709.
92. *Arsatthas*, pargana Khohri, VS 1768/1711 to 1722/1715. The total number of villages in this pargana was 342.
93. *Arsattha*, and pargana Khohri, VS 1769/1712; *arzdashts*, dt. Jeth Sudi 11, Jeth Vadi 3, Asadh Sudi 7 and Asoj Vadi 9, VS 1769/1712.
94. *Arsattha*, pargana Khohri VS 1770/1713 (*rabi*).
95. *Arsattha*, pargana Khohri VS 1771/1713 (*kharif*).
96. *Arsattha*, pargana Khohri VS 1773/1716 (*kharif*), and *Chithi*, dt. Mah Sudi 3, VS 1773/1716.

97. *Arzdasht*, dt. Sawan Vadi 1, vs 1771/1714.
98. *Arzdasht*, dt. Mangsir Sudi 3, vs 1774/1717.
99. *Arzdasht*, dt. Posh Sudi 5, vs 1774/1717.
100. Shiv Das Lakhnavi, *Shahnama Munawar Kalam* (tr.), p. 21.
101. Ashin Das Gupta, 'Trade and Politics in Eighteenth Century India', in D.F. Richards (ed.), *Islam and the Trade of Asia*, Philadelphia, Bruno Carrier and the University of Pennsylvania Press, 1970, p. 189.
102. *Arzdasht*, dt. Sawan Sudi 1, vs 1775/1718.
103. *Daftar Mawazna Khurd*, Toji no. 4, Pargana Bahatri, vs 1775/1718.
104. *Arzdashts*, dt. Sawan Sudi 3 and 5, vs 1775/1718.
105. Vakil Report from Meso Rai to Bishan Singh, dt. 13 Rajab, 31st Regnal year of Aurangzeb.
106. *Arzdashts*, dt. Vaisakh Vadi 14, Jeth Sudi 8 and Mangsir Vadi 2, vs 1744/1687.
107. Churaman received a *mansab* of 1500/500 from Bahadur Shah, the title of Rahdar Khan from Farrukh Siyar and 'Thakur' from Muhammad Shah.
108. *Arzdasht*, dt. Kati Sudi 11, vs 1766/1709.
109. He was present in all the battles: Lahore, Jaju, Khajua, Samugarh, etc.
110. Satish Chandra, *Parties and Politics*, pp. 122-5.
111. See Annexure 2 to Chapter 4.
112. The revenue arrears shown in the *arsathas* of various parganas clearly establish this 'charge' against Churaman.
113. Khohri, Ferozepur, Kama, etc. were re-occupied.
114. U.N. Sharma, *A New History of the Jats*, pp. 244-8.
115. *Arsatthas*, pargana Kotla, vs 1770/1713 and *Khatoot Ahalkaran*, dt. Kati Vadi 10, vs 1771/1714.
116. Satish Chandra, *Parties and Politics*, p. 178.
117. *Arzdasht*, dt. Mangsir Vadi 9 and 10, vs 1775/1718.
118. K. Natwar Singh, *Maharaja Suraj Mal: 1707-1763*, New Delhi, 1981, Vikas Publishing House, 1983, p. 18.
119. *Arzdasht*, dt. Mangsir Vadi 9, vs 1775/1718.
120. *Arzdasht*, dt. Mangsir Vadi 11, vs 1775/1718.
121. Plundering the royal camp in the battle of Hasanpur, instigation of the Bundelas against the *subadar* of Allahabad; harassment of Saadat Khan when he marched against Ajit Singh of Jodhpur and murder of Nilkanth Nagar by Mohkam Singh were some of these actions.
122. William Irvine, *Later Mughals*, vol. II, p. 122.
123. Satish Chandra, *Parties and Polities*, pp. 178-9.
124. V.S. Bhatnagar, *Life and Times of Sawai Jai Singh*, 1688-1743, Delhi, 1974; and K. Natwar Singh, *Maharaja Surajmal*, p. 21.
125. *Arsattha*, pargana Akbarabad, vs 1788/1731.
126. *Arsattha*, pargana Akbarabad, vs 1792/1735.
127. Ibid.
128. *Arsattha*, pargana Bhusawar, etc., vs 1783/1726.
129. *Arsattha*, pargana Sonkhar, vs 1783/1726.
130. *Arsattha*, pargana Bhusawar, etc., vs 1791/1734.
131. *Arsattha*, pargana Khohri, vs 1781/1724.
132. *Arsattha*, pargana Khohri, vs 1783/1726.
133. *Arsattha*, pargana Hindaun, vs 1787/1730.

134. *Arsattha*, pargana Pahari, vs 1781/1724.
135. *Arsattha*, pargana Pahari, vs 1788/1731.
136. *Arzdasht*, dt. Kati Badi 14, vs 1766/1709 and Sawan Vadi, I vs 1771/1714.
137. *Arzdashts*, dt. Asoj Sudi 15, vs 1741/1684 and Asadh Vadi 5, vs 1742/1685.
138. R.P. Rana, 'Agrarian Revolts in Northern India', pp. 287-326.
139. James Tod, *Annals and Antiquities of Rajaputana*, p. 353. According to Tod there were about 16 lineages of the Kachhwaha clan. Rajawats, Khangarots, Narukas, Kalyanots, Valibhadravats, Hamirdeka and Sultanots were some of the prominent lineages.
140. For example there were constant feuds between the Rajawats, Narukas, and the Khangarots during this period.
141. *Arzdashts*, dt. Asadh Sudi 14, vs 1740/1683; Kati Sudi 4, vs 1744/1687; Asoj Sudi 15, vs 1742/1685 and Kati Vadi 6, vs 1759/1702.
142. *Arzdashts*, dt. Asadh Vadi 5, vs 1743/1685 and Asoj Sudi 15, vs 1741/1684.
143. *Arzdashts*, dt. Asoj Sudi 4, vs 1749/1692; Asoj Sudi 15, vs 1742/1685; Kati Sudi 13, vs 1742/1685 and Posh Vadi 13, vs 1743/1686.
144. *Arzdasht*, dt. Posh Vadi 13, vs 1743/1686.
145. *Arzdashts*, dt. Mangsir Sudi 6, vs 1743/1686; Bhadwa Vadi 13, vs 1743/1686 and Kati Sudi 4, vs 1744/1687.
146. *Arzdasht*, dt. Posh Sudi 6, vs 1743/1686. These parganas were: Tonk, Malpura, Toda Raisinghpur, Mauzabad, Naraina, Bhagotgarh, Sherpur, Sarsomp, Boli, etc.
147. *Arzdasht*, dt. Posh Vadi 7, vs 1743/1686.
148. *Arzdashts*, dt. Falgun Vadi 2, vs 1743/1686 and Mah Vadi 11, vs 1743/1686.
149. *Arzdashts*, dt. Falgun Vadi 2, vs 1743/1686 and Sawan Vadi 15, 1743/1686.
150. *Arzdashts*, dt. Falgun Vadi 2, vs 1743/1686 and Posh Sudi 6, vs 1743/1686. Prominent Rajput *zamindars* like Ratan Singh Shekhawat and Sanwal Singh Rajawat were directed to fight Pratap Singh Naruka.
151. See Annexure 1 of Chapter 4.
152. *Arzdashts*, dt. Falgun Sudi 10, vs 1733/1676; Mah Vadi 7, vs 1732/1675; Asadh Vadi 8, vs 1749/1694; Chet Vadi 13, vs 1740/1683; Sawan Vadi 7, vs 1745/1688; Mah Sudi 12, vs 1746/1689 and Sawan Sudi 9, vs 1743/1686.
153. *Arzdasht*, dt. Sawan Sudi 10, vs 1733/1676.
154. *Arzdasht*, dt. Jeth Vadi 14, vs 1740/1683.
155. *Arzdashts*, dt. Chet Vadi 9, vs 1746/1689; Chet Sudi and Sawan Sudi 9, vs 1743/1686 and Bhadwa Vadi 13, vs 1743/1686 and *Amber Record*, dt. Chet Vadi 13, vs 1741/1684.
156. *Arsattha*, pargana Salawad.
157. *Arzdashts*, dt. Falgun Sudi 7, vs 1744/1687; Sawan Vadi 7, vs 1745/1688 and Asoj Sudi 7, vs 1743/1686.
158. *Arzdasht*, dt. Sawan Sudi 9, vs 1743/1686.
159. *Arzdashts*, dt. Sawan Sudi 9, vs 1743/1686; Vaisakh Vadi 11, vs 1749/1692 and Asoj Vadi 3, vs 1751/1694.
160. *Arzdasht*, dt. Asadh Vadi 2, vs 1752/1695.
161. *Arzdasht*, dt. Vaisakh Vadi 11, vs 1749/1692.
162. *Arzdasht*, dt. Jeth Vadi 14, vs 1740/1683.
163. Ibid.
164. *Arzdashts*, dt. Falgun Sudi 5, vs 1752/1695 and Mah Sudi 11, vs 1754/1697.

165. *Arzdasht*, dt. Asoj Vadi 7, vs 1751/1694.
166. Ibid.
167. *Arzdashts*, dt. Bhadwa Sudi 12, vs 1756/1699 and Asoj Vadi 7, vs 1751/1694.
168. *Amber Record*, dt. Bhadwa Sudi 12, vs 1756/1699.
169. Ibid., dt. Asadh Sudi 13, vs 1740/1683.
170. *Arzdasht*, dt. Mah Vadi 2, vs 1773/1716. For example, Dhan Singh Panchanot, an evicted *bhomia* of Malarna came and occupied village Jiwad and started harassing the peasants there. See *arzdasht*, dt. Falgun Sudi 9, vs 1752/1695.
171. *Arzdasht*, dt. Kati Vadi 14, vs 1761/1704. Sayyid Hussain Ali Khan, *faujdar* of Ranthambore, had his *jagir* in pargana Boli. When his *amil* Mehta Trikam Das went to collect revenue, he was beaten up by Sanwal Singh and other Sangram Singhavats. Similarly the Shekhawat *bhomias* of Rewasa and Kasli refused payment of land revenue to the *jagirdar*, Abdullah Khan. See *Arzdasht*, dt. Kati Vadi 14, vs 1754/1697.
172. *Arzdashts*, dt. Mangsir Sudi 6, vs 1743/1684, and *Amber Record*, dt. Posh Vadi 4, vs 1761/1704.
173. *Arzdasht*, dt. Chet Vadi 9, vs 1746/1689.
174. *Arzdasht*, dt. Asadh Sudi 15, vs 1761/1704.
175. *Likhtanq*, dt. Vaisakh Sudi 12, vs 1769/1712 of Raja Raj Singh Kalyanot, a *taalluqdar* of 34-1/2 villages with a total revenue of Rs 11,001.
176. *Arzdasht*, dt. Asadh Sudi 13, vs 1740/1683.
177. *Amber Record*, dt. Mangsir Vadi 10, vs 1765/1709. These parganas were: Hindaun, Sambhar, Tonk, Chatsu, Khohri, Lalsot, Malarna, Udai and Salawad.
178. *Arzdashts*, dt. Jeth Sudi 10, vs 1742/1685 and Asadh Vadi 5, vs 1742/1685. These parganas were Gudha, Behror, Salawad, Chhawa, Saner, Gijarh, Bahatri, Niwai, Lalsot, Dausa, Fagi, Malarna, Bhairana, Udai and Nagar.
179. *Arzdasht*, dt. Bhaiwa Vadi 5, vs 1742/1685. These parganas were: Bhusawar, Mandawar, Naharkhoh, Punkhar, Toda Bhim, Bharkol, Umarni, Sonkhar, Kuthumbhar and Hasanpur. On the other hand the Malpura route was closed due to the conflict between the Khangarot and Naruka *bhomias*. See *arzdasht* dt. Kati Sudi 13, vs 1742/1695.
180. *Arzdasht*, dt. Asadh Vadi 11, vs 1749/1692.
181. *Arzdasht*, dt. Posh Sudi 11, vs 1753/1693.
182. *Arzdasht*, dt. Kati Vadi 2, vs 1753/1693.
183. *Arzdashts*, dt. Asoj Vadi 14, vs 1761/1704 and Jeth Vadi 5, vs 1755/1698.
184. *Arzdashts*, dt. Asoj Vadi 14, vs 1761/1704 and *Amber Record*, dt. Kati Sudi 13, vs 1766/1709.
185. *Arzdasht*, dt. Asadh Sudi 14, vs 1760/1703.
186. Ibid.
187. *Arzdasht*, dt. Vaisakh Vadi 11, vs 1749/1692.
188. C.A. Bayly, *Imperial Meridian*, p. 29, and Muzaffar Alam, *The Crisis of Empire in Mughal North India*, p. 303.
189. *Arzdashts*, dt. Asoj Sudi 15, vs 1741/1684 and Jeth Sudi 10, vs 1742/1685. The parganas were: Malarna, Jhilai, Chatsu, Kol, Rewasa, Kasli, Sonkhar, Kuthumbhar, Boli, Banawar, etc.
190. *Arzdashts*, dt. Falgun Vadi 9, vs 1749/1692; Kati Vadi 14, vs 1761/1704; Kati Vadi 14, vs 1766/1709 and Bhadwa Sudi 12, vs 1756/1699.
191. *Arzdasht*, dt. Asadh Sudi 13, 1740/1683.

192. *Arzdashts*, dt. Chet Sudi 7, vs 1751/1694 and Asadh Vadi 2, vs 1752/1695.
193. *Arzdasht*, dt. Asoj Sudi 8, vs 1754/1697.
194. *Arzdasht*, dt. Kati Vadi 13, vs 1741/1684.
195. *Arzdasht*, dt. Asoj Sudi 15, vs 1741/1684. Parganas were: Bahatri, Bharkol, Valhetta, Khilohra, Hasanpur, Maujpur, Pindayan, Sonkhar, Nagar, Banawar, Mandawar and Bhusawar.
196. *Arzdasht*, dt. Asadh Vadi 5, vs 1742/1685.
197. *Arzdasht*, dt. Jeth Sudi 10, vs 1742/1685.
198. *Arzdasht*, dt. Asadh Vadi 5, vs 1742/1685. Parganas: Gudhala, Bahror, Salawad, Chhawa, Saner, Gijgarh, Bahatri, Niwai, Lalsot, Dausa, Fagi, Malarna, Bhairana, Udai, Nagar and Sonkhar.
199. *Arzdasht*, dt. Mah Sudi 12, vs 1746/1689, Parganas: Gijgarh, Kakrala, Gudha and Toda Bhim.
200. *Amber Record*, dt. Kati Sudi 2, vs 1746/1689.
201. *Arzdasht*, dt. Mangsir Sudi 2, vs 1746/1689.
202. *Arzdashts*, dt. Chet Sudi 10 and Jeth Vadi 6, vs 1740/1689.
203. *Arzdasht*, dt. Kati Vadi 5, vs 1749/1692.
204. *Amber Record*, dt. Posh Vadi 1, vs 1750/1693.
205. *Arzdasht*, dt. Falgun Vadi 13, vs 1752/1695.
206. *Arzdasht*, dt. Asoj Vadi 13, vs 1753/1696.
207. *Arzdasht*, dt. Asoj Sudi 8, vs 1754/1697.
208. *Amber Record*, dt. Jeth Vadi 5, vs 1755/1698.
209. *Arzdasht*, dt. Asadh Sudi 14, vs 1760/1703.
210. *Arzdasht*, dt. Kati Vadi 14, vs 1766/1709.
211. *Arsattha*, pargana Khohri (*rabi*), vs 1770/1713.
212. *Arzdasht*, dt. Asadh Vadi 4, vs 1755/1698.
213. Dilbagh Singh, 'The Role of the Mahajans in the Rural Economy in Eastern Rajasthan', *Social Scientist*, no. 22, 1974, pp. 20-31.
214. Irfan Habib, 'Potentialities of Capitalistic Development in the Economy of Mughal India', in *Essays in Indian History*, pp. 180-232.
215. However, in recent 'revisionist' historiography the role of a centralized Mughal state in providing a propitious environment for trade has been questioned. See C.A. Bayly, 'Epilogue to the Indian Edition', in Seema Alvi (ed.), *The Eighteenth Century in India*, Oxford University Press, 2002, p. 190.
216. *Arzdashts*, dt. Kati Sudi 13, vs 1742/1685 and Mah Vadi 9, vs 1742/1685.
217. *Arzdashts*, dt. Mah Sudi 3, vs 1743/1686 and Posh Vadi 7, vs 1743/1686; Posh Sudi 5, vs 1746/1689 and Sawan Sudi 4, vs 1749/1692.
218. *Arzdasht*, dt. Chet Sudi 4, vs 1743/1686.
219. *Amber Record*, dt. Bhadwa Vadi 9, Vs1742/1685.
220. Ibid., dt. Mah Vadi 9, vs 1742/1685.
221. Ibid., dt. Bhadwa Vadi 3, vs 1741/1684; and *arzdasht*, dt. Kati Vadi 6, vs 1751/1694.
222. *Arzdashts*, dt. Bhadwa Vadi 3, vs 1741/1684; Asoj Sudi 13 and Vadi 2, vs 1751/1694 and Falgun Sudi 7, vs 1760/1703.
223. *Arzdashts*, dt. Chet Sudi 4, vs 1743/1686 and Posh Sudi 6, vs 1743/1686.
224. *Amber Record*, dt. Posh Sudi 11, vs 1753/1696 and *arzdasht*, dt. Mah Vadi 2, vs 1761/1704.

225. *Amber Record*, dt. Falgun Sudi 14, vs 1744/1687.
226. *Arzdasht*, dt. Falgun Vadi 2, vs 1751/1694.
227. *Amber Record*, dt. Bhadwa Sudi 8, vs 1769/1712.
228. Maldhavi Bajekal, 'The State and Rural Grain Market in Eighteenth Century Eastern Rajasthan', *IESHR*, 254 (1988).
229. *Arsattha*, pargana Bayana, dt. vs 1750/1693.
230. *Arsattha*, pargana Kuthumbar, dt. vs 1770/1713.
231. *Arsattha*, pargana Kuthumbar, dt. vs 1774/1717.
232. Ibid.
233. The Ahir peasants of pargana Rinsi revolted along with their own caste's *bhomias*. In village Bhurka the Gujar and Meo peasants followed the *bhomias* of their respective caste in a similar rebellion. See *Amber Record*, dt. Asadh Sudi 4, vs 1722/1665.
234. Ibid.
235. *Arsattha*, pargana Bhusawar, vs 1751/1694.
236. *Arsattha*, pargana Bhusawar, vs 1773/1716.
237. *Arsattha*, pargana Kama, vs 1722/1665.
238. *Arzdashts*, dt. Chet Sudi 7, vs 1751/1694 and Asadh Vadi-2, vs 1752/1695.
239. *Arsattha*, pargana Khohri, vs 1773/1716.
240. *Arzdasht*, dt. Posh Sudi 5, vs 1774/1717.
241. *Arsattha*, pargana Khohri, vs 1773/1716.
242. *Arzdasht*, dt. Mangsir Vadi 5, vs 1750/1693.
243. *Arzdasht*, dt. Posh Vadi 1, vs 1750/1693.
244. *Ain-i-Akbari*, vol. II, pp. 202-3.
245. *Amber Record*, dt. Bhadwa Sudi 15, vs 1749/1692.
246. In the *hasil-firohi* column of the *arsathas* of various parganas, the caste of peasants is mentioned.
247. *Amber Record*, dt. Bhadwa Sudi 15, vs 1749/1692.
248. *Arzdasht*, dt. Asadh Vadi 5, vs 1742/1685.
249. *Arzdashts*, dt. Jeth Vadi 4, vs 1706/1649; Asoj Vadi 7, vs 1751/1694; Falgun Sudi 15, vs 1752/1695; Falgun Sudi 9, vs 1752/1695 and *Amber Record*, dt. Asadh Sudi 13, vs 1740/1683 and Chet Vadi 13, vs 1741/1684.
250. For the caste of the zamindars see Annexure I and the *Ain-i-Akbari*, vol. II (tr.), p. 279. For the caste of the peasants see *arsatha* of the respective parganas for various years.
251. R.P. Rana, 'Everyday Forms of Peasant Resistance'.
252. *Arzdashts*, dt. Mah Vadi 4, vs 1750/1693 and Asadh Sudi 15, vs 1761/1704.

7

Conclusion

The agrarian disturbances that swept the region located between Agra, Delhi, and Ajmer during the late seventeenth and early eighteenth century were inevitably multi-dimensional in character and multi-causal in origin, but it is possible to mark out certain defining features. The smooth functioning of the Mughal state was predicated upon equilibrium of pulls among the three chief components of the system, the *jagirdars*, the zamindars and the peasants. For nearly a century the equilibrium operated more or less satisfactorily from the point of view of *jagirdars* and zamindars, even as the burden was borne by the peasantry. A more or less customarily accepted share of the produce of the peasants' land and labour was distributed between *jagirdar* and zamindar, again along conventionally accepted lines. Such a situation could continue only so long as no element capable of disrupting the equilibrium came to the fore: if, in other words, demand and supply of resources kept pace with each other and each group kept to its defined limits.

In our analysis of the pattern of rural settlements we found that the process of settling new villages was slow and desultory whereas the desertion of existing villages was phenomenal. Such a situation had a limiting impact on agricultural production. We have noted above on the basis of data for agricultural production that this was marked by a strong element of stability rather than any dramatic expansion. Indeed, considering the scale of village desertions, there should have been a tendency towards declining production levels. Long-term price fluctuations were to a large extent the result of influx of money rather than one of real economic changes. But revenue demand was far from stable; its tendency was to rise. As rural society was highly stratified, the fiscal pressure of the state was felt differently by each stratum of the peasantry. The middle ranking peasants, called *paltis,* were the worst affected. Overall quantitative evidence has helped us to establish that the burden of taxes was increasing.

This was the scenario in which each element exerted itself to maintain its subsistence levels; the consequent tensions traversed along several alignments. The peasantry, being subjected to a tightening squeeze, resisted tax in the form of quotidian struggles and armed uprisings of varying intensity. The zamindars, forever uncomfortable at being deprived of the major share of peasant surplus by the *jagirdars*, saw in this as opportunity to establish their supremacy. There is a remarkable expansion of zamindari right at all levels in our region and period. The smaller zamindar sought to become a bigger zamindar and the bigger zamindar sought to become even bigger, and no means were spared towards this end: purchase of zamindaris, taking of lands on *ijara* and sticking on, expulsion of other zamindars from their lands, and, of course, downright violence. The bigger zamindars also attempted to concentrate various shades of authority in their own hands, in a variety of offices: *jagirdari*, *faujdari*, *ijara*, etc.[1] The coalescence of different offices into one person became quite common.

One of the chief supports in such a flux was the caste and clan ties of various zamindars. We have noticed above an extreme manifestation of this support in the case of the Chauhans. There was considerable co-operation among each lineage group for reasons of caste and clan links leading them on to collective aggression. But that was one facet of the endeavour, not the only one. Rebels did transcend caste and clan barriers to launch major group offensives and zamindars of various castes and clans came together. The formation of a multi-caste zamindar front shows increasing awareness among the rebels about the situation. They pooled their resources and together confronted the imperial armies. Therefore the view that the revolts were solely a Jat venture, needs to be corrected. Another aspect of the revolts, though often underplayed, is a skilful use of fortresses (*garhis*) by the rebels as bases of resistance. The making and destruction of *garhis*, was such an important event that it looms large on our sources. These *garhis* were strategically located and well equipped with arms and other necessities of life. It would not be an exaggeration to say that each *thana* of the empire was matched by the *garhi* of some zamindar. There is yet another important item of information which has been overlooked by scholars so far. The rebels very often met in secret conferences where important decisions about defence and offence were taken. Moreover, the rebels frequently exchanged letters and shared information among themselves. Such a network of communication invariably helped the rebels to foil the designs of the imperial strategists. Thus the rebels had devised their own strategies to challenge the military might of the empire, so far intact.

It is these tensions, the off-shoot of expanding zamindaris, that forms the major backdrop of the agrarian disturbances under review. The chief beneficiaries of this flux were 'upstart' but not 'bandit' zamindar groups—the Jats in our region and the Narukas in the neighbourhood. Of these the Jats were to lead on to the formation of a state at Bharatpur. The Narukas laid the foundation of the emergence of their state at Alwar only in the eighteenth century.

In their offensive the Jat zamindars had to seek the support of their fellow caste men among the peasants. Partly as a protest against the rising demand of the state and partly owing to caste solidarity and a shared historical past, the linkages between the two rural groups were forged with considerable ease. In this they were helped by the attitude of the Mughal rulers who could observe no other dimension of the problem except one of law and order, and who sought the solution of the problem in enhancing the number of troopers under the *faujdars*' command. The Mughal emperors as well as the Kachhwaha rulers had made it a habit to use abusive words whenever the Jats were mentioned in their documents. The Jat zamindars apparently knew their constituency well; while Raja Ram and Churaman lost no time in plundering passing merchant carvans, and of course making special targets of the symbols of imperial authority such as *thanas* and treasuries, our evidence never mentions villages being looted by them. Occasionally, they attacked those villages which persisted in their loyalty to the rulers.

Such however is not the case in *sarkar* of Ranthambore where rebel zamindars attacked villages and made off with cattle and agricultural implements. Perhaps the heterogeneity of caste was one reason for this. At any rate, it is worth remembering that no new state was formed in a region where zamindars did not carry peasant support.

Zamindars and peasants very often attacked *qasbas*. These seats of revenue-collectors and the law enforcing authority, invited the wrath of the zamindars and the peasants. Differences in revenue rates on the cultivators of a *qasba* and villages, might have also created a distance between the inhabitants of *qasbas* and villagers. This perhaps accounts for the non-participation of *qasbas* in the uprisings of our region and period. Not a single revolt originated from a *qasba:* all had their origin in the villages. Most of the rebel zamindars mentioned in chapter 4 had their zamindaris in the villages which they began to fortify more assiduously as the Mughal state sent military expeditions against them. When Churaman had conquered the entire pargana of Khohri only *qasba* Khohri and three villages in its vicinity remained under the control of the *amil*. The villages were the real theatre of the armed uprisings while the role of the *qasbas* was to act as a grid of control for the administration.

Participation in the rebellion was not equal. *Chaudhuris* and *qanungos* did not participate. Their integration with the Mughal revenue administration was considerable and they identified more with the administration than with the cause of the rebels. Their interest was better served while working for the administration than by joining the ranks of the rebels. Economically, they were the most privileged group in the countryside. Moreover, they could not gain anything by joining the ranks of the refractory elements. Lastly, the *qanungos* who were largely from the *kayastha* and *bania* castes had more avenues to acquire wealth while operating the revenue machinery. The *chaudhuris* and *qanungos* not only thrived within the framework of the empire but also survived its collapse. How they escaped unscathed is a matter of further research.

As already stated, the *patels* were whole-heartedly with the peasants. All 'deputations' to the imperial or local courts for revenue concessions were led by *patels*. Even in flight and rebellion, the *patels* seem to have played a leading and prominent role. The reasons were many. First, the economic deterioration in the countryside affected the *patels* too. Second, the *patels* of a village were usually the leading members of the dominant caste. In fact, they were best placed to play the role of a link between the rebellious zamindar and peasant. In case of success, they could acquire zamindari rights and thereby consolidate their dominant position within their caste. In the locales of the Jat uprisings, the *patels* definitely played a central role. They became the instrument through which the rebellion of the zamindars and the peasants merged together in the parganas around Agra, Kol, and Khohri. In the Ranthambore *sarkar*, the rebellion of the zamindars and peasants did not however merge. The rebellious zamindars of this region very often 'kidnapped' *patels* and freed them on payment of ransom. Such conflict is missing in the records of the parganas of the Jat revolts.

It has been stated above that the disturbances in our region took place in the context of stable, even declining, production levels. This has an important bearing on the outcome of these disturbances. Clearly the acute tensions in society had not been the result of changes occurring within the production system; all the tensions had as their target a redistribution of surplus collected from the peasants. The classes that were contesting for enhanced shares in the surplus represented age-old property forms, even if the personnel were new. There was thus very little in these disturbances that could lead to amelioration in the miserable condition of peasants. Even the caste affinity that tied the zamindars and the peasants of our region proved ephemeral; it was left to be remembered only in folk tales once the Bharatpur state had been established and the Jat zamindars had acquired the mechanism for collecting surplus much as their Mughal masters once had. Even then, the Jat revolt can be termed successful, as it resulted in the expansion of Jat zamidaris[2] and the creation of a state covering the entire Braj region. In yet another outcome, the establishment of the Bharatpur state accelerated the process of social upgradation of the Jats in the existing caste hierarchy.[3] Rajput titles such as Rao, Thakur and Raja were conferred on many Jat zamindars by the Kachhwaha rulers and later Mughals.[4] The acquisition of political power by a section of the Jats of Braj worked as a catalyst for the Jats of other regions to assert their identity of a marshal caste.[5]

Jats today have a mixed memory of the events associated with the career of the Bharatpur state. Early Jat rebels such as Raja Ram (d. 1688) and Churaman (d. 1721) who heralded the rise of Jat power by driving the Mughals and Kachhwahas out of Braj; are less remembered. Later Jat rulers such as Surajmal (r. 1756-63) and Jawahar Singh (r. 1764-8) are fondly remembered as provider of a marshal identity to the community. However, in the context of political mobilization for achieving reservation quotas, ordinary Jats find the Bharatpur lore increasingly purposeless to preserve in memory. Yet it remains to be sung.

NOTES

1. *Arzdasht*, dt. Bhadwa Vadi 5, vs 1749/1692.
2. Irfan Habib, *Agrarian System*, p. 393.
3. *Sanad Parwana Bahi*, dt. Vaisakh Budi 2, vs 1838/1781, Rajasthan State Archives, Bikaner. In this *Sanad* the Rajputs and the Jats have been recognized as 'Hindu' castes, having equal rights at centres of pilgrimage.
4. *Dastur Komwar*, Register no. 11, Rajasthan State Archives, Bikaner.
5. Nonica Datta, *Forming an Identity: A Social History of the Jats*, Oxford University Press, New Delhi, 1999.

Glossary

The definitions and meanings of the terms given in this glossary reflect the sense in which they are used in the source documents.

abadi	habitation
asami	cultivator, revenue payer
asli	original (used for a village)
awwal	first class soil in terms of productivity
bahat	land under cultivation
banjar	waste land
baqaya	arrears of revenue
barani	rain-fed land
batai jinsi	crop-sharing
begar	unpaid service
begar kotri-ki	*begar* rendered to the *bhomia*
bigha	unit of area equal to 2/5 of an acre
bhara	cess to meet the expenses of transportation of grain
bhent	regular gift paid by the villages to the officials
bhog	grant made for the maintenance of temples
bhom	zamindari tenure
bhomia	local term for zamindar
bohra	money-lender
butayat	corruption of *buyutat*, stores
chahi	land irrigated from wells
chackar	a servant (used for soldiers)
chakla	a territory comprising of a group of *mahals*
chhapparbandi	making of a hut; denoting the settlement of a cultivator.
charas	leather bucket
chiknot	clay-loam
cahri	land under flood
dakhili	dependent village
dam	a copper coin
darobast	entire
dastur	custom; customary revenue rate
dastur amal	revenue schedule for the guidance of revenue officials
dhenkli	wooden scoop, a means of irrigation
dhol	drum

dihangi	a tax collected from the *patels* and *patwaris* until they presented themselves in the *amil's* court, if summoned
diwan	chief minister of a state
diwan huzuri	court of a chief minister/finance minister
dom	second class soil in terms of productivity
dufasli	land twice cultivated in a year
dungar	hill top
dundhari	a variant of the Rajasthani language spoken in the Jaipur area
farah-serina	exactions collected in *sers* appropriated by officials under *batai* system
faslana	tax on crops
gaveti	one who is a permanent resident of a village
garhi	fortress constructed usually by zamindars
gharuhala	land holder with superior rights
girani	dearness
haljota	cultivators
halsal	revenue collection in the current year
hasbul mufasal	realization of revenue according to kharif and rabi harvests
hasil	actual realization of revenue; state's share of the produce of land
hasil-ferohi	penalties imposed by the *amil* or *faujdar* on offenders
hasil ghas	cess on grazing
hasil-Kawarya	levy to raise money for some Purohits
hasil lakri	cess on wood taken from the forest
hundi	bill of exchange
huzuri	court of a ruler
ijara	farming out of revenue of any given source
istamrari	in perpetuity
jagir	assignment of revenue in lieu of salary
jagirdar	holder of a jagir
jama	revenue payable or assessed revenue
jamabandi	total assessment of revenue
jaribana	cess to meet the expenses incurred on the measurement of land
jihat	taxes levied in order to meet expenses incurred in connection with the assessment and collection of land revenue
kamin	menials
kankar	village boundary
khalisa	lands whose revenue goes to the state exchequer
kharara	land of dried up ponds
kharif	autumn harvest

khasra	field book of a village specifying the number of *asamis*, area, the quality of soil and crop grown
khenchal	dispute
kori bhumi ki	a cess realized by the *bhomias* from the traders
kotri	establishment of a *bhomia*
lata-kharach	cess charged to meet expenses incurred on the division of crops
latadori	estimate of crops and measurement of land
laik zaraat	arable land
likhtang	written undertaking
magro	hilly land
mahajan	moneylender and or trader
mal	land revenue
malba	financial pool of a village
mal-o-jihat	mal and jijat taxes merged into one head
mal-zamini	surety
mapa	tax on the sale of commodities
mauza	village
muafiq-jamabandi	revenue realized in accordance with assessment
muchalka	bond
muqarara jama	total expected revenue
mutaliba	state's financial claims outstanding against a jagirdar
muwazana	accounts of produce, revenue, etc. of various years of a particular village or pargana
nadari	indigence
nahri	canal-irrigated (land)
nalbant	share
naniponi	artisans and menials
nankar	revenue-free land grant for subsistence in lieu of service obligation
naraju-raiyat	peasants unhappy with the administration
neel	indigo
nyota	invitation (at the time of marriage ceremony)
pahi	non-resident cultivator
panch	member of a village panchayat
parat	land from which the plough has been temporarily withdrawn
pargana	the administrative sub-division of a *sarkar* under the Mughals
parwana	order, directive
patel	headman of a village
patta	document given to a revenue payer, indicating his obligations
patti	portion of a village

patwari	the village accountant
peshkash	tribute paid to higher-ups
polchi (Polaj)	land under continuous cultivation
potadar	treasurers
punya udik	religious endowment, charitable grant
qanungo	hereditary revenue record keeper of a pargana
rabi	Spring harvest
rahadari	Transit duties
raiyat	cultivators in general
raiyati or *palti*	ordinary peasants
rozindar	daily wager
sadir	expenses to meet the needs of officials on tour
sahukar	banker-cum-trader
sair-jihat	taxes other than mal or land revenue
salami	salutation money paid by villages to officials
sakimi	poverty
sanad	letter of appointment.
sarhi	cess related to the assessment of *zabti* crops
sarikat	in part
sarkar	territorial subdivision of a Mughal province
sehna	watchman
sehngi	cess paid to the watchman
sehngi dihangi	lumpsum payment to watchman
som	third class land in terms of productivity
sor	saline land
suba	province under the Mughals
syalu	*kharif*
taalluqa	connection; a zamindari territory
taalluqdar	holder of *taalluqa*
tagai	agricultural loan granted to cultivator by the state
taka	copper coin.
taqmina	detailed account of the estimate of revenue, crops, and yield of a village
taqsirana	fine on various offences
talbana	cess similar to *dihangi*; paid in lumpsum
tankina	exaction collected in *taka* under the *batai* system
tankhwah	salary
tankhwah jagir	*jagir* in lieu of pay
tapdar	revenue officer of the *tappa*
tappa	sub-division of a pargana
thanadar	officer in charge of a *thana* or police station
thikana	hereditary estate of a Rajput notable
thikanadar	holder of *thikana*
topchi	musketeer

tulai	cess for weighing the grain
udiki	holder of *udik*
ujar	desolate
unhalu	*rabi*
vagdum	cess paid to the *bhomia*, *jagirdar* or *patel* at the time of the marriage of the daughter of a villager
vahda	uproar, fear
van	cotton
var	sugarcane
vasi	*bhomia's* settlement and residence
vasidar	tenants of a *jagirdar* or a *bhomia* working in the *vasi*
vav	exactions of officials in addition to the *jama*
virar	special levy imposed on peasants and *mahajans* to meet miscellaneous expenses
wadh	land allotted to one appointed to protect the village boundary
wadhdar	holder of *wadh*
watan	hereditary dominion of a chief
watan-jagir	hereditary dominion of a chieftain
yaddashti	memoranda
zabitana	cess collected to pay to the measuring parties
zabti	method of land revenue assessment involving the measurement of land and payment of revenue in cash
zortalab	rebellious

Appendix 1 to Chapter 4

TABLE 1: LIST OF REBELLIOUS ZAMINDARS

S.No.	*Name*	*Zamindari Village(s)*	*Pargana(s)*	*Source: Arzdashts*
1	*2*	*3*	*4*	*5*
1.	Vijay Ram & Udai Singh Narukas	–	14 *mahals*	Asadh Vadi 5, vs 1742/1685
2.	Rao Hathi Singh Naruka	Varkhera	Bharkol	Kati Sudi 9, vs 1759/1702
	-do-		Jalalpur & Bharkol	Mangsir Sudi 15, vs 1759/1702
	-do-	12 villages	Bharkol	Jeth Vadi 1, vs 1761/1704
3.	Kishan Singh Naruka	Mal wa & Fatehpur	Maujpur	Bhadon Vadi 5, vs 1749/1692
	-do-	Vachhgaon*	Naharkhoh	Mangsir Sudi 15, vs 1759/1702
	-do-		7 *mahals*	Kati Vadi 6, vs 1759/1702
	-do-		Banawar	Asadh Sudi 14, vs 1760/1703
	-do-	Bishangarh	Bahatri	Falgun Sudi 7, vs 1760/1703
	-do-	Kaithwara	Khohri	Sawan Vadi , vs 1783/1726
	-do-	Many villages	Naharkhoh	Asadh Sudi 4, vs 1787/1730
4.	Rao Fateh Singh Naruka	Kakore*	Kakore	Kati Sudi 4, vs 1744/1687
5.	Pratap Singh Naruka	Soda	Malpura	Asadh Sudi 14, vs 1744/1687
6.	Sudarshan Naruka	–	Dausa	Sawan Sudi 3, vs 1733/1677
7.	Shyam Singh Naruka	Dablula	–	Kati Sudi 13, vs 1742/1685
8.	Jas Karan Naruka	Chhapari	Mauzabad	Jeth Sudi 8, vs 1744/1682
9.	Devi Singh and Pratap Singh Narukas	8 villages	Jalalpur	Bhadon Sudi 13, vs 1749/1692

10.	Guman Singh and Puran Mal Narukas	Many villages	Bharkol & Umarni	Bhadon Sudi 13, vs 1749/1692
11.	Karan Singh Naruka	3 villages	Bharkol	Mangsir Sudi 15, vs 1759/1702
	-do-	Khohra*	Maujpur	-do-
	-do-		Jalalpur & Bharkol	-do-
12.	Sawai Ram Naruka	–	Mandawar	Asadh Sudi 14, vs 1740/1683
13.	Ishwar Singh Naruka	–	Toda Thek	Asadh Sudi 14, vs 1760/1703
14.	Amar Singh Rajawat	Dulheka	Dausa	Sawan Vadi 12, vs 1733/1677
15.	Jait Singh Rajawat	Paharya*	Chatsu	Chet Sudi 1, vs 1740/1683
16.	Kesari Singh Rajawat	Chandlai*	Chatsu	Chet Sudi 1, vs 1740/1683
17.	Mukand Singh Rajawat	Ghasotta	Bhairana	Chet Sudi 1, vs 1740/1683
18.	Sujan Singh Rajawat	Kapriwas*	Bhairana	Asadh Sudi 14, vs 1740/1683
19.	Gopinath Rajawat	Bhadolai	Malpura	Asadh Sudi 13, vs 1740/1683
20.	Daulti Singh Rajawat	Pandan	Malpura	Asadh Sudi 13, vs 1740/1683
21.	Rughnath Rajawat	Kherli-Madan	Malarna	Asoj Vadi 4, vs 1742/1685
22.	Shyam Singh Rajawat	Pilloo-Khera	Boli	Asoj Vadi 4, vs 1742/1685
23.	Mohkam Singh Rajawat	Rughnathpur	–	Mah Vadi 11, vs 1743/1686
24.	Gaj Singh Rajawat etc.	–	Boli	Posh Vadi 7, vs 1743/1686
25.	Devi Singhmal Rajawat	2 villages	Tonk	Asadh Sudi 13, vs 1743/1686
26.	Raj Singh Rajawat	Rajgarh*	Mehamdabad	Mangsir Vadi 7, vs 1744/1687
27.	Guman Singh Rajawat	10 villages	Chatsu	Falgun Sudi 14, vs 1745/1686
28.	Manohar Singh Rajawat	–	Dausa	Asadh Vadi 8, vs 1749/1692
29.	Sawal Singh Rajawat	–	Malarna	Kati Vadi 5, vs 1749/1692
30.	Anand Singh Rajawat	Didwani	Khirni	Kati Vadi 5, vs 1749/1692

(contd.)

TABLE 1 (*contd.*)

1	*2*	*3*	*4*	*5*
31.	Sangram Singh Rajawat	32 villages	Chatsu	Asoj Vadi 7, vs 1751/1694
32.	Kushal Singh Rajawat	Dattwas*	Chatsu	Asoj Vadi 7, vs 1751/1694
33.	Vijay Singh Rajawat	2 villages	Chatsu	Asoj Vadi 7, vs 1751/1696
34.	Sardar Singh Rajawat* S/o Sangram Singh	Vorda	Boli	Falgun Sudi 5, vs 1752/1695
35.	Jorawar Singh Rajawat* S/o Sangram Singh	4 villages	Boli	Falgun Sudi 5, vs 1752/1695
36.	Anand Singh Rajawat* S/o Sangram Singh	–	Malarna	Falgun Sudi 7, vs 1755/1698
37.	Sawal Singh Rajawat* S/o Sangram Singh	Gopalpura	Boli	Kati Vadi 14, vs 1761/1704
38.	Sardar Singh Rajawat Malarna, Boli & Mauzabad	10 villages	Chatsu, Niwai,	Falgun Sudi 9, vs 1752/1705
39.	Kalyan Singh Rajawat	Dewaldha	Malarna	Chet Vadi 11, vs 1752/1705
40.	Madho Singh Rajawat	4 villages	Bhangarh	Asadh Sudi 2, vs 1754/1707
41.	Hari Singh Rajawat	Didawta*	Chatsu	Kati Vadi 14, vs 1754/1707
42.	Kushal Singh and Mohan Singh Rajawat	–	Boli	Kati Vadi 14, vs 1761/1704
43.	Sawal Singh Rajawat	–	Boli	Mangsir Vadi 10, vs 1761/1704
44.	Hari Singh Rajawat	Sumelya*	Niwai	Asadh Sudi 15, vs 1761/1704
45.	Kushal Singh Rajawat	–	Niwai	Kati Vadi 14, vs 1760/1703
46.	Himmat Singh Rajawat	7 villages	Tonk	Kati Vadi 14, vs 1766/1709
47.	Vijay Singh Rajawat	3 villages	–	Kati Vadi 14, vs 1766/1709
48.	Sardar Singh	Nangal-Chhara	Chatsu	Jeth Vadi 11, vs 1775/1718

49.	Sangram Singhawats	4 villages	–	Sawan Sudi 12, vs 1761/1704
50.	Bal Kishan Shekhawat	–	Lalsar	Vaisakh Vadi 14, vs 1744/1687
51.	Pao Jagat Singh Shekhawat	–	Manoharpur	Posh Sudi 6, vs 1746/1689
52.	Ratan Singh Shekhawat	–	–	Posh Sudi 6, vs 1746/1689
53.	Brij Bhan and Inder Bhan Shekhawats	–	Amarsar	Kati Vadi 11, vs 1751/1694
54.	Jagat Singh Shekhawat	–	Kasali	Kati Vadi 14, vs 1754/1697
55.	Kesari Singh Shekhawat	–	Rewasa	Kati Vadi 14, vs 1754/1697
56.	Ajab Singh Chauhan	Mohlai	Gijgarh	Kati Vadi 14, vs 1744/1687
57.	Mohan Das Chauhan	Morhar	Gijgarh	Kati Vadi 14, vs 1744/1687
58.	Rawat Karan Chauhan	–	Gudha	Mangsir Sudi 15, vs 1746/1689
59.	Kirpa Ram Chauhan	Kaloli	–	Jeth Vadi 2, vs 1746/1689
60.	Bihari Ram Chauhan	Mandawar	Liwali	Kati Vadi 9, vs 1746/1689
61.	Sampat Ram Chauhan	4 villages	Liwali	Kati Vadi 9, vs 1746/1689
62.	Ajab Singh Chauhan	Manha	Salawad	Bhadwa Vadi 13, vs, 1743/1686
63.	Chauhans	Morda*	Hindaun	Asoj Sudi 7, vs 1743/1686
	Chauhans	–	Saner	Falgun Sudi 14, vs 1745/1688
	Chauhans	Ugoh, Vagari	Malarna	Chet Sudi 10, vs 1746/1689
	Chauhans	6 villages	Liwali	Kati Vadi 9, vs 1746/1689
64.	Ran Singh Kalyanot	Mahua*	Toda Bhim	Posh Sudi 1, vs 1746/1689
65.	Sawai Ram Kalyanot	Kaladehra	Saner	Asadh Vadi 8, vs 1749/1692
66.	Raj Singh Kalyanot	Pyonkhar*	Toda Bhim	Kati Vadi 4, vs 1753/1696
67.	Chitter Singh Kalyanot	Pipalkhera*	Toda Bhim	Kati Vadi 4, vs 1753/1696
68.	Surat Singh Kalyanot	Hingua*	Toda Bhim	Sawan Vadi 13, vs 1750/1693
69.	Daulat Singh Kalyanot	Pilori	Gudha	Asoj Vadi 13, vs 1753/1694

(contd.)

TABLE 1 (*contd.*)

1	2	3	4	5
70.	Santokh Singh Kalyanot	Patoli*	Toda Bhim	Asoj Vadi 14, vs 1761/1704
71.	Ran Singh Kalyanot	Sikrai*	Toda Bhim	Mah Sudi 12, vs 1742/1685
72.	Un-named Kalyanots	–	Fatehpur, Machilpur	Jeth Vadi 13, vs 1752/1695
73.	Hari Singh Khangarot	Diggi*	Malpura	Asoj Sudi 15, vs 1742/1685
74.	Hari Singh Khangarot	Lawa*	Malpura	Bhadwa Vadi 13, vs 1743/1686
75.	Gopal Singh Khangarot	Ganwar	Malpura	Asadh Sudi 14, vs 1740/1683
76.	Dungar Singh Khangarot	Rojhari, Hirgoda	Bhairana	Chet Sudi 1, vs 1740/1683
77.	Shyam Singh Khangarot	Akroda	-do-	-do-
78.	Kushal Singh Khangarot	Palhuwas*	-do-	-do-
79.	Jagroop Singh Khangarot	Kachner	-do-	-do-
80.	Udai Singh Khangarot	Kinnor	-do-	-do-
81.	Hari Singh Panchanot	Aloda	Udai	Asadh Sudi 13, vs 1740/1683
82.	Bharmal Panchanot	Jaswantpur-Khurd Sahar	-do-	-do-
83.	Than Singh Panchanot	Sikanderapur	-do-	-do-
84.	Pratap Singh panchanot	Muderdu*	-do-	-do-
85.	Shyam Singh Panchanot	Jiharna*	-do-	-do-
86.	Todarmal Panchanot	Varnala*	Malarna	Sawan Sudi 6, vs 1750/1693
87.	Santokh Ram Panchanot	Naroli	-do-	-do-
88.	Gopal Singh Panchanot	Gopalpur	-do-	Chet Vadi 11, vs 1752/1695
89.	Fateh Singh Panchanot	–	Amargarh	Mangsir Vadi 2, vs 1749/1692
90.	Dhan Singh Panchanot	Jiwad*	Malarna	Mah Vadi 2, vs 1773/1677
91.	Suraj Mal Panchanot	Sirsoli, Vichhore*	Behror	Sawan Sudi 11, vs 1775/1718
92.	Ratan Pal Jadon and Surat Singh Jadon	–	Karoli	Kati Vadi 5, vs 1749/1692

93.	Ratan Pal Jadon	Hirapur*, Narainpur	Malarna	Kati Vadi 14, vs 1750/1693
94.	Surat Singh Jadon	8 villages	-do-	Chet Vadi 11, vs 1752/1695
95.	Vakhat Singh Jadon	Kanuhar*	Hindaun	Vaisakh Sudi 11, vs 1752/1695
96.	Ajab Singh Jadon	Motharipur*	-do-	Vaisakh Sudi 11, vs 1752/1695
97.	Ram Singh Bargujar	Khutehta*	Bharkol	Mangsir Sudi 3, vs 1747/1690
98.	Hirday Ram Bargujar	-do-	-do-	Mah Vadi 4, vs 1761/1704
99.	Bargujars	Bhura*	Toda Bhim	Bhadwa Sudi 1, vs 1741/1684
	Bargujars	Malakhera*	Punkhar	Kati Vadi 13, vs 1741/1684
	Bargujars	–	Mandawar	Bhadwa Sudi 1, vs 1741/1684
101.	Surat Ram Shivbhrampota	–	Kot	Kati Sudi 13, vs 1766/1709
102.	Bhav Singh Solanki	–	Tonk	Falgun Vadi 2, vs 1751/1694
103.	Jodh Singh Solanki	Pandana	-do-	Chet Vadi 3, vs 1762/1705
104.	Rawata Mina	Niwoda Jhak	Malarna	Chet Vadi 11, vs 1752/1695
105.	Pahar Singh Sultanot	3 villages	Tonk	Kati Vadi 2, vs 1766/1709
106.	Gopinath Sultanot	6 villages	-do-	Kati Vadi 14, vs 1766/1709
107.	Abhay Singh Balibhadravat	Pihawari	-do-	-do-
108.	Dura Meo	Pahat	Kama	Asadh Vadi 14, vs 1766/1709
109.	Raja Ram Jat	Sansani*	Ao	Chet Sudi 1, vs 1744/1687
110.	Ram Chehar Jat	Soghar*	–	Chet Sudi 1, vs 1744/1687
111.	Churaman Jat	Jagira	Bhusawar	Kati Vadi 11, vs 1766/1709
112.	Amar Singh Chauhan	Khair*	Kol (*tappa* Khair)	Vaisakh Vadi 11, vs 1749/1694
	Nanda Jat			
113.	Jats	Vinani*	Kama	Asadh Vadi Amawasya, vs 1766/1709

Notes: Blank space indicates non-availability of information.
*Indicates a *garhi*.

Appendix 2 to Chapter 4

TABLE 2: PARGANA-WISE DISTRIBUTION OF CASTES

S.No.	Pargana	Zamindar castes/clans	Source: Arzdasht
1	2	3	4
1.	Malarna	Jadon, Panchanots, Rajawats Asadh Sudi 2, vs 1761/1704	Falgun Sudi 7, vs 1755/1698
2.	Udai, Salawad Gudha	Panchanots, Chauhans	Asoj Sudi 9, vs 1740/1683
3.	Bhura	Minas, Gujars	Mangsir Vadi 2, vs 1749/1692
4.	Bayana	Gaurvas, Jats, Panwars	Asoj Vadi 14, vs 1752/1705
5.	Khohri	Jats, Rajputs, Meos	Asadh Sudi 7, vs 1769/1712
6.	Pahari	Jats, Meos	Sawan Sudi 1, vs 1775/1718
7.	Antrauli, Baliram	Jats, Chauhans	Vaisakh Vadi 11, vs 1749/1692
8.	Sonkhar	Jats, Kalyanots, Narukas,	Asadh Sudi 14, vs 1760/1703
9.	Kuthumbar	Jats, Narukas	Asadh Sudi 14, vs 1760/1703
10.	Chatsu*	Amber Raja	Posh Vadi 7, vs 1746/1687
	Dausa	-do-	Mah Vadi 5, vs 1746/1687
	Bairath*	Kachhwaha Raja	Sawan Vadi 7, vs 1746/1687
	Malarna**	-do-	Chet Sudi 10, vs 1746/1687
	Banawar, Mandawar*	-do-	Falgun Sudi 12, vs 1740/1683
	Niwai, Chatsu	-do-	Bhadwa Sudi 12, vs 1756/1699
	Jhilai, Boli, Bhagotgarh*	-do-	Chet Sudi 12, vs 1746/1689

Mauzabad**	-do-	Falgun Sudi 12, vs 1746/1689
Kati Vadi 14, vs 1761/1704		
Mauzabad, Jhak, Bhairana	-do-	Bhadwa Sudi 5, vs 1761/1704
Abhaneri*	-do-	Asadh Vadi 1, vs 1754/1697
Bharkol, Umarni	-do-	Bhadwa Sudi 13, vs 1749/1692
Banawar	-do-	Asadh Sudi 2, vs 1754/1697
Bharkol, Jalalpur,	-do-	Mangsir Sudi 14, vs 1759/1702 and
Khilohra, Vadhera		Kati Vadi 6, vs 1759/1702
Rajore*	-do-	Vaisakh Sudi 10, vs 1762/1705
Khohri	-do-	Chet Sudi 6, vs 1769/1712
Toda Raisinghpur	-do-	Asoj Vadi Amawasya, vs 1742/1685

Notes: * The Amber officials were negotiating with different imperial officials to get the zamindari of these parganas.
** The zamindari of these parganas were under dispute.

Appendix 1 to Chapter 6

TABLE 1: PARGANAS THAT SAW REVOLTS (PERIOD 1650 TO 1735)

Caste/clan of the Zamindars	*Period of the uprisings*	*Total years of revolt*	*Parganas in which the uprisings took place/affected by the uprisings*
Jats	1669 to 1735	65	Bhusawar, Hodal, Palwal, Kama, Sonkhar, Kuthumbar, Banawar, Maujpur, Toda Bhim, Bahatri, Khohri Rana, Pahari, Tapal, Antrauli, Kol, Bayana, Baliram, Hindaun, Fatehpur, Nagar, Harsana, Pindayan, Soghar, Sahar, Mandawar, Alwar, Pawta, Rehlari, Raipur, Akbarabad to Shahjahanabad
Narukas	1680 to 1730	50	Malpura, Fagi, Sonkhar, Toda Raisinghpur, Bharkol, Sherpur, Bhagotgarh, Maujpur, Bahatri, Jalalpur, Naharkhoh, Kuthumbar, Alwar, Banawar, Toda Bhim, Khilohra, Mungona, Baroda Meo, Khohri, Rana, Jhilai, Umarni, Pindayan, Punkhar, Harsana, Sonkhar-Sonkhari, Niwai, Chatsu and Hasanpur
Chauhans	1650 to 1715	65	Udai, Salawad, Hindaun, Saneri, Lalsot, Dausa, Kol, Gijgarh, Kuwawa, Liwali, Behror and Bawal
Kalyanots	1683 to 1715	32	Toda Bhim, Hindaun, Udai, Machilpur, Godhala, Abhaneri, Saneri and Bahatri
Rajawats	1676 to 1718	42	Udai, Malarna, Boli, Dausa, Niwai, Chatsu and Khirni.
Sangramsinghawats	1695 to 1705	10	Chatsu, Niwai, Fagi, Malarna, Lawani, Mauzabad, Saner, Gijgarh and Lawana.
Panchanots	1685 to 1714	29	Malarna, Udai and Salawad
Bargujars	1687 to 1705	18	Bharkol, Banawar, Mandawar and Bahatri

Khangarots	1687 to 1696	9	Udai, Malpura, Toda Raisinghpura, Bahatri and Bhairana.
Shekhawats	1686 to 1693	7	Rewasa, Kasli, Khandela, Kaladehra, Behror and Bawal
Solanki	1694 to 1709	15	Tonk and Niwai
Gujars	1688 to 1695	7	Bhuda, Bayana, Hindaun, Bhusawar, Machilpur and Gudhala.
Minas	1688 to 1698	10	Bhuda, Bayana, Hindaun, Bhusawar and Machilpur
Gaurvas	1688 to 1689	2	Bayana, Hindaun, Bhusawar and Machilpur
Jadams	1692 to 1698	6	Hindaun, Bayana, Malarna and Karoli
Panwars	1683 to 1695	12	Bayana, Hindaun, Malpura and Fatehpur
Meos	1650 to 1713	63	Khohri, Pahari, Kama, Khilohra, Kotla
Vakavats	1692	1	Khohri Rana and Saneri
Tanwars	1703	1	Mewat, Behrawar and Bawal
Nathawats	1686 to 1703	17	Pahari
Mansinghawats	–	–	Chatsu
Sultanots	1698 to 1710	12	Tonk
Valibhadrawats	1698	1	Tonk
Miscellaneous	1683 to 1717	34	Sonkhar, etc. (15 parganas), Malpura to Mewat, Kasli, Saner, Dausa, Tapal, Kol, Hindaun, Abhaneri, Bhairana, Udai, Senganer, Banhetta, Barwara, Nainwai, Niwai, Mauzabad, Chatsu, Jhak and Tonk

Note: This table has been prepared on the basis of the *Arzdashts* and the *Amber Records*. It is possible that all the rebellious acts of the zamindars are not covered by these documents. Hence the duration of their uprisings could have been more extensive than indicated in this table.

Appendix 2 to Chapter 6

TABLE 2: DESCRIPTION OF JAT STRONGHOLDS/*GARHIS*

Fort/Area	*Description*	*Zamindar*	*Location*
1. Sonkh		Raja Ram Jat	16 miles south-west of Mathura 8 miles south-west of Sinsini
2. Mahaban, Kotban, Kosi, Hodal, Chhatta	Heavy Jat Concentration		
3. Govardhan	Jungle between the hills Held in strength by the rebels	Lodha b/o Bukna	12 miles west of Mathura
4. Gantholi	Bands of Jats in the jungle		3 miles west of Govardhan
5. Ao	Jats moving like wolves		16 miles west of Govardhan and 7 miles north-east of Sinsini
6. Sabora	Which nobody had attacked before		6 miles south-west of Sinsini
7. Kasot	Link between Sinsini and Sogor, Abair, Pingora. Region extremely difficult to access	Bukna Jat	8 miles east of Sinsini
8. Vagsariya and Jarara Khair	Doab	Amar Singh Chauhan	
9. Tappal	Moving bands of Jat rebels		12 miles west of Aligarh
10. Rath	Gateway of Khair	Birju and Taula Jat	
11. Abair	Dense forest of thorny trees	Alia Jat b/o Nanda Jat	7 miles west of Kumher
12. Sogor	Dense forest of thorny trees	Sogaria Jats	4 miles south of Abair
13. Rara		Rauriya Jats	6 miles east of Abair

14. Pingora		Fateh Ram s/o Raja Ram Jat	18 miles south-west of Abair
15. Bhatauli	On River Banganga 'junction of the rebel Jats of Bayana and Bhusawar'		8 miles south-west of Nadbai
16. Raisis			4 miles east of Nadbai
17. Helek	Eight *naglas*, i.e. fortified houses		8 miles south of Kumbher
18. Kuthumbar			13 miles north of Bhatauli
19. Daryapur	Three villages	Mandhata	
20. Bhusawar Jharsauli	Kharistan i.e. land of thorns		
21. Nathila			
22. Kesra		Hari Singh	4 miles north of Bhatauli
23. Barah	'A belt of thorny forest 1 *kos* in width and 11 *kos* in length'		
24. Kharahra			Halfway between Bayana and Bhusawar
25. Chinkara	Surrounded by thick forest	Maujjiya Jats	8 miles south of Fatehpur
26. Chapsara	Men, women fought together for the Jat fugitives of Mathura		8 miles north of Sikri
27. Dura			7 miles north-east of Chinkara
28. Arhera	Rebellious village giving stiff resistance		2 miles north of Dura
29. Sarsondha			1 mile west of Rupbas
30. Bawari		Sukha Jat	18 miles west of Chinkara
31. Chhaiya		Sunderman Gujar	
32. Khorasa			4 miles west of Khanwa

(*contd.*)

TABLE 2 (*contd.*)

Fort/Area	*Description*	*Zamindar*	*Location*
33. Makanda	Rebellious	Jats	6 miles south-west of Agra
34. Bargaon	Fugitive Jats hiding here		3 miles west of Jagnair
35. Jawar	The rebels are predominantly Jats in Mahaban, Sadabad Jalesar	Nanda Jat	2 miles north-east of Mursan
36. Nuh	Allies of Nanda Jat	Nuhwar Jats	7 miles north-east of Jalesar
37. Kiharari		Bainilal s/o Nanda	6 miles north-west of Mahaban

Note: *Based on the *arzdashts* written during VS 1740-50 (AD 1683-96).

Bibliography

ARCHIVAL SOURCES*

1. *Arzdashts*, AD 1650 to 1750.
2. *Amber Records*, AD 1650 to 1750.
3. *Arsatthas*:
   Arsattha Mujmil of pargana Bahatri for the years of AD 1665, 69, 84, 86, 88, 89, 96, 97, 1706, 8, 10, 11, 16, 17, 18, 20, 21, 23, 24, and 25.
   Arsattha Mujmil of pargana Jalalpur for the years of AD 1666, 89, 90, 91, 92, 1709, 11, 12, 13, 16, 18, 19, 20, 23, 35, 36, 39, 40, 41, 42 and 43.
   Arsattha Mujmil of pargana Khohri Rana for the years of AD 1664, 66, 1713, 15, 16, 33, 35, 41, 43, 44, 47 and 51.
   Arsattha Mujmil of pargana Hindaun for the years of AD 1713, 14, 17, 20, 21, 23, 24, 27, 28, 30, 32, 33, 34, 46, 47 and 48.
   Arsattha Mujmil of pargana Pahari for the years of AD 1716, 17, 30, 31, 33, 34, 35, 36, 37, 38, 39 and 40.
   Arsattha Mujmil of pargana Toda Bhim for the years of AD 1663, 1713, 14, 15, 16, 17, 18, 20, 21, 30, 31, 32, 33, 34, 35, 36, 37, 42 and 43.
   Arsattha Mujmil of pargana Bhusawar for the years of AD 1716, 27, 30, 31, 33 and 34.
   Arsattha Mujmil of pargana Kama for the years of AD 1665 and 1769.
   Arsattha Mujmil of pargana Udai for the years AD 1712 to 1743.
   Arsattha Mujmil of pargana Chatsu for the year of AD 1664.
   Arsattha Mujmil of pargana Malarna for the year of AD 1665.
   Arsattha Mujmil of pargana Dausa for the years of AD 1665 and 1703.
   Arsattha Mujmil of pargana Sahar for the years of AD 1689 and 1690.
   Arsattha Mujmil of pargana Malpura for the year of AD 1714.
   Arsattha Mujmil of pargana Bayana for the years of AD 1693, 1716, 26, 27, 28, 29 and 30.
   Arsattha Mujmil of pargana Banawar for the year AD 1713.
   Arsattha Mujmil of pargana Ao for the year AD 1693 and 1694.
   Arsattha Mujmil of pargana Kotla for the years of AD 1665, 1713, 1735 and 1736.

Note: *All the documents are dated in the Vikrami Samvat (VS) which is ahead of the common Era by 57 years. I have converted the years of Vikrami Samvat into the years of Christian Era.

Arsattha Mujmil of pargana Niwai for the year of AD 1664.
Arsattha Mujmil of pargana Akbarabad for the years of AD 1731 and 1732.
Arsattha Mujmil of pargana Fagi for the year of AD 1697.
Arsattha Mujmil of pargana Tonk for the year of AD 1708.
Arsattha Mujmil of pargana Maujpur for the year of AD 1714.
Arsattha Mujmil of pargana Kuthumbar for the years of AD 1713 and 1717.

4. *Chithis*. From 1700 to 1750 for parganas Alwar, Mathura, Hindaun, Ghazi-ka-Thana, Pindayan, and Pahari etc.
5. *Dastur Amal*
   Dastur-amal pargana Antela, VS 1784/1727.
   Dastur-amal pargana Niwai, VS 1800/1743.
   Dastur-amal pargana Gijgarh, VS 1794/1737.
   Dastur-amal pargana Sonkhar-Sonkhari, VS 2773/1716.
   Dastur-amal pargana Chatsu, VS 1769/1712.
   Dastur-amal pargana Maujpur, VS 1770/1713.
   Dastur-amal pargana Khohri Rana, AH 1049-50/1642.
6. *Khatoot Ahakaran*.
7. *Likhtang*.
8. *Muwazana Kalan* pargana Hindaun and Toda Bhim.
9. *Ro Naaz-ki* pargana Bawal AD 1664.
10. Miscallenous *Sanads*.
11. *Taqsim* Papers
    Muwazana dahsala, pargana, Hindaun, VS 1790-99 (AD 1733-42).
    Taqsim dahsala, pargana, Punkhar, VS 1787-98 (AD 1730-41).
    Taqsim pandrehsala, pargana, Antela Bhabhra, VS 1706-1720 (AD 1649-63).
    Taqsim dahsala, pargana, Antela Bhabhra, VS 1756-65 (AD 1699-1708).
    Taqsim dahsala, pargana, Bahatri, VS 1761-70 (AD 1704-13).
    Taqsim dahsala, pargana, Udai, VS 1791-1800 (AD 1734-43).
    Taqmina papers are usually found inside the *arsatthas*.
12. *Yaddashtis*
    Hal Bail Jubani Patel, Patwari pargana Chatsu AD 1666.
    Yaddashti Hal Bail pargana, Pindayan AD 1726.
    Yaddashti Pradakhti Gaon pargana Malarna, AD 1723.
    Yaddashti Raqba Hal pargana Kotla, VS 1723/1666.
    Yaddashti Haqiqati Hal pargana Chal Kalana, VS 1722/1665.
    Yaddashti Ghar pargana Wazirpur, VS 1783/1726.
13. *Dastur Komwar*, Register nos. 1, 2, 3, 7, 11 and 23.
14. *Sanad Parwana Bahi*, dt. Vaisakh Budi 2, VS 1838/1781, Rajasthan State Archives, Bikaner.

15. A Descriptive List of the Vakil Reports Addressed to the Rulers of Jaipur, vol. I (Persian), published by the Rajasthan State Archives, Rajasthan, Bikaner, 1967.

PERSIAN SOURCES IN TRANSLATION

Chachnama: An Ancient History of Sindh. Mirza Kalichbeg Fredenbegi, Delhi, Idarah-i-Adabiyat-i-Delhi 1900; rpt., 1979.

Abdul Qadir Badaoni, *Muntkhab-ut-Tawarikh*, tr. W.H. Lowe, vol. II, Calcutta, Asiatic Society of Bengal, 1864–9.

Abul Fazl, *Akbar-Nama,* H. Beveridge, Calcutta: Asiatic Society of Bengal, 1897-1921 (rpt., New Delhi, Low Price Publications, 1993).

Abul Fazl, *Ain-i-Akbari*, ed. H. Blochmann, Calcutta: Asiatic Society of Bengal, 1867-77 (first volume translated by H. Blochmann and revised by D.C. Philott, second and third volumes translated by H.S. Jarrett and revised by Sir Jadunath Sarkar, Calcutta: Asiatic Society of Bengal, 2nd edn., 1927-49) (rpt., New Delhi, Low Price Publications, 1994).

Babur, Zahiruddin Muhammed, *Baburnama*, tr. A.S. Beveridge, London: E.J.W. Gibb Memorial Trust, 1921 (rpt., New Delhi, Low Price Publications, 1995).

Dabistan-i Mazahib, *c*. 1658, ascribed to Muhammad Muhsin Fani, ed. Nazr Ashraf, Calcuta, 1809, Eng. tr. Anthony Troyer and David Shea, *Schools of Religions,* London, 1843. The sections dealing with the religious systems of the Hindus have been reproduced as *Hinduism during the Mughal India of the 17th Century*, Patna, Khuda Bakhsh Oriental Public Library, 1993.

Isardas Nagar, *Futuhat-i Alamgiri,* tr. and ed. Tasneem Ahmad, Delhi, Idarah-i-Adabiyat, 1978.

Jahangir, *Tuzuk-i Jahangiri* or *Memoirs of Jahangir*, tr. Alexander Rogers, ed. Henry Beveridge, London, Royal Asiatic Society, 1909-14 (rpt., Delhi, Atlantic Publishers, 1989).

Sachau, Edward C., ed., *Alberuni's India,* 1st pub. S. Chand & Company 1910, rpt., Delhi, Low Price Publications, 1993.

Sadi Mustaid Khan, *Maasir-i-Alamgiri,* tr. J. Sarkar, Royal Asiatic Society of Bengal, Calcutta, 1947.

Shiv Das Lakhnavi, *Shahnama Munawar Kalam*, tr. S.H. Askari, Patna, Janaki Prakashan, 1980.

VERNACULAR SOURCES

Chaurasi Vaishnavan Ki Varta, Bombay, Khemraj Shrikrishnadas, 1988.

Do Sav Bavan Vaishnavan Ki Varta, Bombay, Khemraj Shrikrishnadas, 1986.

EUROPEAN SOURCES

Bernier, Francois, *Travels in the Mogul Empire* AD *1656-1668*, tr. and ed. A. Constable, 3rd edn. S. Chand and Co. (Pvt.) Ltd., Delhi, 1972.

Manucci, N., *Storia do Mogor* or *Mogul India 1653-1708*, tr. William Irvine, vol. II, Indian Text Series, Government of India, London, 1907-8.

GAZETTEERS

The Imperial Gazetteer of India, vol. VIII, New Edition, Oxford, Clarendon Press, 1908.

District Gazetteer, Alwar by P.W. Powlet, London, Trubner and Co. 1872.

Rajasthan District Gazetteers, Bharatpur, 1971. Directorate of District Gazetters, Govt. of Rajasthan, Jaipur.

Rajasthan District Gazetteers, Sawai Madhopur, 1981. Directorate of District Gazetters, Govt. of Rajasthan, Jaipur.

Land Revenue Settlement of the Gurgaon District by F.C. Canning, Lahore, 1877.

MODERN WORKS

Alam, Muzaffar, *The Crisis of Empire in Mughal North India: Awadh and the Punjab, 1707-1748*, Delhi, Oxford University Press, 1986.

Alam, Muzaffar, 'Aspects of Agrarian Uprisings in North India in Early Eighteenth Century', in S. Bhattacharya and Romila Thapar, eds., *Situating Indian History*, Delhi, Oxford University Press, 1986, pp. 146-70.

Alam, Muzaffar and Sanjay Subramanyam, eds., *The Mughal State, 1526-1750*, Delhi, Oxford University Press, 1996.

Alvi, R.A., 'Persian Documents of the Reign of Aurangzeb', *PIHC*, Dharwad, 1988.

Athar Ali, M., Presidential Address, *PIHC*, 33rd Session, Muzaffarpur, 1972.

——, *The Mughal Nobility Under Aurangzeb*, New Revised Edition, Delhi, Oxford University Press, 1997.

——, 'The Passing of Empire: The Mughal Case', *MAS*, vol. 9. 3, 1975, pp. 385-96.

Bajekal, Madhavi, 'The state and rural grain market in eighteenth century eastern Rajasthan', *IESHR*, 25.4 1988, pp. 444-74.

Bahura, Gopal Narayan and Chandramani Singh, *Catalogue of Historical Documents in Kapad Dwara*, vol. I, Jaigrah Public Charitable Trust, Amber-Jaipur, 1988.

Banga, Indu, *Agrarian System of the Sikhs: Late Eighteenth Century and Early Nineteenth Century*, Delhi, Manohar, 1978.

Bayly, C.A., *Rulers, Townsmen and Bazaars*, North Indian Society in the Age of British Expansion 1770-1870, Great Britain, Cambridge University Press, 1983.

——, *Imperial Meridian: The British Empire and the World 1780-1830*, Delhi, Orient Longman, 1989.

——, 'Epilogue to the Indian Edition', in Seema Alvi (ed.), *The Eighteenth Century in India*, pp. 165-98, 2002.

Bhadani, B.L., 'The Profile of Akbar in Contemporary Rajasthani Literature', *Social Scientist*, vol. 20. 10, 1992, pp. 46-53.

Bhadra, Gautam, 'Two Frontier Uprisings in Mughal India', in Ranajit Guha (ed.), *Subaltern Studies*, vol. II, Delhi, Oxford University Press, 1984, pp. 43-59.

Bhatnagar, V.S., *Life and Times of Sawai Jai Singh, 1688-1743*, Delhi, 1974.

Brown, Peter, *The Cult of Saints*, Chicago, The University of Chiego Press 1981.

Calkins, C. Philip, 'The Formation of a Regionally Oriented Group in Bengal 1700-40', *JAS*, vol. 29, 1970, pp. 799-806.

Chandra, Satish, *Parties and Politics in the Mughal Court, 1707-1740*, Delhi, revd. edn. 2002.

Chandra, Satish, *Medieval India, Society, the Jagirdari Crisis and the Village*, Delhi, Macmillan, 1982.

——, 'Some Aspects of the Indian Village Society in Northern India during the 18th Century', *IHR*, vol. 1.1, 1974, pp. 51-64.

——, 'Role of the Local Community, the Zamindars and the State in Providing Capital Inputs for the Improvement and Expansion of Cultivation', *IHR*, vol. 3.1, 1976, pp. 83-98.

——, 'Some Documents Pertaining to *Zamindari* and *Thikana* Records in the Former Jaipur State', *PIHC*, 29th Session, Patiala, 1967.

Chundawat, P.C., *Maharaja Surajmal Aur Unka Yug*, Agra, Jaipal Agencies Udyog Nagar, 1982.

Das, Banarsi, *Ardhkathanak*, tr. Mukund Lath, Jaipur, Rajasthan Prakrit Bharati Sansthan, 1981.

Datta, Nonica, *Forming an Identity: A Social History of the Jats*, Delhi, Oxford University Press, 1999.

Deloche, Jean (ed.), *Wendel's Memoirs on the Origin, Growth and Present State of Jat Power in Hindustan (1768)*, Pondichery, 1991.

Dumont, Louis, 'The Village Community from Munro to Maine', *Contributions to Indian Sociology*, no. 9, 1966.

Dwivedi, G.C., *The Jats: Their Role in Mughal Empire*, Delhi, Arnold Publishers, 1989.

Eaton, Richard M., 'The Political and Religious Authority of the Shrine of Baba Farid', in Barbara Daly Metcalf (ed.), *Moral Conduct and Authority: The Place of Islam in South Asian Islam*, Berkeley, University of California Press, 1984.

——, *Essays on Islam and Indian History*, Delhi, Oxford India Paperbacks, 2000.

Entwistle, Alan W., 'Rediscovery of Braj', papers published by the International Association of the Vrindavan Research Institute, School of Oriental and African Studies, University of London, *Bulletin XIV*, December 1988.

Fukuzawa, H., *The Medieval Deccan: Peasants, Social System and States: Sixteenth to Eighteenth Centuries*, Delhi, Oxford University Press 1991.

Govinddas, Seth, *Braj Aur Braj-Yatra*, Delhi, Rajkamal Prakashan 1959.

Growse, F.S., *Mathura, a District Memoir*, London, 1874.

Guha, Ranajit, *Elementary Aspects of Peasant Insurgency in Colonial India*, Delhi, Oxford University Press, 1983.

Gupta, Ashin Das, *Indian Merchants and the Decline of Surat c. 1700-1750*, Delhi, Manohar, 1994.

——, 'Trade and Politics in Eighteenth Century India', in D.F. Richards (ed.), *Islam and the Trade of Asia*, Philadelphia, Bruno Cassirer and the University of Pennsylvania Press, 1970.

Gupta, S.P., *The Agrarian System of Eastern Rajasthan* (*c.* 1650-1750), Delhi, Manohar, 1986.

Habib, Irfan, *The Agrarian System of Mughal India 1556-1707*, 2nd revd. edn., Delhi, Oxford University Press, 1999.

——, 'The Eighteenth Century in Indian History', *PIHC*, Calcutta, 1995.

——, *The Economic History of Medieval India – A Survey*, Delhi, Tulika, 2001.

——, *Essays in Indian History: Towards a Marxist Perception*, Delhi, Tulika, 1997.

——, 'A Documentary History of the Gosains (Gosvamis) of the Caitanya Sect at Vrindavan', in Margaret H. Case (ed.), *Govinddeva: A Dialogue in Stone,* New Delhi, Indra Grandhi National Centre for the Arts 1996, pp. 131-60.

——, 'Social Distribution of Landed Property in Pre-British India', *Enquiry*, (Winter), 1965.

——, 'Jatts of Punjab and Sindh', in H. Singh and N.G. Barrier (eds.), *Punjab Past and Present, Essays in Honour of Ganda Singh,* Patiala, Punjab University 1976.

——, 'Economic History of the Delhi Sultanate – An Essay in Re-interpretation', *IHR*, 4, 1977, pp. 92-103.

——, 'Historical Background of the Popular Monotheistic Movement of the 15th and 17th Centuries', in Bisheshwar Prasad (ed.), *Ideas in History*, Bombay, Asia Publishing House, 1969, pp. 6-13.

——, *An Atlas of the Mughal EmpireI*, Delhi, Oxford University Press, 1982.

——, 'Potentialities of Capitalistic Development in the Economy of Mughal India', in Irfan Habib (ed.), *Essays in Indian History: Towards a Marxist Perception*, Delhi, Tulika, 1977.

Hardy, P., 'Commentary and Critique', *JAS*, vol. XXXV, no. 2, 1976, pp. 257-63.

Hasan, S. Nurul, 'Zamindars Under the Mughals', in R.E. Frybenkerg (ed.), *Land Control and Social Structure in Indian History*, First Revised Indian Edition, Delhi, Manohar, 1979, pp. 17-32.

Hasan, S. Nurul et al., 'The Pattern of Agricultural Production in the Territories of Amber (*c*. 1650-1750)', *PIHC*, 28th Session, Mysore, 1966, pp. 244-64.

Hasan, S. Nurul and S.P. Gupta, 'Prices of Foodgrains in the Territories of Amber (*c*. 1650-1750)', *PIHC*, 29th Session, Patiala, 1967, pp. 345-67.

Horstmann, Monika, 'Religious Dignities in the Court Protocol of Jaipur (mid-eighteenth to early nineteenth century), in George Berbemer, Normann Kulke, Tilman Frasch and Jurgen Lutt (eds.), *Explorations in the History of South Asia*, Delhi, Manohar, 2001, pp. 139-55.

——, *In Favour of Govinddevji: Historical Documents Relating to a Deity of Vrindavan and Eastern Rajasthan*, Delhi, Manohar, 1999.

Hussain, S.M., Azizuddin, 'Scarcity of *paibaqi* Lands during Aurangzeb's Reign in the light of Inayat Jung Collection Documents', *PIHC*, 34th Session, 1997.

Irwin, William, *The Later Mughals* (ed.), Jadunath Sarkar, Delhi, Oriental Books Reprint Corporation, 1971.

Khan, Dominique-Sila, *Conversions and Shifting Identities: Ramdev Pir and Ismailis in Rajasthan*, Delhi, Manohar, 2003.

Khan, Iqtidar Alam, 'Muskets in Mawas: Instruments of Peasant Resistance', in K.N. Panikkar, T.J. Byres, Utsa Patnaik (eds.), *The Making of History: Essays Presented to Irfan Habib*, Delhi, Tulika, 2000, pp. 81-103.

——, 'The Nobility under Akbar and the Development of His Religious Policy, 1560-1580', *Journal of the Royal Asiatic Society*, of Great Britain and Ireland, 1968, pp. 29-36.

Khan, Kanwar Refaqat Ali, *The Kachhwahas Under Akbar and Jahangir*, Delhi, Kitab Publishing House, 1971.

Kolf, Dirk H.A., *Naukar, Rajput and Sepoy: The Ethnohistory of the Military Labour Market in Hindustan, 1450-1850*, Delhi, Cambridge University Press, 1990.

Kulkarni, A.R., 'The Indian Village with special reference to Medieval Deccan (Maratha Country)', Presidential Address, *PIHC*, Delhi, 1992.

Leonard, Karen, 'The Hyderabad Political System and its Participants', *JAS*, vol. 30, 1971, pp. 569-82.

——, 'The "Great-Firm" Theory of the Decline of the Mughal Empire',

Comparative Studies in Society and History, vol. 21, no. 2, 1979, pp. 161-7.

MacLean, Derryl N., *Religion and Society in Arab Sindh*, New York, E.J. Brill, 1989.

MacLeod, W.H., *The Evolution of the Sikh Community*, Delhi, Oxford University Press, 1996.

Mayaram, Shail, *Resisting Regimes: Myth, Memory and Shaping of Muslim Identity*, Delhi, Oxford University Press, 1997.

Mittal, P.D., *Braj Ka Samskritik Itihas*, Delhi, Rajkamal Prakashan, 1966.

——, *Braj Sampardayon Ka Itihas*, Mathura, Sahitya Sansthan, 1968.

Moosvi, Shireen, *The Economy of the Mughal Empire c. 1595: A Statistical Study*, Delhi, Oxford University Press, 1987.

——, 'Scarcities, Prices and Exploitation: The Agrarian Crisis, 1658-70', *Studies in History*, I, 1. n.s., 1985, pp. 45-55.

——, 'Aurangzeb's *Farman* to Rasikdas on Problems of Revenue Administration 1665', in Irfan Habib (ed.), *Medieval India* I, pp. 197-208, 1992.

Moreland, W.H., *The Agrarian System of Moslem India*, 2nd edn, Delhi, 1968.

Mukherji, Tarapada and Irfan Habib, 'Akbar and the Temples of Mathura and its Environs', *PIHC*, 48th Session, 1987.

——, 'The Mughal Administration and the Temples of Vrindavan during the Reign of Jahangir and Shahjahan', *PIHC*, 49th Session, 1988.

Mukherji, Tarapada and Irfan Habib, 'Land Rights in the Reign of Akbar (The Evidence of the Sale-Deeds of Vrindavan and Aritha)', *PIHC*, 50th Session, 1989-90.

Mukherjee, S.N., 'The Idea of Village Community and British Administrators', *Enquiry*, N.S., vol. III. 3, 1971, pp. 56-67.

Mukhia, Harbans, 'Illegal Extortions from Peasants, Artisans and Menial in Eighteenth Century Eastern Rajasthan', *IESHR*, vol. XIV. 2, 1977, pp. 231-45.

Nath, R., 'Sri Govinddeva's Itinerary from Vrindavana to Jayapura, *c.* 1534-1727', in Margaret H. Case (ed.), *Govinddeva – a Dialogue in Stone*, Delhi, 1996, pp. 161-83.

Natwar Singh, K., *Maharaja Surajmal: His Life and Times, 1707-1763*, Delhi, Vikas, 1983.

Pearson, M.N., 'Shivaji and the Decline of the Mughal Empire', *JAS*, vol. XXXV, no. 2, 1976, pp. 221-35.

Perlin, Frank, 'State Formation Re-considered', *Modern Asian Studies*, vol. 19, nos. 3, 4, 1985.

Pradhan, M.C., *The Political System of the Jats of Northern India*, London, Oxford University Press, 1966.

Prasad, Pushpa, 'Akbar and the Jains', in Irfan Habib (ed.), *Akbar and His India*, Oxford India Paper Books, 2000, pp. 97-108.

Qanungo, K.R., *History of the Jats*, Delhi, Sunita Publications, 1925, rpt., 1987.

——, *History of the House of Diggi* (written in 1963) (ed.) S.S. Ratnawat, and published by the Centre for Rajasthan Studies, University of Jaipur, 1997.

Rana, R.P., 'Agrarian Revolts in Northern India during the late 17th and early 18th centuries', *IESHR*, vol. 18. 3-4, 1981, pp. 287-326.

——, 'A Dominant Class in Upheaval: The Zamindars of a North Indian Region in the Late Seventeenth and Early Eighteenth Centuries', *IESHR*, vol. 24.4, 1987, pp. 395-410.

——, 'Everyday Forms of Peasant Resistance in Eastern Rajasthan (c. 1660-1750)', *Social Science Probings*, vol. 15. 3-4, 2003, pp. 41-62.

Raychaudhury, Tapan, 'The Agrarian System of Mughal India', *Enquiry*, N.S., vol. 2.1, 1965, pp. 92-121.

Raychaudhuri, Tapan and Irfan Habib (eds.), *The Cambridge Economic History of India,* vol. I, *c. 1200-1750*, Orient Longman in association with CUP, 1982.

Richards, J.F., *The Mughal Empire* (The New Cambridge History of India1.5), 1993.

——, 'The Imperial Crisis in the Deccan', *JAS*, vol. XXXV, 1976, pp. 237-56.

——, 'The Islamic Frontier in the East: Expansion into South Asia', *JAS*, no. 4, October 1974, pp. 91-109.

Sarkar, Jadunath, *History of Aurangzeb*, vol. III, 3rd edn., Calcutta, Orient Longman, 1952; rpt., Bombay, Orient Longman, 1974, Chapter XXXV.

——, *Fall of the Mughal Empire*, 4 vols., Hyderabad, Orient Longman Ltd., rpt., 1991.

Scott, James C., *Weapons of the Weak, Everyday Forms of Peasant Resistance.*, Delhi, Oxford University Press, 1990.

Sharma, S.R., *The Religious Policy of the Mughal Emperors*, 3rd edn., Agra, S.L. Agarwala, 1972.

Sharma, U.N., *A New History of the Jats*, Jaipur, Mangal Prakashan, 1977.

Siddiqi, N.A., *Land Revenue Administration Under the Mughals (1700-1750)*, Bombay, Asia Publishing House, 1970.

Singh, Chetan, *Region and Empire: Punjab in the Seventeenth Century,* Delhi, Oxford University Press, 1991.

——, 'Conformity and Conflict: Tribes and the 'Agrarian System' of Mughal India', *IESHR*, vol. 25, no. 3, 1988, pp. 319-40.

Singh, Dilbagh, 'Role of Mahajans in the Rural Economy of Eastern Rajasthan during the Eighteenth Century', *Social Scientist*, vol. 2, 1974, pp. 20-31.

——, 'Caste and Structure of Village Society in Eastern Rajasthan during the Eighteenth Century', *IHR*, vol. 2, 1976, pp. 299-31.

——, *The State, Landlords and Peasants: Rajasthan in the Eighteenth Century*, Delhi, Manohar, 1990.

Smith, W.C., 'Lower Class Uprisings in the Mughal Empire', *Islamic Culture*, vol. 10, 1946, pp. 21-40.

Stokes, Eric, *Peasant and the Raj: Studies in Agrarian Society and Peasant Rebellion in Colonial India*, Delhi, S. Chand, 1978.

Streausand, Douglas E., *The Formation of the Mughal Empire*, Delhi, Oxford University Press, 1989.

Subrahmanyam, Sanjay, 'The Mughal State-Structure or Process? Reflections on recent western historiography', *IESHR*, vol. XXIX, no. 3, July-Sept. 1992, pp. 291-321.

Thapar, Romila, 'The Scope and Significance of Regional History', Presidential Address to the Punjab History Conference, Patiala, 1976.

Tod, Col. James, *Annals and Antiquities of Rajasthan*, Delhi, Motilal Banarsidass, 1971.

Vaudeville, Charlotte, *Myths, Saints and Legends in Medieval India*, Delhi, Oxford India Paperbacks, 1999.

Wills, C.U., *A Report on the Land Tenures and Special Powers of Certain Thikanadars of the Jaipur State*, 1935.

Ziegler, Norman P., 'Rajput Loyalties During the Mughal Period', in J.F. Richards (ed.), *Kingship and Authority in South Asia*, Delhi, Oxford University Press, pp. 242-84.

Index